GW00672136

SHARE THE GOOD NEWS

NATIONAL DIRECTORY FOR CATECHESIS IN IRELAND

Share the Good News

NATIONAL DIRECTORY FOR CATECHESIS IN IRELAND

Irish Episcopal Conference

VERITAS

First published 2010 by
Veritas Publications
7–8 Lower Abbey Street
Dublin 1, Ireland
publications@veritas.ie
www.veritas.ie

Copyright © Irish Episcopal Conference, 2010

ISBN 978 1 84730 258 8

10 9 8 7 6 5 4 3 2

The material in this publication is protected by copyright law. Except as may be permitted by law, no part of the material may be reproduced (including by storage in a retrieval system) or transmitted in any form or by any means, adapted, rented or lent without the written permission of the copyright owners. Applications for permissions should be addressed to the publisher.

A catalogue record for this book is available from the British Library.

Scripture taken from the New Revised Standard Version Bible: Catholic Edition copyright © 1993 and 1998 by the Division of Christian Education of the National Council of Churches of Christ in the United States of America. Used with permission. All rights reserved. All documents of Vatican II taken from A. Flannery (ed.), *Vatican Council II: Constitutions, Decrees and Declarations* (New York/Dublin: Costello Publishing/Dominican Publications, 1996). All other Vatican documents © Libreria Editrice Vaticana. Quotes from *Catechism of the Catholic Church* © 1994 Libreria Editrice Vaticana (Veritas, 1994). Lines from 'Ceasefire' from *Collected Poems* by Michael Longley, published by Jonathan Cape. Reprinted by permission of The Random House Group Ltd. Lines from 'Hospitality in Ireland' in A *Drinking Cup: Poems from the Irish* by Brendan Kennelly, published by Allen Figgis, 1970. Excerpts from 'The One' by Patrick Kavanagh are reprinted from *Collected Poems*, edited by Antoinette Quinn (Allen Lane, 2004), by kind permission of the trustees of the estate of the late Katherine B. Kavanagh, through the Jonathan Williams Literary Agency. Lines from 'Send Us Forth in Love' by Paul A. Tate, Epiphany Publications, Georgia. Reprinted by permission of the author. Acknowledgement and thanks is given to the following for use of their photographs: Dermot Nester, pp. 100, 193, 221; John McElroy, p. 126; Parish of the Travelling People, pp. 152, 175; Trócaire: p. 159; National Chaplaincy for Deaf People, pp. 173, 220; St Joseph's Training Centre, Ennis, p. 176. iStock images, pp. 57, 82. All other photographs courtesy of Gareth Byrne. Acknowledgement and thanks is given to the following for use of images of their artwork: Leo Clancy, p. 166; Sr Paula Kiersey, p. 222; Miriam Gogarty, p. 227. Acknowledgement and thanks is given to the following for use of their illustrations: Bill Bolger, p. 4; Jeanette Dunne, p. 141.

The publisher has endeavoured to contact all sources regarding photographic work contained herein; please contact the publisher should we have failed to give due acknowledgement, and we will endeavour to rectify this in all future prints.

Design & Typesetting by Colette Dower
Printed in the Republic of Ireland by Hudson Killeen, Dublin

Veritas books are printed on paper made from the wood pulp of managed forests.
For every tree felled, at least one tree is planted, thereby renewing natural resources.

Contents

Abbreviations

ACCC	*Adult Catechesis in the Christian Community*
AG	*Ad gentes*
CA	*Centesimus annus*
CCC	*Catechism of the Catholic Church*
CD	*Christus Dominus*
CIC	*Codex Iuris Canonici (1983)*
CL	*Christifideles laici*
CPMS	*Consecrated Persons and Their Mission to Schools*
CS	*The Catholic School*
CSDC	*Compendium of the Social Doctrine of the Church*
CSTTM	*The Catholic School on the Threshold of the Third Millennium*
CT	*Catechesi tradendae*
CV	*Caritas in veritate*
DCE	*Deus caritas est*
DI	*Dominius Iesus*
DV	*Dei Verbum*
EE	*Ecclesia in Europa*
EMCC	*Erga migrantes caritas Christi*
EN	*Evangelii nuntiandi*
ETCS	*Educating Together in Catholic Schools*
EV	*Evangelium vitae*
FC	*Familiaris consortio*
FD	*Fidei depositum*
FR	*Fides et ratio*
GCD	*General Catechetical Directory (1971)*
GDC	*General Directory for Catechesis (1997)*
GE	*Gravissimum educationis*
GS	*Gaudium et spes*
HFH	*Handing on the Faith in the Home*
LG	*Lumen gentium*
NA	*Nostra aetate*
NMI	*Novo millennio ineunte*
PDV	*Pastores dabo vobis*
RCIA	*Rite of Christian Initiation of Adults*
RDECS	*The Religious Dimension of Education in a Catholic School*
RH	*Redemptor hominis*
RMat	*Redemptoris Mater*
RM	*Redemptoris missio*
RP	*Reconciliatio et paenitentia*
SC	*Sacrosanctum concilium*
SCar	*Sacramentum caritatis*
SRS	*Sollicitudo Rei Socialis*
SS	*Spe salvi*
TMA	*Tertio millennio adveniente*
UUS	*Ut unum sint*
UR	*Unitatis redintegratio*
VS	*Veritatis splendor*

Preface

It is with a strong sense of gratitude for the blessing that Jesus Christ has been in the life of Irish people down through the centuries that the Irish Episcopal Conference publishes this *National Directory for Catechesis in Ireland*. We are convinced that the gifts of goodness, healing and peace that Christ offers the Church and all peoples today have the power to teach us, and future generations, how to live generous, just and committed lives with one another in God's all-embracing love:

> I know the plans I have for you, says the Lord, plans for your welfare... to give you a future with hope... When you search for me, you will find me; if you seek me with all your heart. (Jeremiah 29: 11-13)

In the spirit of the Second Vatican Council, and of the pastoral attentiveness to catechesis with which the Church has concerned itself since, *Share the Good News* seeks to encourage renewal within the Catholic community in Ireland as it endeavours to make the Good News of Jesus Christ more fully known and available to all. It does so, as pointed out in the Introduction to the Church's *General Directory for Catechesis*, by situating catechesis within the call to evangelise, taking account of the particular circumstances and needs of the local Church, and by helping people to appropriate the content of the faith as presented in the *Catechism of the Catholic Church*. This National Directory provides the Irish Church with a framework indicating principles and guidelines for evangelisation, catechesis and religious education today, and motivating us to study and research all the means available to bring the Gospel to life anew every day. *Share the Good News* has been reviewed and approved, according to established norms, by the Vatican's Congregation for the Clergy and Congregation for the Doctrine of the Faith.

The Irish Episcopal Conference wishes to acknowledge and support the wonderful catechetical work that is ongoing, the length and breadth of the country, and the great variety of faith development initiatives for adults as well as for young people that are emerging North and South. It is difficult to express adequately our gratitude to all those who contribute to the Church's catechetical ministry in parishes, schools, groups and communities, as well as in their homes and at diocesan and national levels. We invite you, wherever you may be on life's journey, to take this opportunity to open yourself again to the mystery and message of Jesus Christ. Guided by the Holy Spirit, let us enter, once more, into energetic proclamation and discussion of the Gospel. Together we can find the resources necessary to build on the time and talents we have been given by the Living God and so make the coming decade a period of great catechetical renewal.

We extend our profound thanks to Dr Gareth Byrne, writer and editor of this important text, to his Advisory Group, Linda Kiely and Brendan O'Reilly (successive National Directors for Catechesis), Roger Maxwell, Raymond Topley (RIP) and Grainne Wilson, for their ongoing commitment, and to the final editing team, Dr Byrne, Bishop Martin Drennan and Professor Brendan Leahy. We congratulate all the members of the Episcopal Council for Catechetics for overseeing this project with enthusiasm. We offer our gratitude also to the many hundreds of people nationwide who wrote in response to the invitation for submissions, to those involved professionally in theological, catechetical, religious education and pastoral ministry who gave of their rich experience, to diocesan advisers and other diocesan and national catechetical and education groups and associations, to priests, members of religious congregations and of lay communities and organisations, and all those individuals who have continued to offer their wisdom and insight. Particular thanks to the Episcopal Commissions/Councils for Doctrine, Education, Theology, Pastoral Renewal and Adult Faith Development, Liturgy, Justice and Peace, Missions, and Emigrants, for their generous contributions. Special thanks to Veritas for the preparation and production of this very attractively presented text.

This *National Directory for Catechesis in Ireland* speaks from the heart of the Church with love. It is particularly timely in seeking to address the specific catechetical issues that arise in the Irish context now, at the beginning of the twenty-first century. It acknowledges the many questions about Christ and his message that are alive in Irish society and in the Church in Ireland today. We hope that it will encourage all who are searching for the deepest meaning of life and love to turn toward Christ who educates us to live truly, compassionately and with integrity in the presence of our ever-loving Father.

We trust that this Directory will have a wide circulation. It is essential reading for those engaged in catechetical and other faith development initiatives at every level of the Church in Ireland. We invite all those who are interested in sharing the Good News, to study, reflect, pray and act upon this document, as individuals and as communities of faith, so that together we may grow ever closer to the Lord.

We pray that the same Holy Spirit who gave courage and voice to the prophets and apostles will guide us, too, in all our efforts. May Mary, ever faithful, intercede for us in the wonderful work of making her Son more fully known to all.

✠ Seán Brady
Archbishop of Armagh
Primate of All Ireland

✠ Diarmuid Martin
Archbishop of Dublin
Primate of Ireland

✠ Dermot Clifford
Archbishop of Cashel & Emly

✠ Michael Neary
Archbishop of Tuam

CONGREGATIO PRO CLERICIS

Prot. N. 20102546

In a letter of 13 October 2008, His Eminence Seán Baptist Brady, President of the Conference of Bishops of Ireland, having received the previous consent of the Bishops of Ireland, presented the text of the *National Directory for Catechesis in Ireland* for the necessary 'recognitio' of the Holy See, in accord with the provisions of the Apostolic Constitution *Pastor Bonus* n. 94, can. 775 §2 of the *Code of Canon Law* and the *General Directory for Catechesis* n. 282.

The text was examined, as required, by both the Congregation for Clergy and the Congregation for the Doctrine of the Faith, within the terms of reference of their particular competencies. Having received the integrated observations of the aforementioned Congregations, His Eminence Cardinal Brady, by a letter of 30 August 2010, presented the revised text of the National Directory, with the previous approval of the Conference of Bishops of Ireland.

Accordingly, this Congregation for the Clergy hereby grants the requested 'recognitio' in accord with the above mentioned authority, to the text entitled *Share the Good News: National Directory for Catechesis in Ireland*, as presented on 30 August 2010.

With the granting of this 'recognitio', integrating the required modifications, this text will become the 'definitive text' of *Share the Good News: National Directory for Catechesis in Ireland*. Any subsequent revisions will require that the necessary approval be obtained, in accord with the law.

Given at the Seat of the Congregation for the Clergy
8 Septmber 2010
Feast of the Nativity of the Blessed Virgin Mary

Cláudio Cardinal Hummes
Prefect

✠ Mauro Piacenza
Titular Archbishop of Vittoriana
Secretary

Glóir don Athair,
Agus don Mhac,
Agus don Spiorad Naomh.
Mar a bhí ó thús,
Mar atá anois,
Mar a bheas go brách,
Le saol na saol.
Áiméan.

Introduction

1. The Christian faith, like the Word of God, is something alive and active.[1] Christ has set our hearts on fire.[2] Like so many in the gospel stories, we too have heard Jesus Christ calling us. He continues to reach out, drawing near to us in our own particular places. He is conscious of each person in their need and he addresses us personally. This is his way. He has come among us in our humanity and he remains with us always. Of the sick man at Bethzatha he asks with intent: 'Do you want to be well again?' (John 5:6). He surprises the Samaritan woman at the well, and upsets his companions, when he makes a request of her: 'Give me a drink' (John 4:7). And to the rich young man, on whom he looked lovingly, he offers an unanswered challenge: 'Come, follow me' (Mark 10:21). Despite our weakness and the inadequacies of our efforts, we too have felt his closeness and known his care. He has touched our very being. As in Galilee two thousand years ago, Jesus Christ offers us, now, healing and forgiveness, comfort and challenge, the tenderness and pain of all-embracing love, and a peace in God's presence rooted in commitment to one another and to whole-hearted service of our neighbour.

Prompted by the Holy Spirit, we seek to live our faith in Jesus Christ and become the supportive and unified community of disciples that he calls us to be. We are convinced that knowing Christ's love for us can change our lives, convert our hearts and transform our world. As members of his Church, we trust in the power of Christ's love to prevail over our human limitations and, even in confusing and turbulent times, we reach out with Jesus Christ to serve the world and one another. True Christian faith can renew all things and lead us to live in love with Christ, now and for ever.

[1] See Heb 4:12a.
[2] See Lk 24:32.

2. The years since the Second Vatican Council have seen a tremendous effort in the Church worldwide to express for our times the centrality of evangelisation and catechesis in the life and mission of all members of the Church. *Gravissimum educationis* (1965), the Council's Declaration on Christian Education, together with its other documents, set the scene for this reflection. The *General Catechetical Directory* (1971), called for at Vatican II,[3] *The Rite of Christian Initiation of Adults* (1972), Pope Paul VI's *Evangelii nuntiandi* (1975), and Pope John Paul II's *Catechesi tradendae* (1979) and *Redemptoris missio* (1990), all contributed enormously to a renewal in understanding of how we proclaim the faith. The *Catechism of the Catholic Church* (1992) added a rich and comprehensive exposition of the content of Christian faith. In its wake, the new *General Directory for Catechesis* (1997), bringing the original 1971 document up to date, created a synthesis of all that had been achieved.

The value of the local Church providing a National Directory for Catechesis has been stated repeatedly.[4] A national Directory of this kind spells out the vision, organisation and planning involved in evangelisation and catechesis within the particular situation of the local Church. It applies the principles and foundations highlighted in the *General Directory for Catechesis* to the local context or contexts. It addresses the specific issues arising in that situation. The *Catechism of the Catholic Church* makes it clear that those who seek to deepen the understanding of Christian faith must develop 'catechetical methods required of different cultures, age, spiritual maturity, and social and ecclesial condition'.[5] The *General Directory for Catechesis* calls for local catechetical directories as well as local catechisms, and the formulation of a 'programme of action' to determine the objectives, the means of pastoral catechesis and the norms governing it. This process, it notes, should be completed with reference to local needs, while remaining in harmony with the universal Church.[6]

This *National Directory for Catechesis in Ireland* seeks to lay down a framework and principles, suited to local needs in Ireland, for the presentation of the Good News of Jesus Christ. It does so with enthusiasm and joy, for to know Christ and to experience in him the love of God, revealed to us in our time by the kindness of the Holy Spirit, is to come to a whole new way of life, lived in faith, hope and love. This National Directory for Catechesis is not a catechism, a programme or a theological explanation of all that might be contained in a catechism. It does not seek to offer a particular catechesis on the many and varied themes uncovered here. It contents itself, instead, in pointing to the *Catechism of the Catholic Church*, the complete statement of the Catholic Faith, and searching out sure ways of making the treasures to be found there more readily available to people in Ireland today.

[3] See *CD* 44.
[4] See *CD* 44; *GCD* 1, 77; *GDC* 11, 282.
[5] *CCC* 24.
[6] See *GDC* 281-283.

This is an opportune time to encourage members of the Catholic Church in Ireland to become engaged in renewed reflection, leading to a reinvigorated approach to teaching the Faith and sharing the Gospel. The preparation of this Irish National Directory for Catechesis is only the beginning of this process. It follows the model and principles laid out by the *General Directory for Catechesis*, seeking to establish guidelines upon which catechesis and all forms of faith development can best be pursued by the Church in Ireland. As a result of various consultation processes undertaken in its preparation, it hopes to reflect and encourage good practice at all levels of evangelising action within the Catholic Church in Ireland. It seeks to help members of the Church to speak confidently of the Gospel message, which we have always cherished in Ireland and yet are still only coming to know. It sets us on a journey as a pilgrim Church,[7] searching for new ways to encourage all to seek Christ. It entices us to pause with him awhile, to come to understand more fully the power of his love, and to meet him face to face.[8]

3. Chapter 1 of this *National Directory for Catechesis in Ireland* reviews the situation today in Ireland, North and South, as the context within which we proclaim in words and action the Good News given to us by Jesus Christ. The rapid pace of change experienced in most societies across the world today, if anything, seems to be even more apparent in Ireland: new understandings, new infrastructure, new forms of communication, new initiatives all around. New peoples, new cultural dispositions and, for Irish society, new religious traditions are now part of our day-to-day experience. The complexity of the world in which we live is evident. Yet, amidst uncertainty and insecurity, the Christian faith is good news for people today. Our processes and programmes focused on education in Christian living must be relevant to as many of them as possible and to the circumstances of their lives.

Chapter 2 presents the main purpose of this reflection: conversion to Christ and the ongoing faith development that can take place at a whole series of levels throughout our lives, from cradle to grave, on our journey to the fullness of the Kingdom of God. Evangelisation is a lifelong process that admits of a series of moments which may be isolated for the purpose of reflection but which are interconnected as part of the continuum of life. Initial proclamation, Christian initiation, catechesis, religious education (at least from the perspective discussed below), new evangelisation and theological reflection all

[7] See *NMI* 8-13.
[8] See *NMI* 16-28.

have a part to play in the continuing lifelong education in faith that characterises Christian commitment. All the efforts of the Church in this area, under the inspiration of the Holy Spirit, indicated within these distinct but interrelated headings, we draw together using the comprehensive title 'faith development'.

In Chapter 3, we consider the essential framework around which we live our Christian lives. Our starting point and underlying logic is the pedagogy of God. God's love is revealed to the world in every time and place, most particularly in Jesus Christ, calling each one of us to a response in faith. Christian faith is understood as a way of life, and the close connection between educational methods and the content of faith is noted. Particular significance is attached to choosing methodology that suits the specific circumstances of those interested in learning about Christian faith and developing their faith life. The Deposit of Faith and hierarchy of truths revealed in salvation history and taught by the Church is presented in a concise manner. The four themes set out in the *Catechism of the Catholic Church*, and dealt with there in detail, are also indicated here: the Profession of Faith; the Celebration of Christian Mystery; Life in Christ; and Prayer in the Christian Life. The chapter concludes with reflections on the search for Christian unity as an essential disposition of Christian living, on the challenge of bringing the Gospel into dialogue with the culture of our time, and on the need for respectful inter-religious and inter-cultural dialogues.

Chapters 4, 5 and 6, together, consider the types of learning appropriate within the Irish Church so as to attend to the real faith needs of people. Chapter 4 addresses the primary question of adult catechesis and ongoing faith development. All levels of evangelisation are considered. Once again today, there is need for an initial proclamation of the Gospel to those who do not know Jesus Christ. There can be no presumption, however, on any of our parts that we have come to a point in our lives where we no longer need to seek a deeper understanding of our religious faith. In Chapter 5, the faith formation of children and young people is explored. Sharing faith with a new generation is understood as the work of home and parish, supported by schools. The positive contribution of the education systems in Ireland, and of generations of teachers, in establishing an

appreciation of the significant place of religion in life, is acknowledged. The partnership between home, parish and school in the Christian initiation, religious education and ongoing catechesis of young people is reviewed. Chapter 6 invites an inclusive approach that addresses the needs of those who require specific attention and specialised forms of faith development: among others, those who are socially deprived, people with special needs, the Deaf Community, the Travelling People, newcomers of every kind, and people living with serious illness.

Chapter 7 is the culmination of this Directory, bringing together, under the format of objectives and indicators, all that has emerged in this reflection. The objectives set out the policy to be pursued over the coming years according to local needs and possibilities. The indicators are steps along the way, which, when achieved, suggest progress toward the realisation of the particular objective. These objectives and their indicators are designed to ensure that the core catechetical values espoused in this Directory are encouraged nationally, at diocesan and parish level, in Catholic schools and third-level colleges, and within Catholic lay communities and organisations. This formula is used in order that implementation is given high priority. It provides the basis upon which evaluation can take place locally at regular intervals. The Directory itself should be reviewed within ten years. It should be revised according to the new needs and new questions that its own implementation will have helped bring to the surface.

4. The *National Directory for Catechesis in Ireland* is a document for implementation and discussion among all the members of the Catholic Church in Ireland. It seeks to support all those responsible at diocesan and national levels, particularly bishops, in their role as leaders of the faith community. It encourages parents, guardians, grandparents, godparents and sponsors, and all family members, in their primary responsibility of sharing faith in the home with the coming generations. It endorses the efforts of priests, deacons, parish pastoral councils, pastoral workers and others, at parish, groups of parishes and deanery levels. It celebrates the commitment of school principals, teachers, religious educators, school chaplains, boards of management, patrons and trustees, as well as diocesan advisers for religious education. It recognises the tremendous

efforts of religious congregations over the years to provide for the faith needs of the young, the poor and the marginalised. It looks forward to the energetic contribution of new lay communities and groups in building up the faith in Ireland.

The *National Directory for Catechesis in Ireland* will require time to be fully digested and put into action. It is to be hoped that it will not be read merely once, and then put off to one side and forgotten. We should all feel encouraged to come back, again and again, to the Directory, as a source of inspiration and direction. Each day, we can become more aware of the enlightening influence that informed and reflective faith can have in life. We can find more time, even in our busy lives, for prayer, study and conversation around faith. We should desire the same kind of knowledge and confidence in this area as we require of ourselves in many other matters. Readers of this Directory may wish to begin by focusing on their own particular area of interest, but they are encouraged, also, to realise that they are part of a bigger picture. A renewed adult faith that grapples with all the realities of life is possible, but it does require attention and effort beyond what we receive as children. We must learn to own our faith and become ambassadors for Christ in a world that has good reason to question, but sometimes prefers an easy cynicism to the challenge of love.

5. The style employed in the writing of this document seeks to be comprehensive yet accessible. Documents of the universal Church are relied upon. It is hoped that the language used is simple, clear, inclusive and relevant. Where a passage from another author is quoted, it is given as written. There is an attempt to involve the reader personally. As well as the text itself, highlighted quotations, explanations and ideas are designed to draw the reader or group of readers into reflection and prayer. Images are also used to help readers to reflect on the different ways in which God touches into our lives each and every day. Captions are not provided, because what is important is the atmosphere created as one is drawn into contemplation of God's presence, rather than knowledge of where the place is or who the person might be. These pauses are calculated to help readers assimilate the themes addressed, engaging them deeply at a variety of levels. They are also intended to provide starting points for group discussion and to open the Christian community to Christ's call to love. We take this opportunity to invite people to become involved in a process of catechetical reflection and pastoral action, on the basis of this document. The text is itself a tool for evangelisation. It invites the reader to journey personally with Christ within the developing community that is the Church and, in the power of the Spirit, to contribute to its growth. All of us can be good news, living and sharing the Gospel with one another and with the world, in what we say and do and are.

It is hoped that the approach outlined will encourage all those who have responsibility for evangelisation initiatives and for catechetical planning in the Church in Ireland. The Directory seeks to renew adults in their faith and to ensure that the faith is shared with coming generations. It provides the basis upon which future programmes can be designed for differing contexts, and  will, we believe, be invaluable for those writing textbooks and creating resources for home, parish and school. It suggests parameters within which priests, men and women religious, Faith Development Coordinators and other pastoral workers, diocesan advisers, parish ministers and volunteer catechists, principals and teachers in Catholic primary schools, and principals, religious educators and school chaplains in post-primary schools can be trained. The dialogue in faith that this Directory gives rise to will be the foundation upon which the future of the Catholic community in Ireland will be built. It will require substantial resourcing, both in terms of personal time and financial commitment. We are convinced that when the Christian community understands the value of sharing its faith and growing in faith, new resources will be found.

6. We would like to conclude this introduction by noting our hope that this Directory will be an instrument that contributes in its own way to peace, reconciliation and new hope in Ireland. We see the Directory as an invitation to all people to enter into dialogue about the meaning for us today of the Christian heritage that has been passed on from previous generations. We are confident that honest discussion of Christian faith, and careful consideration of its impact on our lives, will offer all of us, including those who find themselves in times of doubt, an opportunity to contribute to renewal in the Church.

While this Irish National Directory for Catechesis is a document of the Catholic Church, we hope that it will also encourage committed ecumenical, inter-religious and inter-cultural dialogue on this island. As we in the Catholic Church reflect on our faith, the discussion the Directory gives rise to will, we trust, contribute to a respectful dialogue with those of other Christian denominations, with whom we share so much in common. The ecumenical journey that we are involved in should be recognised as

one of the great adventures of our time, as we learn to support one another in living committed Christian lives.

The invitation to dialogue is also made to those of other religions who believe in God, suggesting an exchange of ideas based on openness, informed understanding and mutual respect. There is so much, we believe, that can be learned, one from the other, about life lived in God's presence.

To those who do not profess belief in God, we also express the hope that we might enrich one another and together come to new understanding on our journey through life. Informed debate will help us all to grow in mutual human respect and genuine care for one another.

We have confidence that under the inspiration of God the Holy Spirit, the Christian message has something to say to everyone. Our deep-felt hope is that new ways of expressing our faith will renew us, contribute positively to the up-building of our world, and bring inner strength and lasting peace to all. For the Christian, faith is always a journey undertaken in the tender and caring friendship of the Risen Christ, whom we seek to imitate in this life and follow into the everlasting life that is God's unending love.

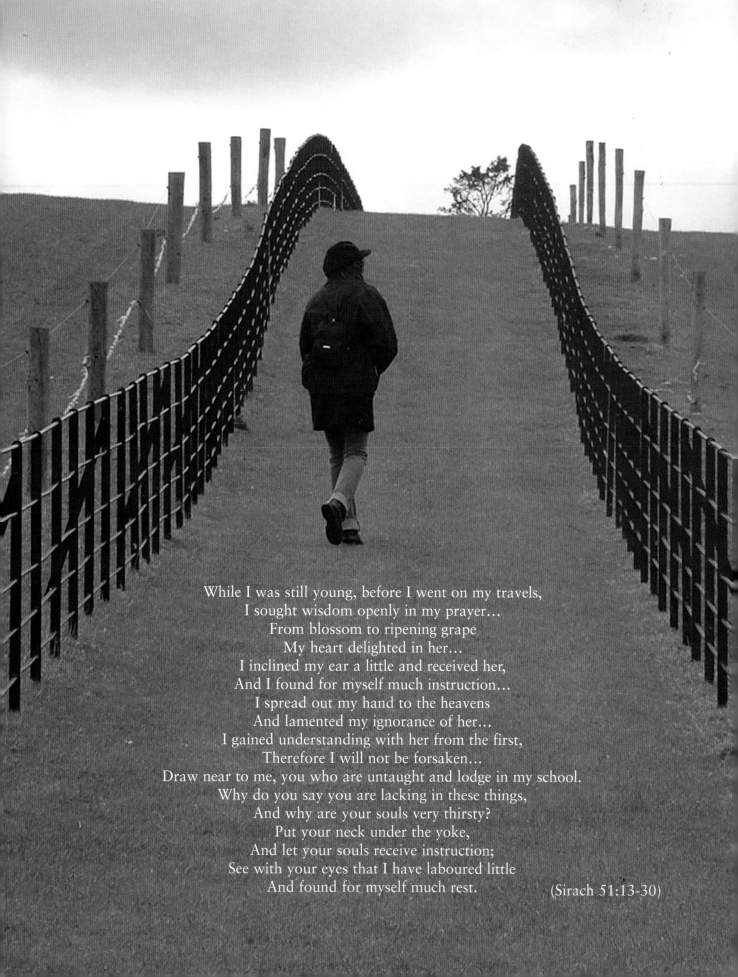

While I was still young, before I went on my travels,
I sought wisdom openly in my prayer...
From blossom to ripening grape
My heart delighted in her...
I inclined my ear a little and received her,
And I found for myself much instruction...
I spread out my hand to the heavens
And lamented my ignorance of her...
I gained understanding with her from the first,
Therefore I will not be forsaken...
Draw near to me, you who are untaught and lodge in my school.
Why do you say you are lacking in these things,
And why are your souls very thirsty?
Put your neck under the yoke,
And let your souls receive instruction;
See with your eyes that I have laboured little
And found for myself much rest.

(Sirach 51:13-30)

SECTION A
THE IRISH CONTEXT

CHAPTER 1

Living the Gospel in Ireland Today

7. One day after praying alone, Jesus Christ asked his disciples: 'Who do the crowd say that I am?' ... 'Who do you say that I am?'[1] The first of these questions could be answered by offering the opinion of others, but the second is deeper. It implies personal relationship. Who do *you* say I am? Who am I for *you*? Jesus' closest disciples had been inspired by what they saw in him and by his vision of how life could be lived: 'You are the Messiah of God', Peter responds, the Anointed One, the one we had been waiting for, the one in whom is all our hope. As Pope Benedict remarks: 'Being Christian is not the result of an ethical choice or a lofty idea, but an encounter with an event, a person, which gives life a new horizon and a decisive direction.'[2] The friends of Jesus became committed to the Lord because they came to know him and his love for them. They saw his commitment to them and to those most in need, his care for the poor, his love for sinners, his ability to change people's lives by his compassionate presence, his challenging stories, his healing words and works. They recognised, too, the most central reality in his life, his close bond to his Father in heaven. He prayed, personally, constantly, intensely, living always in conversation with the One who continually loves the world, and all its people, into life. Their perception of everything around them changed. There could be no going back. 'In Jesus Christ, who allowed his heart to be pierced, the true face of God is seen.'[3]

The same Jesus Christ is alive and active in our world now, crucified but risen from the dead, present always, and by the power of the Holy Spirit continually revealing God's face, helping us to glimpse God's steadfast love for us: 'In Jesus we contemplate beauty and splendour at their source ... the truth of God's love in Christ encounters us, attracts us, delights us.'[4] Jesus Christ gave his first disciples the courage to live in a new way and he seeks to encourage us now to follow his Gospel and, by its power,[5] to transform our lives, our culture, our value systems. He invites us, like the disciples, to come to him, to learn from him, to be healed by him. Brought to

[1] See Luke 9:18-20.
[2] *DCE* 1.
[3] Benedict XVI, *Youth Vigil Address at Marienfeld*, Cologne, 20 August World Youth Day 2005.
[4] *SCar* 35.
[5] See Romans 1:16.

new life by the power of the Gospel, touched by the peace and joy of knowing Jesus, the disciples sought to share the gift of his transforming love with everyone they met. Their mission was clear: they would bring this good news to the world, the news of Christ's astonishing intervention in their lives, and how with his witness to God's concerned and caring love, and by his cross and resurrection, he had changed them for ever. Even death has been conquered; it no longer has any dominion over him.[6]

The extraordinary power of Jesus' gift of love is revealed in the last hours of his life on earth. At the Last Supper, he gives his disciples his Body and Blood to eat and drink. His Body is to be given up for them and his Blood poured out for them so that sins may be forgiven; that is, so that evil may be overcome. On Calvary, the full meaning of this is made clear in the shocking suffering and death that he endured in order to show them the love greater than which no one has[7] and which is stronger than everything we fear. This is the transforming love that changes everything:

> In their hearts, people always and everywhere have somehow expected a change, a transformation of the world. Here now is the central act of transformation that alone can truly renew the world: violence is transformed into love, and death into life ... To use an image well known to us today, this is like inducing nuclear fission in the very heart of being – the victory of love over hatred, the victory of love over death. Only this intimate explosion of good conquering evil can then trigger off the series of transformations that little by little will change the world.[8]

8. The Christian today, graced by the Holy Spirit, is the bearer, too, of this life-giving, dynamic and transforming presence, Jesus Christ, who calls us to live our lives inspired by his life, his truth, his way. We are never alone. Jesus brings us beyond ourselves into a whole new world of loving relationship with God, with our neighbour, with our community, with society and with all of creation: 'Union with Christ is also union with all those to whom he gives himself.'[9] Because Jesus Christ is good news, the Christian today, and the Christian community, can be good news too, called to mission, sharing the gift of Christ, carrying hope to a world that seeks continuously to know, to understand, to live fully and to love.

As we begin this reflection, we observe that the vast majority of people living on the island of Ireland continue to be Christian and that a great number of them are Catholic. In the 2006 census, 86.83 per cent of the population recorded their affiliation to the Catholic Church.[10] In the European Values Study, 1999-2000,[11] a figure of 87.8 per cent was noted, while 40.3 per cent in Northern Ireland identified themselves as Roman Catholic.

[6] See Romans 6:9.
[7] See John 15:13.
[8] Benedict XVI, *Eucharistic Celebration Homily at Marienfeld*, Cologne, 21 August World Youth Day, 2005. See also *SCar* 11.
[9] *DCE* 14.
[10] See Central Statistics Office, Census 2006. Available from *www.cso.ie*
[11] See *The European Values Study* (1999-2000). Available from *www.ucd.ie/issda/*

On the other hand, it is clear that large numbers of Irish Catholics struggle to find a correlation between their faith and life: knowledge of their faith and religious practice is clearly declining among Catholics in the younger generations, particularly the youngest age-groups; and the teaching of the Catholic Church is frequently distrusted and thought to be out of touch. Young adults, in the urban centres  particularly, where increasing numbers of Irish people live their lives, are becoming generally absent from Church life, living often with cultural influences that are at best indifferent to religion. Accepting that many people question the concept of faith as well as the Church's teaching role, and also the possibility of any form of authority, this Directory seeks, in love, and with respect, to open up a dialogue about all these things with those who are committed, with those who are interested, with those who are alienated, and with those who are coming to consider these questions for the first time.

The Irish Christian Tradition

Who is God
And where is God,
Of whom is God,
And where His dwelling?
Has He sons and daughters,
Gold and silver,
This God of yours?
Is He ever-living?
Is He beautiful...
Is He in heaven
Or on earth?
In the sea, in the rivers,
In the mountains,
In the valleys?
Speak to us
Tidings of Him:
How will He be seen,
How is He loved,
How is He found?
Is it in youth
Or in old age
He is found?[12]

9. St Patrick, in response to the question put to him, according to legend, by the Celtic princess Eithne, speaks indeed of a beautiful God, 'the God of all things', who is revealed in the person of Jesus Christ. The same enquiry has been made, again and again, to Irish Christians down through the centuries, and it is still being asked of the Church in Ireland today: 'Who is God?' ... 'What does knowing Jesus tell us about God and about ourselves?'

When St Patrick and other missionaries came to Ireland, they were conscious of having reached the furthest ends of the known world. They were following the command of Jesus: 'You will be my witnesses in Jerusalem, in all of Judaea and Samaria, and to the ends of the earth' (Acts 1:8). The Gospel, as is well known, was received early in Ireland and, alone among all the countries of Western Europe, without martyrdom. The early Christians built up local communities of faith through monastic settlements that became centres of life and learning, open to all. In everything they did, they sought the protection of God's power in Jesus Christ:

The arms of God be around my shoulders...
The sign of Christ's cross on my forehead...
The work of God's church in my hands...
A home for God in my heart...[13]

[12] Stokes and Whitley, *The Tripartite Life of St Patrick* (London: Eyre and Spottiswoode, 1887), p. 100.
[13] *Breastplate of St Fursa*, traditional, translation F. Mullaghy.

The early Irish Church adapted itself quickly to the cultural realities, seeking to inculturate the Gospel in its new context. Many of the religious traditions of the people were adapted, allowing the Gospel to find new expression. Traditional sites and celebrations were transformed in the light of Christ. The natural wonder of the people, their closeness to nature, their understanding of community, their celebration of death and awareness of the other world, were all seized upon to explain the closeness of God.[14] Indeed, the love of God, Father, Son and Holy Spirit, was experienced as Good News for all. And Christ was as near as the door.

ST PATRICK'S BREASTPLATE

Christ be with me, Christ within me,
Christ behind me, Christ before me,
Christ beside me, Christ to win me,
Christ to comfort and restore me.
Christ beneath me, Christ above me,
Christ in quiet, Christ in danger,
Christ in hearts of all that love me,
Christ in mouth of friend and stranger.
I bind unto myself the name,
The strong name of the Trinity;
By invocation of the same, The Three in One and One in Three;
Of whom all nature hath creation,
Eternal Father, Spirit, Word;
Praise to the Lord of my Salvation –
Salvation is of Christ the Lord! Amen.

St Patrick's Breastplate,
ascribed to St Patrick, translation C. F. Alexander.

The work of those who transcribed the gospels, preserving them in beautiful books, of the stone-carvers who produced the magnificent Irish High Crosses, and of those who worked precious metals into wonderful vessels for the celebration of the Mass, bears witness to the treasure the Irish people realised they had found and were happy to celebrate. Texts attributed to St Patrick and other early Irish saints were held in high esteem, and the Christian message was taught widely. Scripture and the Eucharist were central, providing and sustaining intimacy with the Lord. Music and art, ritual, silence and penance, all had their special place.

[14] See J.J. Ó Ríordán, *The Music of What Happens: Celtic Spirituality, A View from the Inside* (Dublin: Columba, 1996).

The 'Golden Age' of Irish Christianity, as it has been called, produced an extraordinary enthusiasm in Ireland for the mission to bring the Gospel back to the heart of Europe. The 'white martyrdom' of the Irish monks saw them leaving home and family for ever, to proclaim Jesus Christ risen, alive and available to all. The early Irish missionary monks, among them Colman, Colmcille, Columbanus, Fergal, Gall and Killian, continue to inspire Europe today. Their lives speak of generosity and courage, of a deep love for the Gospel and an unswerving trust in Christ's care and love for them, wherever they travelled.

While particularly conscious of native influences on Irish Christianity, we should also keep in mind the impact of successive waves of immigration through the centuries. The arrival of Viking, Norman, English, Scots and Huguenot peoples, whether welcome at the time or not, helped to create a rich diversity in the ethnic, linguistic and religious life of Ireland.

10. The Irish experience of Christianity is not without times lived in darkness and division, oppression and violence, poverty and sometimes even famine. A great love for Jesus and for Mary, his mother, the mother confided in deeply by Irish people down through the ages, has brought consolation to many in times of despair. The advent of the Reformation also left its mark upon Ireland, and for many, even today, our understanding of ourselves, our family affiliation to one Christian church or another, as well as our politics and our social commitments, emanate from places deep in our history. The impact of religious affiliation on the many divisions on the island of Ireland needs to be fully addressed. Reconciliation within a divided Christianity, and within Irish society, remains one of the most pressing requirements of our day in Ireland.

With the return of those who had studied secretly on the European Continent because of the Penal Laws in Ireland, a variety of spiritualities was introduced. The flourishing, in the eighteenth and nineteenth centuries, of so many Irish congregations of religious women and men, focused on the provision of aid to the poor, the sick, the uneducated and those in other forms of need, brought renewed impetus to Christian community life and charitable service in Ireland.

As a result of the 'national schools' initiative, set in motion in 1831, Catholic parish schools emerged throughout the country.

These schools have continued to make an enormous contribution to education in Ireland from that date down to the present time. The second half of the nineteenth century saw great emphasis on Catholic identity. In this period, and for most of the twentieth century, extraordinary numbers of young Irish men and women joined the priesthood and religious life, dedicating their whole lives to Christ and to their neighbour. At this time, Irish Christianity looked out beyond itself and became, again, a major force in the Universal Church's missionary endeavour to the world and all its peoples.

The second half of the twentieth century was influenced particularly by the deliberations of the Second Vatican Council (1962-65), which sought to renew the Christian spiritual life. It did so by returning to the fundamentals of the Gospel, in order to explore, in the light of Christ, issues for the Church that had come centre stage at the time of the Council. Three key aspects of the reflection undertaken at Vatican II are significant in understanding the dramatic influence of the Council: the renewal of the liturgy, helping Catholics to participate knowingly, actively and fruitfully in the celebration of the sacraments and especially the Mass;[15] a renewed ecclesiology based on the rediscovery of the concept 'People of God', the community of the followers of Christ, indicating that all the faithful, whatever their particular role, share fully in the salvific mission of the Church;[16] and a renewed emphasis on the need for an ongoing dialogue between the Church and the world. This, the Council recognised, calls for a receptive reading of the 'signs of the times' in the light of the Gospel,[17] thereby imbuing the everyday activities of men and women with deeper meaning.[18] 'The Second Vatican Council indicated that the mission of the Church in the contemporary world consists in helping every human being to discover in God the ultimate meaning of his existence.'[19]

PONTIFICAL COUNCIL FOR JUSTICE AND PEACE

COMPENDIUM OF THE SOCIAL DOCTRINE OF THE CHURCH

VERITAS

11. Due recognition should be given to the promising things that are happening within the Church in Ireland at the beginning of the twenty-first century: an extraordinary interest in sacred Scripture, particularly *lectio divina*, prayer groups of all kinds, Perpetual Adoration in many parishes, the hunger among some lay Catholics for adult education and their willingness to participate in courses for ministry, the emergence of parish pastoral councils and parish pastoral workers, the development of priestly fraternities, the restoration of the permanent diaconate, the refocusing of their commitments by congregations of religious women and men, the contribution of new ecclesial movements, the efforts of the Conference of Religious in Ireland and outreaches of the Bishops' Conference in tackling poverty and social justice, the invaluable

[15] See *SC* 11.
[16] See *LG* 9.
[17] See *GS* 11.
[18] See *GS* 40-41.
[19] *CSDC* 567.

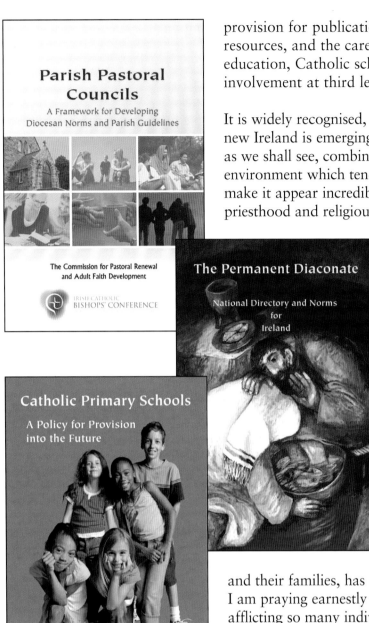

provision for publication of Catholic books and resources, and the careful way in which Catholic education, Catholic schooling and Catholic involvement at third level is debated.

It is widely recognised, however, that in many ways a new Ireland is emerging in which a variety of influences, as we shall see, combine to create a new cultural environment which tends to challenge faith and even make it appear incredible. The fall in vocations to the priesthood and religious life has been dramatic. The disturbing problem of child sexual abuse in all its dimensions has raised so many questions and left Irish Catholics ashamed and disorientated by what has happened in the Church. The abuse of children and vulnerable young people, particularly by priests and religious, has had a devastating impact on the lives of many, for which the Church in Ireland has expressed its deepest sorrow and regret. Pope Benedict, writing to the Catholics of Ireland, and speaking of his grief to the victims of abuse and their families, has said: 'In solidarity with all of you, I am praying earnestly that, by God's grace, the wounds afflicting so many individuals and families may be healed and that the Church in Ireland may experience a season of rebirth and spiritual renewal'.[20] With safeguarding policies, procedures and personnel now in place, we hope to reassure young people and their families, that children, who occupy a central place in the teaching of Jesus Christ, 'will find an active and warm welcome in the Church carried on according to the highest standards of best practice in safeguarding children'.[21]

The Christian community is in continuous dialogue with the world and with the circumstances and needs of people according to the times in which they live. Christians today, seeking always to remain faithful to Jesus Christ, must grapple with philosophies and beliefs, with political and economic strategies, with achievements and failures, which seek to hold sway over us and manipulate us and our future. The Christian tradition, constant but ever new, has spoken with an Irish voice to people in the past. It can do so again, and with something new and vital to say to the younger generations too.

[20] Benedict XVI, *Pastoral Letter of the Holy Father Pope Benedict XVI to the Catholics of Ireland*, 19 March 2010, 13.
[21] The National Board for Safeguarding Children in the Catholic Church, *Safeguarding Children: Standards and Guidance Document for the Catholic Church in Ireland* (2008), p. 8.

INVESTIGATE AND REFLECT:
ELEMENTS OF IRISH CHRISTIAN SPIRITUALITY

- A spirituality in harmony with nature, accepting it, respecting it, in love with it, even in its more violent expressions.
- A natural religious spirit in the people.
- A faith firmly rooted in the Sacred Scriptures, known and loved by the people.
- A great love for and devotion to the person of Jesus Christ, especially in his passion and at the Mass.
- A corresponding love for Mary, the angels and the saints – above all, for Mary as Mother of God.
- The quality of *muintearas* – the community, communion, friendship, relationship, kindness, connection with the Lord and his household in this present world and in the world to come.
- The combining of a strong notion of 'localness' with a deep sense of communion with the Body of Christ at a universal level.
- Hospitality as a living expression of the Gospel – the guest is none other than the living Christ.
- Penance and self-denial as means of entering into the death of Jesus Christ.
- The phenomenon of pilgrimage.
- A close bond of unity with the dead, giving a sense of fidelity to and continuity with the past.

Adapted from J.J. Ó Ríordán, *Irish Catholic Spirituality: Celtic and Roman* (Dublin: Columba, 1998), p. 11.

New Culture, New Challenges

Fulfilling Our Potential

12. Today, with an evolving peace process and a greater realisation of their individual potential by many people, Ireland is full of promise. At the same time, Irish society remains vulnerable to global economic instability and local financial mismanagement. In Northern Ireland and in the Republic, there are renewed efforts to reconcile and cherish people's diverse identities, to establish a climate of openness and to encourage people to play a full part in creating a just and equitable society. As the Catholic Bishops of Northern Ireland have stated: 'Peace and reconciliation, to a large extent, depend on respect for cultural diversity in a climate that promotes openness and communication. This respect must be carefully cultivated and will only develop where those who want peace and reconciliation work together in harmony and with purpose.'[22] Forgiveness and

[22] Catholic Bishops of Northern Ireland, *Building Peace: Shaping the Future* (Armagh: Catholic Bishops of Northern Ireland, 2001), p. 11. See also John Paul II, Messages for World Days of Peace, 1979-2005. Available from *www.vatican.va*

understanding are essential if we are to begin again and establish renewed trust:

'I get down on my knees and do what must be done And kiss Achilles' hand, the killer of my son.'[23]

The new confidence that we gained in the past two decades made Ireland an attractive destination for those in emerging countries who were looking for work and a way of life they could not find at home. Their contribution in recent years has supported our development, adding new colour and life to Irish society. Yet many of the social issues that Ireland has in the past struggled to tackle, remain current: dignified work and fair pay, employment and emigration, improved care for the sick and the elderly, better literacy and numeracy skills, appropriate housing and nutrition.

Overcoming Social Exclusion

13. Irish society is becoming more aware of problematic social situations that need to be given serious and urgent attention. The danger of a rural decline and a worsening regional imbalance between east and west is ever more real. In urban centres, the development of ghettos, where poverty, unemployment, crime and imprisonment are part of everyday reality, requires earnest attention. Child poverty, child care and the circumstances of those who have work but remain poor, are recognised as issues that need to be resolved.[24] Fraud of one kind or another, violence, racism, 'gangland warfare' and murder have become an increasing and troublesome part of Irish life. The culture of alcohol abuse, drug-taking and drug-pushing calls for immediate and ongoing action.[25] Suicide, particularly among young men, is now a worrying feature of Irish society. Murder-suicide within families has also become a shocking phenomenon.

Social exclusion, inequality and injustice are still evident in our society. The Christian community, in good times and in difficult moments, reflecting on the social teaching of the Church and seeking to put it into action, is always looking for innovative ways to help achieve what is good and true and just.[26] The gifts present and available among the members of the Church, and in society generally, are immeasurable. Creative ways of unlocking and employing these rich resources are continually being sought. At the same time, there is a need to be vigilant that evil, sin and human

[23] M. Longley, 'Ceasefire', *Collected Poems* (London: Jonathan Cape, 2006).
[24] See Justice Commission, Conference of Religious in Ireland (Cori). Available at *www.cori.ie/justice*; Vincentian Partnership for Social Justice, *One Long Struggle: A Study of Low Income Families* (2000).
[25] See Irish Commission for Justice and Social Affairs, *Violence in Ireland: Towards an Ecology of Peace* (Dublin: Veritas, 2008).
[26] See *CSDC*; P. Corkery, *Commentary on the Compendium of the Social Doctrine of the Church* (Dublin: Veritas, 2007). See also, Council for Justice and Peace, available from *www.catholicbishops.ie*

weakness do not overpower the potential for doing good, as we strive to contribute to a society built on transparency, honesty, responsibility and justice. The Christian community continues to believe in the power of Jesus Christ, not only to open the human heart to the things that really matter, but also to set the human spirit free.

Ecology, the Sciences and Technology
14. The doing of justice and the pursuit of peace are inconceivable without being grounded in respect for the integrity of creation. We can only understand human reality within the network of relationships in which human life is lived. Ecology, reflection on the relationship between human beings and the earth, is preoccupied today with the consequences of reckless disregard for the natural environment. We are, daily, more aware of the immensity and beauty, yet fragility and vulnerability, of the universe in which we are rooted, and of the power and gracious generosity of God:

> From the greatness and beauty of created things
> comes a corresponding perception of their Creator.
> (Wisdom 13:5)

Many, however, are alarmed to see the uses to which some extraordinary scientific and technological discoveries are being put, with wholly negative effects on the natural world. The pollution of land, water and air, the destruction of the rainforests, the erosion of the soil and the loss of fresh sources of water, as well as the spread of deserts, are causes of great concern worldwide. Species extinction, climate change and the depletion of natural resources[27] are causing us to stop and think. The horrifying consequences for the biosphere of the use of weapons of mass destruction, whether nuclear, biological or chemical, can hardly be imagined. As the relatedness and interconnectedness of all things becomes clearer to us, we contemplate the threat of a great collapse.

The Christian tradition understands all creation as the gift of God. God's ongoing creative activity includes not only the work of origins but that of salvation and consummation as well. The potential of human nature has been fully realised in the mystery of Jesus Christ, the Son of God and Son of Mary, risen from the dead. He is the cosmic Christ, Lord over all creation (Philippians 2:5-11). In him all things have been created anew (1 Corinthians 15:45ff). Humankind, our world, all creation, is in need of

[27] See Irish Catholic Bishops' Conference, *The Cry of the Earth: A Pastoral Reflection on Climate Change* (Dublin: Veritas, 2009).

healing and of wholeness, the salvation in Christ to which he calls all things. Christian spirituality does not seek escape from this world to God. It is rather a way in and with the world to God.[28]

15. The relationship between the sciences and religion is one of the great challenges of our time. Contemporary dialogue is beginning to show signs of hope that an imaginative conversation between scientific disciplines and religion is possible. Scientists and theologians meet regularly to discuss mutual interest in, for example, cosmology, evolution and genetics. There are indications that scientists have become more sensitive to religious questions and that those who are religiously committed are actively engaging with the implications of modern

science and technology. Theology and science can be understood as offering compatible rather than contradictory explanations. One discipline does not exclude another. The stories of creation in the Book of Genesis, for example, serve a different function from standard scientific theories. They are not meant to offer a scientific explanation but reveal God as Creator and source of human life.

Both science and religion have to battle continually against 'category mistakes' and the move toward fundamentalism, a tendency to overplay one's hand and claim more for one's discipline than is warranted. Those, for example, who indulge in 'scientism' claim that science is competent to explain everything, providing us with the only reliable answers. Religious fundamentalism is equally certain, rejecting the findings of science and reason where they clash with a literal interpretation of the Bible or other religious texts. Today, religion and the sciences can best be understood as interacting and complementary disciplines, neither in unrelenting conflict nor totally independent of one another.[29]

Understanding Culture

16. Culture is one of those concepts that can be difficult to grasp, even though we speak about it constantly. This in a sense reflects what has been called the 'postmodern world' in which we live today, adrift without any one overriding narrative or story to define who we are and what we believe in. Contemporary usage of the term 'culture' generally falls into one of two understandings: Culture with a capital C, meaning the conscious frontiers of creative freedom and exploration, and culture with a small c,

[28] See Z. Hayes, 'Creation', M. Downey, *The New Dictionary of Catholic Spirituality* (Collegeville, Minnesota: The Liturgical Press, 1993), p. 241.
[29] See F. McCarthy and J. McCann, *Religion and Science* (Dublin: Veritas, 2003), pp. 31-42.

culture-as-ordinary, indicating a focus on our ways of life as embodying our priorities, values, meanings, and so on.[30] Ireland in recent years has made great contributions to Culture in such fields as literature, film and music. But it is the second meaning that we are interested in here, as we consider how we interpret our everyday lives within a variety of influences and carriers of meaning. It is on this level that the lived culture is a hidden persuader, impacting as much on our self-images and assumptions as on our explicit ideas.

In the past, in Ireland as elsewhere, it was generally understood that there was a specific culture within which people lived in a particular country or place, permeated by a core set of meanings and values that helped to define it. Today, we are influenced by many external sources, often with contradictory value systems, expressing changing and conflicting interpretations of life.

Coping with change is never easy, and all societies find it especially difficult to integrate rapid change. When everything seems to be changing at the one time, it can appear almost impossible to find our way and steer a steady course through complexity and confusion. Yet life today, in our postmodern world, seems to be defined by change. In such a society, security is easily lost, and loneliness can go hand in hand with a frenetic lifestyle.[31] The culture of our time can, at its best, provide us with a set of resources for constructing an understanding of life lived in an unsettled world, shaping us as we build strategies for reflection and action that address the demands of the present. The Church, today, must explore its tradition and its cultural contribution, seeking to build on the gift we have been given, as we shall see in Chapter 3. We must learn to dialogue with an ever-changing human reality, in order to incarnate in new ways the meaning of life as we understand it in Jesus Christ. First, we must analyse the culture in which we live, so that we can better enter into conversation with it.

PAUSE FOR THOUGHT: COMPLEX CULTURAL VOICES

In a situation of change, each person may find themselves with different cultural voices within them. Ireland, for instance, lived with a largely pre-modern culture as far as the Sixties, before making a rapid move into modernity and, after an unusually short stay in that framework, seems to have moved into the complex fragmentation of post-modernity. Such a passage from pre-modern omnipresence of anchors to modern autonomy, and then to post-modern diversity, has created a very different context for all the major decisions of life.

M.P. Gallagher, 'Religious Readings of Our Culture', *Studies* 94(2005), p. 144.

[30] See M.P. Gallagher, 'Religious Readings of Our Culture', *Studies* 94(2005), p. 141.
[31] See M.P. Gallagher, 'Christian Identity in a Postmodern Age: A Perspective from Lonergan', D. Marmion (ed.), *Christian Identity in a Postmodern Age: Celebrating the Legacies of Karl Rahner and Bernard Lonergan* (Dublin: Veritas, 2005), pp. 145-61.

Diversity: Welcoming Newcomers

17. Within the Irish cultural landscape, one of the clearest examples of change is the emergence in recent years of an influx of migrants of one kind or another; newcomers who, with the greater movement of peoples, have arrived in Ireland for work, seeking economic stability, and sometimes escaping persecution and oppression. Very quickly, Ireland has become a multicultural society, with significant intercultural issues to be addressed. Ethnic, cultural and religious diversity, although always present in Ireland, has, as a result of the European and global community to which we now firmly belong, become a reality as never before.

POETIC REFLECTION: WELCOMING THE STRANGER

God in Heaven!
The door of my house will always be
Open to every traveller.
May Christ open His to me!

B. Kennelly, 'Hospitality in Ireland',
A Drinking Cup: Poems from the Irish (Dublin: Allen Figgis 1970), p. 19.

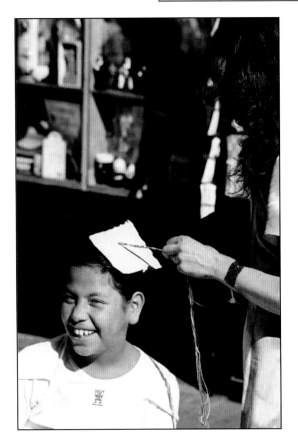

In local communities, our intercultural future is recognised. Processes to ease integration are being put in place. Tensions can arise, particularly where ghettos are allowed to be established. Talking about multiculturalism is not enough. A concerted effort needs to be made to ensure that newcomers, and the rest of Irish society, are not exploited for financial or other gain. Looking to the experience of other countries, open and transparent discussion, the development of adequate policy, and the implementation of that policy, are important elements in building up confidence and security for all in this new situation.

For the Church, newcomers are a gift and a challenge. The variety of people coming to live and work in Ireland, some from a Catholic tradition, provides us with new resources and new experiences. In turn, these people also require resources, which we may struggle to provide. The Catholic Church welcomes them and offers them not just hospitality but love. It offers them a home, a community of faith, within which to belong:

Today's situation thus requires of pastoral workers and host communities, in other words, of the Church, loving attention to 'people on the move' and to their need for solidarity and fellowship... This calls for well-designed forms of welcome and pastoral activity, that is, continuous, thorough and adapted as closely as possible to the actual situation and specific needs of the migrants.[32]

It is possible that the Irish Catholic tradition, humble and aware, enriched by its newcomers, can reach out once more in confidence, not just to those who have come to live in Ireland but, through them, and through Irish people residing abroad, to a world searching for something more than material riches.

PERSONAL REFLECTION: ALL THAT GOD IS DOING IN OUR MIDST

The Church at this moment may be likened to the disciples on the road to Emmaus (Luke 24:13ff). Like them, we continue to speak with one another about all that God has been doing in our midst. Like them, we are on the road, in via, amidst a journey, and, like them, many of our expectations have been unsettled. As our tightly held expectations are disturbed, the gift of the Lord's presence, the power of the Spirit, is ours to receive, and the Lord is in our midst, no less than on the road to Emmaus – as companion on the journey, as teacher, as guide and, especially, in the Blessing and Breaking of the Eucharistic Bread.

Cardinal R. Mahoney and the Priests of the Archdiocese of Los Angeles, *As I Have Done for You: A Pastoral Letter on Ministry* (Chicago: Liturgy Training Publications, 2000), p. 76.

Globalisation and Communications Technology

18. The world has become, in some senses at least, a global community. Economic crises in one part of the world can, as we know, become global phenomena. There are great possibilities, however, of growing closer to people all over the world. We can learn from one another and from our rich cultural inheritances. The globalisation of our world can strengthen solidarity among peoples and support understanding among nations. Yet conflict remains and wars continue unabated. Local difficulties, built up sometimes over centuries, cannot be overcome without genuine and generous efforts on the part of all. In Northern Ireland, especially, we know this well. There is much to be done to achieve justice, reconciliation and peace in our world.

The term 'globalisation' has, unfortunately, come to describe a particular consumerist and materialist mentality, sweeping across the world in recent years, often undermining the values and way of life that people have struggled, over centuries, to establish in their societies. Economic realities are given precedence over people and

[32] *EMCC* 11.

their stories. However, as Pope John Paul II explained, 'There are collective and qualitative needs which cannot be satisfied by market mechanisms. There are important human needs which escape its logic. There are goods which by their very nature cannot and must not be bought or sold.'[33]

The unprecedented expansion in information and communications technologies in recent years has contributed enormously to the global atmosphere being created in our world. The development of such sophisticated technology has, no doubt, revolutionised life in Ireland. It has also had a considerable impact on Ireland's place in the world. The benefits derived from technological advances should be welcomed, but technology must not be seen as an end in itself. Instead, modern forms of information and communications technology should be recognised as instruments to improve the quality of human life and freedom. New technological advances should be judged in accordance with their benefits for the human person and for the building up of human society. A concerted effort worldwide to promote justice, especially for the most poor, is essential. The Church recognises its responsibility in this regard:

> The Christian message does not inhibit men and women from building up the world, or make them uninterested in the welfare of their fellow human beings: on the contrary it obliges them more fully to do these very things.[34]

19. Today, various forms of communication, from television and print media to the Internet, websites and chat-rooms, carry messages to the general public or to specialised participants. Any form of communication not only presents a message, but chooses how to amplify it, what perspective to speak from and what angles to highlight. Sometimes it distorts the message, either knowingly or unknowingly. Simply to recognise the vast reality of multimedia communication today is to alert people to the need to maintain a critical view of what is being offered. All of us need to be aware of

[33] CA 40.
[34] GS 34.

and attend to the bias that can be ingrained in messages transmitted by various forms of media communication, dependent often on commercial interests, and the power both these media and their messages have to reach into our lives, even at times unnoticed. As the *Compendium of the Social Doctrine of the Church* puts it:

> The essential question is whether the current information system is contributing to the betterment of the human person; that is, does it make people more spiritually mature, more aware of the dignity of their humanity, more responsible or more open to others, in particular to the neediest and the weakest. A further aspect of great importance is the requisite that new technologies respect legitimate cultural differences.[35]

GROUP DISCUSSION: THE INFLUENCE OF GLOBALISED ELECTRONIC COMMUNICATIONS

Radio and television play a historical unprecedented role in dominating the symbolic environment of modern life from early childhood. They begin to socialise children, almost at the same time as family influences are activated, taking over much of that basic master narrative role once occupied by other cultural institutions and sources of identity – religion, class, nationality, family, workplace, locality – that have declined in influence in proportion to the growing power of the media and the leisure industry – and the consumer lifestyles in which both are bound up in this period of late capitalism. Powerful flows of messages and images in both fiction and non-fiction genres now tell most of the stories, most of the time. Through these dense networks of narrative, Irish people create their own sense of identity, their awareness of unity and feelings of difference, and create their place in an increasingly globalised world. Through the media-driven streams of discourse surrounding us daily, rooted in our lifeworld, we shape our conceptions of reality and spin out the collective 'common sense' which underpins everyday life. This forms the basic tissue of the prevailing sense of communality. This may be the electronic media's most powerful and important effect.
F. Corcoran, *RTÉ and the Globalisation of Irish Television* (Bristol: Intellect Books, 2004), p. 17.

---

20. The traditional communications media (radio, television, newspapers and magazines), in Ireland as elsewhere, often seem slow to be creative, in a positive sense, when it comes to covering religion and religious issues. Granted, it can be challenging to know how best to report on the personal, community and service dimensions of religion, particularly if there is a lack of knowledge of religion, or an attempt to portray it using a 'political grid' or a reliance entirely on a conflict model.[36] The dominant media image

[35] *CSDC* 415.
[36] See B. O'Brien, 'Irish Media and Irish Religion', *Studies* 94(2005), pp. 123-30.

of the Church, out of step in a forward-moving, virtual and global world, is often very different from the significant experience of community, meaning and inspiration Catholic faith provides for many in their lives. Today, Church Communications Officers, nationally and in dioceses, can make a significant contribution by providing support to media personnel. Those who have reflected deeply on the significance of religious faith in their own lives can often speak eloquently too, opening up new ways of thinking for others. There is great opportunity here for all to step out into the deep, particularly in light of the variety of possibilities associated with contemporary forms of multimedia communication. A mutually respectful dialogue should be looked forward to. This does not preclude criticism of the Church or of religion, but asks that any critique would be based on genuine knowledge and follow fair procedures.

At the time of the death of Pope John Paul II, many people experienced an approach to communications, both from the media and from members of the Church, that indicated wonderful new possibilities. It was a moment when people from all over the world, realising how touched they were by the loss of such a fatherly figure, were helped by the media to increase their knowledge and understanding of the Church, of its ministry and message, and of the dedicated commitment John Paul had shown even in times of physical frailty. It became a moment of personal involvement for many people, young as well as not so young, drawn together to keep watch, as it were, at the bedside of a close family member. A new way of being a global family was experienced, of a worldwide community of care and compassion, of being united not in a sudden tragic loss, but in a solemn yet uplifting celebration of life lived to the fullest.

Church and State in Dialogue
21. It is argued by some that, among the changes taking place in Irish society, religion is on the retreat. Ireland is certainly grappling with secularisation, the definition of society in a purely 'this-worldly' manner, having expressed itself as a deeply religious society for so long. A plurality of cultures and of religious affiliations is part of most societies worldwide today. Relations between the political sphere and the religious sphere are, therefore, often hotly contested. Such relations must be built on true freedom giving rise to what Pope Benedict has termed 'a serene and positive dialogue', in which the role of religion as well as the benefits of the modern secular State are acknowledged and respected:

> It is fundamental, on the one hand, to insist on the distinction between the political realm and that of religion in order to preserve both the religious freedom of citizens and the responsibility of the State towards them; and, on the other hand, to become more aware of the irreplaceable role

of religion for the formation of consciences and the contribution which it can bring to – among other things – the creation of a basic ethical consensus in society.[37]

Secularism, the most radical form of secularisation, an attempt to exclude God and religion from culture and from public life, represents a radical and profound break not only with Christianity but, generally, with the religious and moral traditions of humanity. It can also reduce our perception of the human person, presenting humanity simply as a product of nature and, as such, not really free at all. Pluralism, on the other hand, at its best upholds positive respect for and interest in the quest for truth engaged in by individuals and faith communities and other groups in society. There can be the danger, however, that a pluralist approach will be pushed toward acceptance of a relativist ethos, refusing to make any judgement between opinions as to what is true and just. This, too, diminishes our understanding of the human person and the search for meaning and truth.

The Christian community, for its part, must engage in real dialogue with society, never becoming closed in on itself.[38] The Church is open to all that is good and true in society and welcomes the authentic values promoted by the culture of our time, such as scientific knowledge, technological advancement, human rights, religious freedom and democracy. It must take every opportunity to contribute to the cultural and moral growth of society, entering into ongoing and mutually beneficial conversation with the State:

> This is the task that is before us, a fascinating adventure that is worth our effort, to give a new thrust to the culture of our time and to restore the Christian faith to full citizenship in it.[39]

STARTING POINT: THE WORLD OF REASON AND
THE WORLD OF FAITH

I would suggest that the world of reason and the world of faith – the world of secular rationality and the world of religious belief – need one another and should not be afraid to enter into a profound and ongoing dialogue, for the good of our civilisation.

Religion, in other words, is not a problem for legislators to solve, but a vital contributor to the national conversation.

Benedict XVI, Meeting with the Representatives of British Society,
Including the Diplomatic Corps, Politicians, Academics and Business
Leaders: Address of His Holiness Benedict XVI,
Westminster Hall, 17 September 2010.

---

[37] Benedict XVI, *Welcome Ceremony and Meeting with Authorities of State: Address of His Holiness Benedict XVI,* Elysée Palace, Paris, 12 September 2008.
[38] See GS 11, 44.
[39] Benedict XVI, *Fourth National Ecclesial Convention: Address of His Holiness Benedict XVI,* Verona, 19 October 2006.

PHILOSOPHICAL DISCUSSION: PLURALISM VERSUS SECULARISM

To count as pluralist, religious believers must not, in public stances on issues directly affecting citizens not belonging to that group, rely solely on religious-based reasons. But, by the same token, secular humanists may not, if they are to count as properly pluralist, insist on confining public reasoning on policy issues to non-religious forms of discourse. Despite what some people appear to think, pluralism can't be identified with secularism. Today, there are many people in Ireland who appear to believe that pluralism means excluding religion from the public domain, so that it is all right to be influenced (as a citizen or legislator) by Mill, or Marx, de Valera or Mrs Thatcher, but not by Jesus or Mohammed. Often, the impression given by the media is that a pluralist society is by definition a secular society, so that it is wrong that the ethos of any religion should, in any way whatsoever, be reflected in the civil law.

S. Murphy, 'Cultures, Pluralism, and Religious Faith', *Studies* 92(2003)365, p. 36.

22. Contemporary researchers and commentators are beginning to find that religion does not disappear when its power is denied. Instead, it emerges in fresh expressions finding new ways to

highlight the deepest search of humankind for what is true and beautiful and good. Often when traditional forms of religion are denied, a different form of interest in the spiritual emerges.[40] Many now recognise that renewed interest in a variety of spiritualities, alternative religions, sects, cults and similar movements may indicate discontent not only with previous understandings of religious affiliation, but also with the meaning provided by secular culture. In Ireland, too, the recent rise in New Age spiritualities may represent a protest against the drift toward growing individualism, fragmentation and consumer orientation within contemporary Irish culture. The Church and society must learn to engage with the questions and searchings that people express through a range of spiritual activities. Many sociologists of religion point out that the abandonment of

[40] See J. Finnegan, 'Postmodern Spiritualities and the Return to Magic: A Theological Reflection', *Milltown Studies* 39(1997)1, pp. 5-26.

organised church religion when it occurs does not generally signify a move to irreligion, but rather to informal privatised religion, and its transfer from the public realm to the realm of private feeling and belief. Evangelisation must always, therefore, have a double focus: the evangelisation of the individual, and the evangelisation of culture. Such evangelisation of culture requires of us to find room once more for religion, appropriately, in the public square.

> POETIC REFLECTION:
> LOOKING AT LIFE ANEW
>
> Green, blue, yellow and red –
> God is down in the swamps and marshes
> Sensational as April...
> A humble scene in a backward place
> Where no one important ever looked
> The raving flowers looked up in the face
> Of the One and the Endless, the Mind that has baulked
> The profoundest of mortals. A primrose, a violet,
> A violent wild iris...
> Prepared to inform the local farmers
> That beautiful, beautiful, beautiful God
> Was breathing his love by a cut-away bog.
> P. Kavanagh, 'The One', *Collected Poems* (Allen Lane, 2004).

Witnessing to the Power of the Gospel

23. The challenge set out for the Church in Ireland today is in some ways the same as it has always been: How do we proclaim the love of God that we have experienced in Jesus Christ and in one another? How do we witness to the transformation that the love of Jesus Christ effects in us by the way we live? Today, however, we have the added responsibility of finding ways to proclaim and witness to Christ, and live with him, in a world that has changed so rapidly and continues to change, a world that seems out of control and often appears hesitant about the spiritual, moral and religious dimensions of human life.

This first chapter provides a starting point, presenting an initial socio-cultural analysis which highlights the changing context in Ireland, within which we seek to make the Gospel real and alive to one another today. In so doing, it suggests the need, in a time

when change can be expected to accelerate at pace, for an ongoing analysis of social and cultural developments, such that each particular context is understood as fully as possible. Such analysis will allow the reality within which people lead their lives to be acknowledged and discovered. It will encourage those who are committed to the Gospel to present it in such a way that people who find themselves attracted by Jesus Christ may more easily grasp its power. If a sustained dialogue between faith and culture is to take place in Ireland, the importance of socio-cultural analysis must be understood by all interested parties and embraced wholeheartedly.

24. Openness to dialogue with all, based on the ideals of human dignity, human good, human rights, justice and respect, is an important starting point for any discussion. Into this conversation, the Christian will always bring the message of

Jesus Christ, in whom God and humankind are united. Building on good work already taking place, and on the ongoing efforts of so many who quietly confirm others in their faith, we as Church must listen and reflect together on the experience of life as we live it. The visit of Pope John Paul II to Ireland in 1979 saw an extraordinary outpouring of Christian faith, owned, celebrated  and encouraged. Today, affirmation for one another and support, within the Christian community, is particularly necessary. Church gatherings of one kind or another, diocesan assemblies, youth events, pilgrimages to Knock, Lough Derg and Croagh Patrick, and ecumenical meetings, at Glenstal and Greenhills for example, can be very supportive. The real encouragement of lived witness lifts us up and helps us to see together new possibilities born out of relationship with Christ.

PAUSE FOR THOUGHT: COMPLEX CULTURAL VOICES

Nothing is more encouraging, more comforting, than to hear the message of God's unending love. The Christian message, after all, begins and ends with the command to live and preach love.

More than anything else, people seek and need affirmation and confirmation in their lives. Only rare persons are so certain of themselves that they live without affirmation. There is simple affirmation: 'The work you do is good and helpful.' 'You are a great parent.' 'I understand it is difficult, but keep going.' 'What a lovely smile you have.' 'You inspire me in ways you will never know.' 'You are making a difference. Don't stop.' The list goes on. Each of these smaller affirmations is part of a web of larger affirmations that is carved out of the belief that life has meaning, that each one of us is loved and forgiven. Sharing this gospel message is the deeper and more fundamental act of encouragement.

T. C. Fox, 'Evangelization from the Inside Out:
Bringing Faith to the Young', *Human Development* 26/4(2005), p. 25.

A renewed understanding of community in the Church, and in the world, is central to our search for meaning, embracing, supporting and encouraging the individual as she or he comes to belong to a vision of love in Christ. New language must be found, too, in order to speak clearly and be heard easily by the people of our time, especially the young. Our celebration of the liturgy and the sacraments, as well as our service of our neighbour, especially the poor, must encourage belonging and participation. We will need to find new ways to help people to create the space in which to reflect and pray. We need to come to realise, too, that our faith is a lifelong project, supporting us at moments of transition and challenge, as well as in the everyday life we lead, building up the community of communities that is the Church.

**SMALL GROUP DISCUSSION:
A COMMUNITY OF COMMUNITIES**

Faith in today's secularised world will always need community to sustain it. Community will not just be one uniform institution, but a community of communities, with each community experiencing and sharing its particular path towards God. Christian communities of faith will be places where the mystery of God's love will be celebrated, as revealed in the person of Jesus Christ, who gave himself up that we could be free, that we could be the persons God created us to be, freed from the bonds of egoism and enabled to mirror God's love in our relations to other.

The organised structure of such faith communities will be different to what we know in Ireland today. But I am sure that they will be strong communities, even though they will be formed by and led by weak human beings. It is the gratuitous love of God which changes us and charges us for mission, not ourselves, not the institution. When we realise that, then we can rise above our own limited personal spirituality, rise above the conformity of institution, then we can be fully free to take the leap of faith, to risk our lives knowing that God's love will sustain us.

D. Martin, 'Imagining the Future for Organised Religion', H. Bohan and G. Kennedy (eds), *Imagining the Future: Our Society in the New Millennium* (Dublin: Veritas, 2005) p. 76.

The 50th International Eucharistic Congress in Dublin in 2012 may be seen as a unique catechetical opportunity to uncover again, give thanks for and celebrate the deepest meaning of Christian community focused on the risen presence of Christ at the heart of our lives and of our outreach in love to all.

PRAYERFUL REFLECTION:
CONFIDENCE TO LET GOD'S LOVE BE KNOWN

Lord Jesus Christ, we live in a world of great beauty and also of great confusion. We thank you for your presence with us in all of that. Help us, your Church, to seek answers to the many questions that trouble people today and to be faithful to your word in our searching. Help us also to have a real tenderness and compassion for each person as she or he is, so that no one will ever feel excluded from your presence and your love by the way we live or the way we teach and preach. Help us to know that the greatest gift we have for our world is you, our loving Lord and Saviour, and give us the confidence to let your love and your healing power be known to everyone.

J. Doherty, *Do You Want to Be Well Again?*
Thoughts and Prayers at Times of Sickness (Dublin: Veritas, 2005), p. 80.

SECTION B
UNDERSTANDING
THE GOOD NEWS

CHAPTER 2

Evangelisation, Catechesis and Religious Education

25. The Church exists in order to *evangelise*;[1] that is, to proclaim in words and action the Gospel, the Good News revealed to us in Jesus Christ, through the grace of the Holy Spirit, that we are loved by God for all eternity. Everything else, for the Christian, rests on this. When the fact of being loved by God is experienced, understood and cherished by the person, efforts to explain the teaching of Jesus Christ and the challenge he presents us with makes sense in a whole new way. The Church's ongoing endeavour to know and love Christ, following as disciples in his footsteps toward the full realisation of God's Kingdom, becomes a way of life that is fully and personally embraced.

The Revelation of God's Love

26. Religion, for Christians, is not a 'blind search for God'.[2] It is a relationship, a response of faith to God revealed to us in human history and in our times too.[3] God reaches out to us in all our ups and downs, calling each person into ongoing and deepening conversion. We are invited to know and love God and to allow God's grace to shape our lives.[4] We, too, can grow into a relationship of intimate love with God.[5]

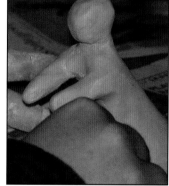

SCRIPTURAL REFLECTION:
YOU ARE PRECIOUS IN MY EYES

Thus says the Lord: 'I have called you by name, you are mine. When you pass through the waters I will be with you; and through the rivers, they shall not overwhelm you; when you walk through fire you shall not be burned, and the flame will not consume you. For I am the Lord your God, the Holy One of Israel, your Saviour... you are precious in my eyes and honoured, and I love you. Fear not, for I am with you.'

(Isaiah 43:1-5)

---

[1] See *EN* 14.
[2] See Acts 17:27.
[3] See *DV* 2-4; *TMA* 6.
[4] See *CCC* 238-267.
[5] See *GDC* 3.

God's plan of love is accomplished not only by self-revelation but also by revealing what is possible for humankind – our true vocation and dignity. God offers salvation to all. God calls us to become, together, one family, working in common purpose, in communion with God and with one another.

Scripture tells us that God uses human events and words to reveal His loving and saving plan down through the ages, drawing us into understanding 'by means of the events of salvation history and the inspired words that accompany them'.[6]

God's love, experienced in liberation from slavery, for instance, and continuously made known to the Chosen People of Israel by the prophets, has been fully revealed in Jesus Christ, the eternal Word of God come among us. By both his 'deeds and words'[7] Jesus Christ reveals to us the inner life of God lived in Trinitarian love: one God, three persons, Father, Son and Holy Spirit. The gift of Jesus, first given to Mary, is the greatest expression of God's love for humankind: 'For God so loved the world that he gave his only Son, so that everyone who believes in him may not perish but may have eternal life' (John 3:16). Jesus also discloses the fullness to which every human person is called. In Jesus, God speaks to us and we speak intimately and personally to God, newly revealed to us by Jesus, as 'Abba', our loving Father: 'Just as God in Christ speaks to humanity of himself, so in Christ all humanity and the whole of creation speaks of itself to God – indeed, it gives itself to God.'[8]

SALVATION IN JESUS CHRIST

Evangelisation will also always contain – as the foundation, centre and, at the same time, summit of its dynamism – a clear proclamation that, in Jesus Christ, the Son of God made man, who died and rose from the dead, salvation is offered to all men, as a gift of God's grace and mercy. And not an immanent salvation, meeting material or even spiritual needs, restricted to the framework of temporal existence and completely identified with temporal desires, hopes, affairs and struggles, but a salvation which exceeds all these limits in order to reach fulfilment in a communion with the one and only divine Absolute: a transcendent and eschatological salvation, which indeed has its beginning in this life but which is fulfilled in eternity.

EN 27.

---

27. To ensure that the Gospel, the Good News of humanity's salvation in Jesus Christ, is preached to the whole world until the end of time, Jesus directed his disciples to go out to 'all the nations' (Matthew 28:19-20). He founded the Church on the apostles, sending the Holy Spirit from the Father to be its inspiration and guide.[9] Nurtured and led by the same Spirit, God continually at work in the world, the Church interprets the Word

---

[6] *GDC* 38.
[7] *DV* 2, 4, 17.
[8] *TMA* 6.
[9] See *LG* 2.

of God in the particular context of each new generation. Together, we seek to transform human life in the power of God's love made known to us abundantly in Jesus Christ. We seek to confirm our capacity for love, also revealed to us fully in Jesus.

The community of Christ is deeply conscious of the presence of Mary in its midst and at its centre. The whole of her life, graced from beginning to end, is recognised as a faith-filled response to God's call, saying 'yes'[10] and giving 'Life to the world'.[11] The Mother of Jesus, the Mother of the Son of God, having accepted a new mission from Jesus on the Cross,[12] is embraced, too, as our mother, the mother of all believers, the Mother of the Church. She is fully human, 'a women of strength, who experienced poverty, suffering, flight and exile',[13] the first disciple, sharing with all other human persons the need for salvation in Christ. Mary continues to inspire the women and men of today, becoming herself a symbol of hope for the pilgrim Church's life on earth.[14] Woman of faith, woman of hope, woman of love, completely at home with the Word of God; we have experienced the gift of her goodness, the unfailing love that she pours out from the depths of her heart.[15] With Mary, who receives the Word, embodies the Word and lives the Word, the Church also receives, embodies and witnesses to the Word of God, day by day.

It is through the sacraments of initiation, Baptism, Confirmation and the Eucharist, that we begin and sustain a lifelong journey in love with Christ and with the community of his love. As members of the Church, we recognise our ongoing need for conversion and reconciliation on this journey. We become witnesses, one to the other, of God's saving presence in our lives. For Christians, all of human life, its joy and hope, its grief and anguish,[16] is lit by the expectation we carry in our hearts as heirs of all that belongs to the Son.[17] Faith heightens the happiness and sorrow, the gifts and losses we experience in life. It never seeks comfort in ignoring or turning away from all that life teaches. Christian faith engages with life, as it is lived day by day, in communion with Jesus Christ, 'the light of humanity',[18] with his Blessed Mother and with all those 'who shine with his light and so guide us along our way'.[19]

SMALL GROUP DISCUSSION:
GROWING INTO THE GOSPEL

The Gospel is conserved whole and entire in the Church: the disciples of Christ contemplate it and meditate upon it unceasingly; they live it out in their lives; they proclaim it in their missionary activity. As the Church lives the Gospel she is continually made fruitful by the Holy Spirit. The Spirit causes her to grow constantly in her understanding of the Gospel, prompts her and sustains the task of proclaiming the Gospel in every corner of the world.   *GDC* 43.

[10] See Luke 1:38.
[11] *LG* 53.
[12] See *SS* 50.
[13] Paul VI, *Marialis Cultus* 37.
[14] See *RMat* 25-37.
[15] See *DCE* 41-42
[16] See *GS* 1.
[17] See Gal 4:7.
[18] *LG* 1.
[19] *SS* 49.

Education in the Love of God

28. Developed over the centuries, the Catholic understanding of education shares with many other education philosophies the idea that education is rooted in the development of the human person

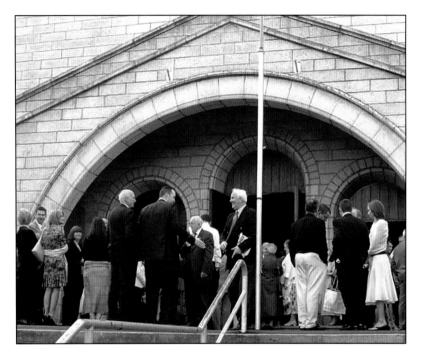

from within. It is directed toward the growth of the whole person[20] in the context of relationship with God in Jesus Christ. A Catholic vision seeks to sustain and enhance people's capacity to discover the meaning of life in the context of God's love. Such an anthropology, such an understanding of the meaning of being human, confirms the person's dignity as an individual, while supporting them in their relationships with God and with others. It encourages us, therefore, to contribute to our community's growth and development, rather than be focused simply on self. Anthropologies based on autonomy, independence and self-sufficiency are prominent today and, as such, often see no need for religion. These understandings of human reality are always in need of being balanced by anthropologies founded on relationality, interdependence and transcendence. When our understanding of humanity is based in relationship with God and with one another, we will be open to hear the liberating, saving and loving Word of God. 'The ultimate aim of Catholic education is the full growth of the individual, a fully alive person for self and others, in communion with Christ.'[21] Love should indeed be 'the distinguishing mark of Christ's disciples'.[22] The work of Catholic education is a work of hope and love which 'helps individuals to be ever more human, leads them ever more fully to the truth, instils in them growing respect for life, and trains them in right inter-personal relationships'.[23]

> Only a humanity in which there reigns the 'civilisation of love' will be able to enjoy authentic and lasting peace.[24]

Searching in true freedom is a humanising action that opens the person up to the mystery of being and the reality that surrounds us. 'In fact, education must be seen as the acquisition, growth and possession of freedom', seeking 'to free the person from the conditionings that prevent him or her from fully living as a person,

[20] See CS 29.
[21] Catholic Bishops of Northern Ireland, *Proclaiming the Mission: The Distinctive Philosophy and Values of Catholic Education, An Executive Summary* (Armagh: Catholic Bishops of Northern Ireland, 2001), p. 8.
[22] SRS 40.
[23] EV 7.
[24] John Paul II, *Message for the 2004 World Day of Peace*, 10.

to form him/herself into a strong and responsible personality, capable of making free and consistent choices'.[25] Such education to freedom is a preparation for the gift of faith, allowing the person space within which to hear the voice of God and come to know God more fully: 'Belief is a fruit of grace and liberty.'[26] Indeed, the Church 'is called to fashion a new history, gift of God and fruit of human freedom.'[27]

SEARCHING IN FREEDOM: CREATING SPACE FOR GOD

Here are some practical suggestions for creating space to allow yourself hear the voice of God speaking in your life:

- Re-commit yourself to gathering consistently with the parish community on Sundays and Feast Days.
- Discover how to pray with scripture, using Ignatian meditation, *lectio divina*, or other recognised methods.
- Learn to reflect on and pray the Stations of the Cross.
- Participate in Taizé-style 'Prayer around the Cross'.
- Take some time to pray before the Blessed Sacrament.
- Walk alone with God in the mountains, by the sea, in a local park.
- Connect with the love of God in Jesus Christ through devotion to the Sacred Heart.
- Engage a spiritual director or *anam chara*.
- Learn to pray the Rosary, meditating on the mysteries it recalls.
- Participate in the Liturgy of the Hours/the Prayer of the Church.
- Become involved with a new ecclesial movement, parish prayer group or collaborative ministry team.
- Participate in a pilgrimage or visit a holy place.

Presenting the Message of Jesus Christ

29. As followers of Jesus Christ, we recognise ourselves to be 'a pilgrim Church sent on mission'.[28] The Gospel scts us free, inviting us to carry the light of Christ to others. Guided by the Holy Spirit, the Christian community continually seeks to live and to proclaim the Word of God, expressing it in human words and deeds, giving it new life. It does so conscious of the conversation in faith that ecumenical[29] and inter-religious dialogues necessitate.[30]

A number of guiding principles for presenting the Gospel message have been highlighted in the *General Directory for Catechesis*:

[25] *CPMS* 52.
[26] *GDC* 156.
[27] *EMCC* 37c.
[28] *GDC* 107.
[29] See *GDC* 86; *RM* 50.
[30] See *GDC* 86; *RM* 55.

- The Gospel message is *christocentric*. It is centred on the person of Jesus Christ, who not only transmits the Word of God: he *is* the Word of God.
- The perspective is always *trinitarian*, focused on God's love, and leading to profession of faith in God, Father, Son and Holy Spirit.
- *Salvation* in Jesus Christ, from all oppression, sin and evil, is central to the Good News.
- *Liberation* for the poor, for those who hunger, who suffer, who weep, justice, is a core concern of the Gospel of Jesus Christ and of our ministry to the world.
- The message is *ecclesial* in that it originates in the Church's confession of faith, it echoes the faith lived by all the people of God and it nourishes their bond of unity.
- It is *historical*, reflecting a constant 'memory' of the saving events of the past, in the light of which we, as Church, interpret the present events of history and await with joyful hope the coming of our saviour, Jesus Christ.
- The Gospel message is *incarnational*. It reaches out to dialogue with human culture, just as Jesus did. The Gospel seeks to inculturate his message, in all its integrity, within each culture and for every generation.
- The *integrity* of the Gospel requires a gradual presentation of the entire treasure of the authentic Christian message.
- The Gospel message is *harmonious* and *comprehensive*, providing a coherent and living synthesis of faith.
- The proclamation of the Gospel message seeks to be a profoundly *meaningful* event for each one of us. It sets out to illuminate the whole of life and put the human person in communication with Jesus Christ.[31]

GROUP DISCUSSION:
PRINCIPLES FOR PRESENTING THE GOSPEL

In your group, discuss the meaning, requirements and responsibilities emerging from the ten principles highlighted above for presenting the Gospel message. Are there others that you would consider worthy of particular mention?

Good News for All People

30. 'Evangelisation is the most powerful and stirring challenge which the Church has been called to face from her very beginning.'[32] When we have understood God's love for us in Jesus Christ, a lifelong journey begins, in which we seek to let the *euaggelion* – the

[31] See *GDC* 97-117.
[32] *VS* 106.

'Good News' of Christ's loving life, ministry, passion, death and resurrection – speak in our hearts. The Gospel is good news for all, particularly those who are lost, poor, forgotten or excluded. Pope Paul VI is clear on this: 'The Gospel message is not reserved to a small group of the initiated, the privileged or the elect but is destined for everyone.'[33]

Sharing the Good News is an essential part of who we are and of who we are becoming. It is not an optional extra: 'Every person has the right to hear the "Good News".'[34] We are called to bring the values and demands of the Gospel into every sphere of our human life and activity. Each day, we live in Christ's love and bring him with us for others wherever we go. We have a gift with which to gift others – Jesus Christ. 'The community must always be fully prepared in the pursuit of its apostolic vocation to give help to those who are searching for Christ.'[35]

SCRIPTURE: THE CALL TO EVANGELISE

I will give you as a light to the nations, that my salvation may reach the ends of the earth. (Isaiah 49:6)

Do not say 'I am only a youth'; for to all to whom I send you, you shall go, and whatever I command you, you shall speak. Be not afraid of them, for I am with you to deliver you. (Jeremiah 1:7-8)

Jesus turned and saw them following, and said to them 'What do you seek?' and they said to him, 'Rabbi... where are you going?' He said to them, 'Come and see.' (John 1:38-39)

'Feed my lambs...feed my sheep... Follow me.' (John 21:15-19)

PAUSE FOR REFLECTION: GOD TRUSTS US SO MUCH

We always want a God who is going to fix our problems, but God is saying, 'I'll give you the strength so you become one of those who work with others to bring peace to our world...' It's up to you and me, but God will give us strength... God trusts us so much; God wants us to become men and women who can receive forgiveness and give forgiveness, who can receive wisdom and give wisdom. Jesus kneeling before his disciples is a revelation of Jesus kneeling at our feet saying 'I trust you, I believe in you, I love you' and calling us to stand up and work for love.

J. Vanier, *Encountering 'The Other'* (Dublin: Veritas, 2005), pp. 60-61.

[33] *EN* 57.
[34] *RM* 46.
[35] *RCIA* 9.

Evangelisation, in the broad sense spoken of by the Catholic Church since Vatican II, encompasses ministry to the faithful, ministry to a divided Christianity and ministry to those outside the Church. It has been suggested that evangelisation can, therefore, be engaged with in three different contexts: It can be spoken of as *pastoral evangelisation* when it is addressed to the faithful to lead them to an ever deeper knowledge of the mystery of Christ; as *ecumenical evangelisation* when addressed to a divided Christianity with a view to promoting unity of truth; and as *missionary evangelisation* when addressed to those who do not know of the Good News, inviting them to a conversion of heart and acceptance of Christ.[36]

As we reach out to share our treasure with the world, we must be alert, always, to the need for ongoing pastoral evangelisation

within the Church itself. 'We cannot preach conversion unless we ourselves are converted anew each day.'[37] We need to be reminded continuously of the centrality of reflection and conversion among the People of God. How else can the Church retain the freshness, vigour and strength necessary in order to proclaim the Gospel with credibility: 'She is the community of believers, the community of hope lived and communicated, the community of brotherly love; and she needs to listen unceasingly to what she must believe, to her reasons for hoping, to the new commandment of love.'[38]

The mission to evangelise is never to be understood as a personal cause. We undertake it in the name of the Church and of Christ. Pastors and lay members of the parish community should be constantly united in nourishing the gift of communion among all the faithful. Communion and evangelisation are of one piece: 'Communion leads to mission and mission itself to communion.'[39]

[36] See F.-V. Anthony, 'The Concept of "Evangelisation" in the General Directory for Catechesis', G. Choondal (ed.), *Introducing the General Directory for Catechesis* (Bangalore: Kristu Jyoti Publications, 2004), p. 49.
[37] *RM* 47.
[38] *EN* 15.
[39] *CL* 31; see also *GDC* 48.

The power of evangelisation will find itself considerably diminished if those who proclaim the Gospel are divided among themselves in all sorts of ways... The Lord's spiritual testament tells us that unity among his followers is not only the proof that we are his but also the proof that he is sent by the Father. It is the test of the credibility of Christians and of Christ himself. As evangelisers, we must offer Christ's faithful not the image of people divided and separated by unedifying quarrels, but the image of people who are mature in faith and capable of finding a meeting-point beyond the real tensions, thanks to a shared, sincere and disinterested search for truth. Yes the destiny of evangelisation is certainly bound up with the witness of unity given by the Church.

EN 77.

31. Evangelisation, we should always remember, can only be undertaken with a humble spirit and with a deep sense of respect for people and communities, for 'the fruit of the Spirit is love, joy, peace, patience, kindness, goodness, faithfulness, gentleness, self-control' (Galatians 5:22-23). Proclaiming the Gospel entails patient listening and willingness to enter into honest dialogue 'always taking the person as one's starting point and always coming back to the relationships of people among themselves and with God'.[40]

Evangelisation should be understood as a 'rich, complex and dynamic reality, made up of elements, or one could say moments, that are essential and different from each other, and that must all be kept in view simultaneously'.[41] A variety of terms are used to explain these various moments, depending on the situation and needs of people. Only appropriate processes should, of course, be employed, so that the Gospel is always freely given and freely received. Initial proclamation, Christian initiation, catechesis, religious education, new evangelisation and theological reflection are all elements that can contribute to the faith development of members of the Church, depending on their particular needs at a particular time along their faith journey. These moments are not to be too strictly differentiated one from another. There is an interplay between them, a lively relationship that acknowledges the requirements of individuals and faith communities, recognising their need for ongoing encouragement along the way as they develop a mature faith and become fully evangelised.

[40] *EN* 20.
[41] *CT* 18; see also *EN* 17-24; *GDC* 49.

Initial Proclamation

32. Let us consider in the first instance the person who has no knowledge of Jesus. *Initial proclamation* (or missionary evangelisation) refers to that moment when, through the intervention of another, an individual for the first time is introduced to, recognises and begins to identify with Jesus Christ.

Initial proclamation brings the person 'into the love of God, who invites him to enter into a personal relationship with himself in Christ'.[42] Initial proclamation brings about conversion, when those who have not previously encountered Christ, or have dismissed him, open their heart to his love.[43] Sometimes it is a simple word offered, an experience of neighbourly love, or the witness of life on the part of a companion or an acquaintance that enables the person to see Jesus in a new light. As Pope Benedict points out: 'A Christian knows when it is time to speak of God and when it is better to say nothing and let love alone speak. He knows that God is love (cf. I John 4:8) and that God's presence is felt at the very time when the only thing to do is to love.'[44] By our actions, our words, our prayer, our example of love, we can be credible, if imperfect, witnesses to Christ. 'The Kingdom of God is now. This is the time for people to extend their hand to take hold of their salvation.'[45]

The Church also uses the term *pre-evangelisation*[46] when referring to a type of initial proclamation that, in bringing the person to consider the deepest meaning of life, helps them, over a period of reflection, to be prepared to meet Jesus. For several reasons, including lack of opportunity, negative experiences and preoccupation with other matters, many people cannot see the value of making God a priority in their lives. They can, however, readily understand the significance of trust, reconciliation, solidarity and love. This is true, too, of very young children. Reflection on such matters tills the earth and prepares the ground, so that when the seed of Christ's message is sown, there is the possibility of its being fully recognised, supported and cared for. By

[42] *AG* 13.
[43] See *GDC* 61; *EN* 52-53; *RM* 44.
[44] Benedict XVI, *DCE* 31c.
[45] Synod of Bishops Special Assembly for Oceania, *Jesus Christ and the Peoples of Oceania: Walking His Way, Telling His Truth, Living His Life* (Vatican City: The General Secretariat of the Synod of Bishops and Libreria Editrice Vaticana, 1997), 18.
[46] See *EN* 51; *Message of the Holy Father Pope John Paul II for the VII World Youth Day*, Vatican, 24 Nov 1991.

raising the person's interest and thoughtfulness about life, a sense of the religious dimension of our lives can be awakened. Themes investigated in different ways by philosophy, science and the arts,[47] for instance, can, for many, open up avenues toward a deep understanding of the mysteries of the world, of human life and of God. Pre-evangelisation can be relevant for people of all ages and stages of life, including children in Catholic schools. We should never presume that the soil has already been prepared when we seek to plant a precious seed.

Christian Initiation

33. In the earliest centuries of the Church's existence, adults were initiated into membership of the Church after extended periods of enquiry and growth. Today, the ancient, and now revitalised, *Rite of Christian Initiation of Adults* (RCIA), restored, revised and adapted to local traditions worldwide, as requested by the Second Vatican Council,[48] provides us with the framework for adult Christian Initiation. The *Rite of Christian Initiation of Adults* 'is designed for adults who after hearing the mystery of Jesus Christ proclaimed, consciously and freely seek to enter the way of faith and conversion as the Holy Spirit opens their hearts'.[49] It outlines the process by which an adult, newly converted to belief in Jesus Christ, is brought, after a journey of instruction and formation in the Christian life, to an explicit profession of faith and to celebration of the sacraments of initiation, Baptism, Confirmation and the Eucharist, preferably at the Easter Vigil.[50]

The RCIA indicates and explains the steps of a journey which, it is envisaged, will take place over four continuous periods: 'the precatechumenate, the period for hearing the first preaching of the Gospel (RCIA 36-40); the period of the catechumenate, set aside for a thorough catechesis, *that is instruction and formation,* and for the rites belonging to this period (RCIA 75-104); the period of purification and enlightenment (Lenten preparation), designed for a more intense spiritual preparation, which is assisted by the celebration of the scrutinies and presentations (RCIA 125-197); and the period of post-baptismal catechesis called 'mystagogy', marked by the new experience of sacraments and community (RCIA 234-241).'[51] A fuller discussion of adult initiation and faith development takes place in Chapter 4.

Since the early Christian era, there developed in the Church the tradition of baptising newborn or young children into the faith that their family has considered precious. Awareness of God's love, revealed in Jesus Christ, has led parents and grandparents over the centuries to engage in sharing the light of Christ with new generations. The rights and responsibilities of parents, parish and school in initiating children into the Catholic faith, through preparation for and celebration of Baptism, Confirmation and the Eucharist, are discussed in Chapter 5.

[47] See *EN 51.*
[48] See *RCIA 2.*
[49] *RCIA 1.*
[50] See *GDC 59.*
[51] *RCIA 7.*

This National Directory for Catechesis, in highlighting the RCIA for Ireland today, invites local Christian communities to see themselves, once more, as missionary communities, listening to the needs of today's people, and reaching out simply and humbly to proclaim Christ by the way they live their lives. The Christian community must be prepared, as well, to accompany those who, over a period of time, are living through the catechumenate, either formally as adults or informally, but no less intensely, as children. The Christian community must also be ready to be a place of welcome for all those who are seeking to become more fully integrated into a living, praying, serving, loving community of faith. Adults and young people who have been baptised, confirmed and who have received the Eucharist, need to know that they belong within and are supported in faith by their parish community.

Catechesis

34. Catechesis, mentioned above, is central to the life and mission of the Church, offering instruction and formation in the faith and bringing members of the Christian community to maturity in that faith. It is distinct from that initial proclamation or first conversion-bringing evangelisation which introduces the Gospel to a person who does not know Christ. 'Catechesis, "distinct from the primary proclamation of the Gospel",[52] promotes and matures initial conversion, educates the convert to the faith and incorporates him into the Christian community.'[53]

According to Pope John Paul II, catechesis has the twofold objective of maturing initial faith and of educating the follower of Jesus Christ into a deeper and more systematic knowledge of the person and message of Christ.[54]

[52] CT 19.
[53] GDC 61.
[54] See CT 19.

REFLECTION AND DISCUSSION:
KEY DEFINITIONS OF CATECHESIS

Catechesis is the term to be used for that form of ecclesial action which leads both communities and individual members of the faithful to maturity of faith.

(GCD 21)

The definitive aim of catechesis is to put people not only in touch, but in communion and intimacy with Jesus Christ.

(GDC 80)

Catechesis is that particular form of the ministry of the word which matures initial conversion to make it into a living, explicit and fruitful confession of faith.

(GDC 82)

By deepening knowledge of the faith, catechesis nourishes not only the life of faith but equips it to explain itself to the world.

(GDC 85)

Catechesis prepares the Christian to live in community and to participate actively in the life and mission of the Church.

(GDC 86)

The model for all catechesis is the *Rite of Christian Initiation of Adults*, described above. In fact, for the community of the Church, the catechesis of adults is the chief form of catechesis. All other forms are oriented toward it: 'The *organising principle*, which gives coherence to the various catechetical programmes offered by a particular Church, is attention to adult catechesis. This is the axis around which revolves the catechesis of childhood and adolescence as well as that of old age.'[55]

In this strict sense, catechesis is entered into by adults who are on the journey to becoming fully Christian, or by parents with their children, whom they have gifted with Baptism and are seeking to initiate fully into the Christian way of life through Confirmation and participation in the Eucharist.

35. The term 'catechesis' has, however, in a broader sense, been used to signify all that the Christian community undertakes, verbally and non-verbally, to educate one another in the Christian faith. Catechesis aims to make our Christian faith become 'living, conscious and active'.[56] It seeks to enable the Word of God to enliven us at our deepest levels – affective and active as well as cognitive. The aim of catechesis is to help the Christian to reach spiritual, liturgical, sacramental and apostolic maturity.[57] The catechetical endeavour draws the person into a deeper understanding, celebration and participation in the mystery of the life, death and resurrection of Jesus Christ, opening up for us new

[55] GDC 275.
[56] CD 14.57
[57] See *RDECS* 69.

life in the Holy Spirit as children of God our Father in the community of the Church.

The assumption of Christian faith, at whatever level of integration, is essential to catechesis, forming the distinction between catechesis and other types of religious education. 'Catechesis takes place within a community living out its faith.'[58] It presupposes some level of Christian faith, of initiation or continuing commitment to a community of believers, particularly one's parish community, and an attempt to live out faith in life. It suggests that the person has found a home, or is finding a home, in the Church, and sees himself or herself as a member of the Body of Christ, united with Christ. It seeks to provide for those who are *believers* and those who are *searchers* or *doubters* within the faith community.[59] It presumes both an initial conversion and openness to ongoing conversion. Catechesis is a complex endeavour, even when it is said that faith is presumed:

> This means that 'catechesis' must often concern itself not only with nourishing and teaching the faith but also with arousing it unceasingly with the help of grace, with opening the heart, with converting, and with preparing total adherence to Jesus Christ on the part of those who are still on the threshold of faith. This concern will in part decide the tone, the language and the method of catechesis.[60]

36. Traditionally, four signs of commitment, already noted in the Acts of the Apostles as attributes of the early Christian community, have been highlighted as characteristic of Gospel living.[61] As such,

[58] *RDECS* 68.
[59] See G.J. Holohan, *Australian RE: Facing the Challenges* (National Catholic Education Commission, 1999), p. 28.
[60] *CT* 19.
[61] See Acts 2:42-47.

they are recognised as central to catechesis. Any expression of Catholicity in Ireland today may usefully engage these themes as a means of examining its own vigour and direction:

- Proclaiming and witnessing to the Gospel message *(kergyma/martyria)*.
- Building up a caring Church community based on Gospel values *(koinonia)*.
- Celebrating faith in worship, prayer and through liturgical participation – in communion with God, in Jesus Christ, and with one another *(leitourgia)*.
- Service to neighbour, particularly the most poor and most vulnerable, the work of justice *(diakonia)*.[62]

**PRAYERFUL REFLECTION:
DEVOTION TO THE APOSTLES' TEACHING**

They devoted themselves to the apostles' teaching and fellowship, to the breaking of bread and to the prayers. And all who believed were together and had all things in common; and they sold their possessions and goods and distributed them to all, as any had need.

(Acts 2:42, 44-45)

The classical starting point for catechesis has always been the four constant themes traditionally addressed in Catholic catechisms, which also form the structure around which the *Catechism of the Catholic Church* has been arranged. A brief overview of these themes, carefully explained in the Catechism, is offered in Chapter 3 of this Directory:

- The Profession of Faith (the Creed)
- The Celebration of Christian Mystery (the Sacraments)
- Life in Christ (the Beatitudes and Commandments)
- Prayer in the Christian Life (the Lord's Prayer)[63]

Both these schemes are useful in themselves, but the *General Directory for Catechesis*, drawing on both these traditions, speaks in all of six fundamental tasks for catechesis as it endeavours to help us to know, celebrate and contemplate the mystery of Christ:

1. **Promoting knowledge of the faith** – initiating and deepening our knowledge of the faith in order to nourish our faith-life and equip us to explain it to the world.
2. **Liturgical education** – celebrating our communion with Christ through his saving presence in the sacraments, particularly in the Eucharist.

[62] See *DCE*, 20-25.
[63] See *FD* 2.

3. **Moral formation** – motivating us to service of God and neighbour, leading to practical action in accord with the demands of the Gospel.

4. **Teaching to pray** – inviting us to learn to pray with Jesus Christ, turning with him to the Father in adoration, praise, thanksgiving, confidence, entreaty and awe.

5. **Educating for community life** – preparing us to live as part of the Christian community, building it up and committing ourselves energetically to the ecumenical dimension of renewal within the Church.

6. **Missionary initiation** – equipping ourselves to participate actively in the life and mission of the Church, witnessing day by day to what intimacy with Jesus Christ has meant in our lives and opening ourselves to inter-religious dialogue.[64]

37. Catechesis, then, is 'a very remarkable' moment in the whole process of evangelisation.[65] It builds upon initial proclamation and leads to a genuinely personal faith. It seeks to assist 'the renewal to which the Holy Spirit ceaselessly calls the Church, the Body of Christ'.[66]

A very helpful clarification, offered by Pope John Paul II in *Catechesi tradendae*, highlights four lessons for catechesis, from the Church's experience through the centuries, which can usefully be kept in mind:

● Just as from the perspective of human rights every human being has the right to seek religious truth and adhere to it freely, from the theological point of view every baptised person has the right to receive from the Church instruction and education enabling him or her to enter on a truly Christian life.

● The more the Church locally and universally gives catechesis priority, the more she finds in catechesis a strengthening of her internal life as a community of believers and of her external activity as a missionary Church.

● Catechesis is a work for which the whole Church must feel responsible and must wish to be responsible.

[64] See *GDC* 85-86.
[65] *CT* 18.
[66] *FD* 3.

● Catechesis must always seek to renew itself, broadening its concept, revising its methods, searching for suitable language and utilising new means of transmitting the message.[67]

Religious Education

38. Religious education is a process that contributes to the faith development of children, adolescents and adults. Religious education helps people to develop religious ways of thinking, feeling and doing, which give expression to the spiritual, moral and transcendent dimensions of life and can lead to personal and social transformation. Religious education can also teach people to think profoundly, allowing them to make free and consistent choices in the way they live their religious, and other, commitments.

Religious education can take place within a Church context or outside that context. In fact, there is a great variety of models, sponsors and circumstances within which religious education can take place in today's world. It is important, therefore, to understand what form of religious education is being spoken of within a particular context. Inter-cultural, inter-religious and inter-ethical issues abound in the increasingly pluralist context that we inhabit today. Religious education, wherever it takes place, should always, however, be carried out in a way that supports the faith life of the Catholic student, strengthening the harmony between what is known, who one is becoming and how one lives one's life.

The Catholic school welcomes pupils of various faiths and none. In the Catholic school, building on the academic preparation and professional expertise of its religious educators, religious education will never simply be a general study of religions, their history, traditions and customs. A purely phenomenological approach, comparing one religion with another without any regard for the faith life of students, their families and the faith community to which they belong, is inadequate. Rather, religious education, as generally defined in Ireland, encourages Catholic students and others to engage with religious questions from within the context of

[67] See *CT* 14-17.

their own lived religious faith. Their own experience and faith journey is respected by the teachers, and their commitment to the religious tradition of their family is supported.

Religious education always has a formational aspect: The degree of emphasis placed on different religions may vary according to the context in which the religious education takes place, but all religious education is formative in nature, allowing students to become aware of and respond to the transcendent dimension of their lives.[68] It should 'contribute to the spiritual and moral development of the student'.[69]

39. The ethos within which religious education takes place, therefore, is crucial. In the Catholic home, in the Catholic parish, in the Catholic school, and wherever the religious education of Catholic students takes place, it should be within a context that supports and informs the Catholic faith of these students. In the Catholic primary school, religious education and formation will also contribute to the preparation of Catholic students for sacramental initiation. Religious education in the Catholic school, therefore, will always be understood as seeking to encourage and support the Catholic faith commitment of its Catholic students. This should be one of the hallmarks of a Catholic school and should always be openly acknowledged as such by management, teachers, parents and students.

Religious education offered in a Catholic school, particularly at post-primary level, as well as supporting Catholic students in their faith, may find itself facilitating discussion not only among Catholic students, but also between them and students of a variety of faiths, as well as those who may not be committed to a religious interpretation of life. Religious education holds open the possibility of helping all people to grapple, within their own reality, with crucial questions central to life and to living, playing its part in personal faith formation if the young person is open and interested and supported in following this through in their lives.

[68] See A. Hession, 'Clearing the Ground: Religious Education in Catholic Primary Schools', P. Kieran and A. Hession (eds.), *Children, Catholicism and Religious Education* (Dublin: Veritas, 2005), p. 34.
[69] Ireland, Department of Education and Science, *Junior Certificate: Religious Education Syllabus* (Dublin: The Stationery Office, 2000), p. 5.

> ### GROUP DISCUSSION:
> ### OPENING WINDOWS OF WONDER
>
> It needs to be said that Catholic education is not about control but about offering a vision of life inspired by Jesus of Nazareth; is not about indoctrination but about opening windows of wonder and igniting a search for wisdom; is not something exclusive to Catholics but inclusive and welcoming towards all to 'come and see'; is not sectarian but radically ecumenical and formally committed to inter-religious dialogue.
>
> D.A. Lane, 'Challenges Facing Catholic Education in Ireland',
> E. Woulfe and J. Cassin (eds), *From Present to Future: Catholic Education in Ireland for the New Century* (Dublin: Veritas, 2006), p. 135.

From the perspective of the Christian community, religious education and catechesis, which specifically seeks to bring Christian people to a 'maturity of faith', are distinct but complementary activities. Each contributes to the development of the person, but in different ways.[70] For the person of faith, religious education can help to reinforce catechesis already received. It can also be supportive of catechesis currently offered.

The Catholic community welcomes the acknowledgement of and provision for the spiritual and moral dimensions of education in all schools in Ireland. It deeply appreciates the encouragement in schools of forms of religious education that support the Catholic faith of Catholic children and young people. Such religious education contributes to ensuring that the education of these young people is life-giving. A detailed discussion of religious education in Irish schools, both primary and post-primary, and of the differences between them, follows in Chapter 5.

The New Evangelisation

40. Evangelisation addressed to those who have already been initiated into the Church but who have lost their deep sense of commitment to Jesus Christ and connection with the Christian community is often referred to as *the new evangelisation*. The term suggests renewed outreach to those who have already encountered Christ and been catechised but have become distanced from him and from his Church. This form of pastoral evangelisation is particularly conscious of the need, especially in the traditionally Christian Western world, to dialogue with what have been termed the postmodern cultural realities of our time. Sometimes where the faith has long been sown, entire groups of the baptised have strayed from their initial commitment. Some have lost their faith. They live lives removed from their baptismal call and no longer consider themselves as belonging to the Christian community. Many in Ireland, while not having made any such formal decision, drift in their faith, attending church only on significant family occasions. Such people, including adults, young people and children, can be offered opportunities for a new evangelisation under the inspiration of the Holy Spirit, upon whom all our efforts depend: a new approach, which Pope John Paul described as 'new in ardour, methods and expression'.[71] They will more likely be affected, and caused to think again, not by words alone but by the witness of those who truly live their Christianity: 'new evangelisation will show its authenticity and unleash all its missionary force when it is carried out through the gift not only of the word proclaimed but also of the word lived.'[72]

[70] See G.J. Holohan, *Australian RE*, pp. 31-2.
[71] John Paul II, 'Discourse to the Bishops of CELAM', 9 March 1983, *Insegnamenti* VI, I (1983), 698.
[72] *VS* 107.

PAUSE FOR THOUGHT:
SUMMONS TO THE NEW EVANGELISATION

Over the years, I have often repeated the summons to the *new evangelisation*. I do so again now, especially in order to insist that we must rekindle in ourselves the impetus of the beginnings and allow ourselves to be filled with the ardour of the apostolic preaching which followed Pentecost... This passion will not fail to stir in the Church a new sense of mission, which cannot be left to a group of 'specialists' but must involve the responsibility of all the members of the People of God. Those who have come into genuine contact with Christ cannot keep him for themselves, they must proclaim him.

NMI 40.

41. Within Irish society today, the different situations of three distinct groups should be kept in mind:[73]

- those who are fervent in their faith and in Christian living who belong to a local Christian community with adequate or developing ecclesial structures, but who require ongoing nourishment;
- the baptised who have lost their sense of the faith and who are in need of some form of new evangelisation;
- and with so many migrant people coming to live in Ireland, the situation, unknown here for many centuries, of people for whom Christ and the Kingdom of God remain unfamiliar.

As the Church in Ireland, we cannot be content to imagine one global catechetical scenario. We are obliged to address the entire panorama of faith situations and their interrelationship: 'Each of them influences, stimulates and assists the others.'[74] All of us need to learn from one another and keep one another in mind. A mutual enrichment can take place between the mission *ad intra* (within the Church) and the mission *ad extra* (beyond the Church). Particular situations require particular responses, but all evangelising action should be seen as a unity.

Pope Paul VI taught that the evangelisation of people must always be complemented by the evangelisation of culture(s). In an often quoted phrase, he advised: 'The split between the Gospel and culture is without doubt the drama of our time, just as it was of other times.'[75] Cultural change in Ireland in recent times, as discussed in Chapter 1, has been dramatic in its influence on our expression of Christian faith in Ireland. Our Christian heritage does not, it is sometimes claimed, have the vitality necessary to impact on the hearts of individuals and on our society as it had in the past. Yet it is only if the Gospel is proclaimed vigorously that new forms of culture, emerging in Ireland today, can be enlightened and regenerated by an encounter with Jesus Christ. It is only then

[73] See *GDC* 58; *RM* 34.
[74] *RM* 34.
[75] *EN* 20.

that new generations will come to hear his message in a language that speaks to them:

> How are they to call on one in whom they have not believed? And how are they to believe in one of whom they have never heard? And how are they to hear without someone to proclaim him? And how are they to proclaim him unless they are sent? As it is written, 'How beautiful are the feet of those who bring good news!'
>
> (Romans 10:14-15)

SEND US FORTH IN LOVE

Send us forth as your blessing, Lord!
Change our hearts and enliven our spirits!
Send us forth as your blessing, Lord!
Send us forth, in love!
Send us forth, in love!

Paul A. Tate, *Send Us Forth in Love* © 2004
(4900 Markim Forest Lane, Sugar Hill, GA 30518).

Theological Reflection

42. As well as the new beginning and ongoing renewal indicated by new evangelisation, a further and very significant moment within the overall evangelising processes ongoing in the Church is referred to as *theological reflection* (also known as theologising or doing theology): the educated and up-to-date reflection of committed members of the People of God, lay, religious and clerical, which presumes and follows on from their faith commitment, leading to just and loving action as members of the Church. Theological reflection does not separate itself in any sense from the everyday questions and struggles associated with Christian living but builds on the mature witness and faithfulness of those who are devoted to Christ and to the Church. Theologising is essentially an ecclesial activity, a 'loving reflection' on the wisdom that resides in a believing community.[76] Informed deliberation that takes place in small Christian communities, parish groups, associations and movements of adult Christians, is an all-important contribution to theological reflection.

PERSONAL REFLECTION: SMALL CHRISTIAN COMMUNITIES

Within the Church, do you belong to any group/s? Where do you have the opportunity to share your faith personally with others? Would you consider initiating a group in your parish who would meet for prayer, reach out to those in need, prepare the community liturgy, support the bereaved or help those initiating their children in the faith? Would you be prepared to share elements of your faith, formally or informally, with others? Under what circumstances would you consider taking a theology course?

[76] See E. Conway, 'Theology in Ireland: Changing Contours and Contexts', D. Marmion (ed.), *Christian Identity in a Postmodern Age: Celebrating the Legacies of Karl Rahner and Bernard Lonergan* (Dublin: Veritas, 2005), pp. 115-36.

Mature theological study and reflection has not always been highlighted within our faith communities in the past. Often, little was offered, or sought, to enable committed Catholics to come together in theologically reflective mode. The mature Christian who has been fully catechised and come to a strong sense of personal discipleship, committed to Christ and his Church, by developing expertise and skills, and by engaging in academic study, can contribute enormously to the ongoing conversion and growth of that local Christian community. Led by the Holy Spirit, he or she can become an informed agent as well as a subject of catechesis within that community and beyond it. With the help of ongoing education and training, dedicated members of the Church in Ireland can contribute in a variety of ways, perhaps not yet fully discerned, to the life of the Christian community.

The welcome growth in the education and training of lay Catholics and the promotion of the study of theology, both formally at third

level and more informally as adult learning, is a sign of vitality and hope not to be underestimated. Once the person begins to engage with theology, which is best done with the support of a parish or other faith community, a journey of discovery is entered upon. The study of theology engages the person in an often difficult reflection, wrestling to discover the essence of truth, and more, to live by truth. It can change people's lives, drawing them into a real conversion of heart. Formal academic theology, such as Scripture, Systematic Theology, Moral Theology, Liturgy, Pastoral Theology, Catechetical Theology, Canon Law, as well as the study of Philosophy and Church History, should be seen to be at the service of that theological action-reflection that continues within the Christian community. The parish community is always interested in the theological education of its committed parishioners. It should be willing to travel with and support those studying theology, discussing with them possible opportunities for engaging in practical service within the parish.

PAUSE FOR REFLECTION:
THEOLOGY AS A WAY OF LIFE

Doing theology involves the religious conversion of the whole person. I have seen this conversion in many people. It begins with a growing passion for and commitment to the theological enterprise itself. The human flourishing to which it gives rise, is, in my experience, remarkable. It produces people who are intellectually confident, morally mature, who think for themselves, and are not prisoners of received ideas. For many it may not be an easy journey; but the dialogue and exchange which is characteristic of that journey leads for the most part to reflection and shared prayer and ultimately to an experience that is life-transforming.

The dialogical element is important to this process because theology is about more than providing answers to questions. It is about locating oneself within a particular tradition of questioning and exchange. And it is precisely because students of theology can locate themselves within the Christian tradition and narrative that they are normally able to appropriate the gospel faith and make it their own. This is growth in holiness. What may have started as a search for knowledge becomes a way of life, a lens through which to view the world.

O. Maloney, contribution to 'The Value of Theology',
The Furrow 53(2002)6, pp. 327-8.

Faith Development Overview

43. The term 'faith development' is employed, as the overarching term, in this National Directory for Catechesis, to encapsulate all the different approaches to ongoing education available to people from the beginning of their journey into Christian faith and throughout a lifetime of growth in that faith. Faith development includes initial faith formation, but suggests that formation in faith is lifelong and does not achieve its end except, finally, in Jesus Christ. It acknowledges that a person's faith can evolve and mature, guided by the Holy Spirit, throughout their experience of life. Building on what has gone before, Christians are continually invited to develop further the intensity of their faith, the intimacy of their friendship with Christ and the strength of their love for God and for their neighbour.

The term 'faith development' embraces all the various moments and possibilities indicated above, seeking to acknowledge and respond appropriately to the initial proclamation, Christian initiation, catechesis, religious education, new evangelisation and theological reflection needs of people in Ireland today. 'Faith development' is a term that suggests energy, dynamism and lifelong commitment in helping people come to know and live more fully their Christian faith. It takes into account dialogue with the different social, educational and cultural contexts encountered.

Approaches and methodologies suited for those who are only getting to know Jesus Christ, for those who are journeying with him, and for those who have been members of the Church for many years but have identified their need for continuing faith education, are all encouraged within what is intended by faith development.

'Faith development', as an all-inclusive term, allows us to treat together, under one heading, when appropriate, all the necessary and nuanced meanings that terms such as initial proclamation, initiation and catechesis, for example, suggest but cannot individually fully contain. Those who are charged with faith development, therefore, within a particular Christian community, whether at parish or inter-parish level, at deanery, diocesan, regional or national level, will need, as we shall see in Chapters 4, 5 and 6, to be adequately educated and trained in discerning, together with those in leadership roles, what forms of faith development are necessary, appropriate and of value for particular individuals, groups and communities. They may be called upon to use a wide variety of approaches in order to respond to the particular faith needs present within their community, so that Jesus Christ may dwell in all our hearts and draw us daily more and more into the all-embracing love of his Father.

SCRIPTURAL MEDITATION:
TO KNOW THE LOVE OF CHRIST

For this reason I bow my knees before the Father, from whom every family in heaven and on earth takes its name. I pray that, according to the riches of his glory, he may grant that you may be strengthened in your inner being, with power through his Spirit, and that Christ may dwell in your hearts through faith, as you are being rooted and grounded in love. I pray that you may have power to comprehend, with all the saints, what is the breadth and length and height and depth, and to know the love of Christ which surpasses knowledge, so that you may be filled with the fullness of God.

(Ephesians 3:14-19)

CHAPTER 3

Our Faith: The Gospel Alive

44. We tend to think of faith first of all, perhaps, as an assent to doctrines; in other words, our mind's acceptance of statements of the Church's teaching. But faith, hope and love are 'theological virtues', meaning that they concern primarily our relationship with God and affect our relationships with one another. We believe first of all not in statements, however important and central, but in God, and we believe not only with our minds but with our whole selves. A Christian understanding of faith is, as we have seen in Chapter 2, Christocentric and Trinitarian. Christian faith flows from a deep appreciation for and connection with the Living God, revealed as Three in One: shown by the actions of God as Creator, whose love for us is open to discovery in all of life; fully uncovered in and through the incarnation, life, death and resurrection of Jesus Christ, the Son of God; and made known through the Holy Spirit, poured into our hearts, speaking to us and guiding us.

Growing in Faith

45. United with God in Jesus Christ, the Christian makes of his or her life one continuous act of faith, hope and love. Faith that flows from a Christocentric and Trinitarian understanding is intrinsically relational, committed to communion with God and with one another. While Christian faith is very much a personal act, it is also, as we saw in Chapter 2, always historical and ecclesial. It links believers with one another and with all who, down through the ages, have responded to the call of Jesus Christ, particularly the saints, living their faith out in the Body of Christ, the Church. Such faith offers the possibility in Jesus Christ of salvation from sin and

liberation from its consequences. It prompts conversion, commitment and belonging. It is a synthesis of believing, acting, giving, trusting, empathising, knowing and loving. Christian faith is incarnational, reaching out to dialogue with human culture. It is a unity presented gradually but always authentically. It is comprehensive, enlightening all of human experience, and offers meaning to all of life. Christian faith is a gift from God, Father, Son and Holy Spirit, that reaches into every aspect of our humanity:

> Faith is relationship with God...
> Faith is our assent to what God tells us...
> Faith is a gift from God...
> Faith is a free response to God's gift...
> Faith is active...
> Faith is communal...
> Faith has a content...
> Faith challenges us to work for the reign of God...[1]

[1] See C. Maloney, F. O'Connell and B. O'Reilly, *Alive-O 8: Teacher's Book* (Dublin: Veritas, 2004), pp. [11]-[12].

PARISH PASTORAL COUNCIL:
LEARNING THROUGH PARTICIPATION

Reflect and celebrate with those who are most active in your parish. How are they nurtured in their faith? What can be learned about faith development from the variety of ways in which others have grown in faith:

- Priests, religious and pastoral workers, in reflecting on their daily contact with people at a variety of religious and spiritual levels.
- Liturgy groups, in preparing parish liturgical celebrations.
- Ministers of the Word and extraordinary ministers of Holy Communion, in preparation for and celebration of the liturgy.
- Choirs and musicians, in choosing and providing liturgical music.
- Financial and administration people, in dealing with parish structures.
- Those who do the small things that keep a parish running, in their quiet way.
- Members of Catholic-school boards of management, in contributing to the education of young people.
- Groups at the service of those in need, in what they have learned of people and society.
- Prayer groups and communities, in how they support one another within the wider parish community.

46. Within a complex understanding of the faith journey, and therefore of education in faith, it is useful for us to focus directly here, in this chapter, on the content of our faith and its proclamation in our world. In doing so, we should first be clear that the Church does not encourage any false division between content and method.[2] Both need careful attention. In catechesis, as in other forms of education, content and method must be correlated and interactive. We cannot focus on one and not on the other. They are always woven together.

Catechetical content provides a subject matter to be engaged with by catechist and learner in a variety of possible ways, in a variety of particular environments, and within the overall context that is Ireland today. A suitable approach must be chosen for every circumstance: 'adequate to the nature of the message, to its sources and language, to the concrete circumstances of ecclesial communities as well as to the particular circumstances of the faithful to whom catechesis is addressed.'[3]

[2] See *GDC* 149.
[3] *GDC* 149.

Good choices have to be made continuously 'suited to the conditions of the hearers and adapted to the circumstances of the times'.[4] We believe that, through the deeds and words of Jesus Christ, God speaks to our concrete human experiences. 'The principle of "fidelity to God and fidelity to man" leads to the avoidance of any opposition or artificial separation or presumed neutrality between content and method.'[5] Catechesis and other forms of faith development, when they pay attention both to the Word of God and to the experience of people's lives, will have a much greater chance of opening the individual's and the community's heart to God's hope and love here and now.

FAITH DEVELOPMENT GROUP: CONTENT AND METHOD

At the preparation stage of any faith development initiative, give time to consider methodology as well as content. Who are the learners and what are their needs? What about those leading the interaction, their different styles and skills? What form of communication do you envisage between learner and facilitator: prayerful reflection, lecture, discussion, action-based approach, small-group work, creative methods such as music, art, pottery, meditation? What about the environment, the space you will be in? What about the issues in society at this moment that might impinge on the particular subject matter you are choosing? Is the subject matter useful and relevant to the people you are planning for? Are you already in contact with your likely participants? How are you going to let them know what is happening, and how much reflection are you putting into preparing something worthwhile for them? Does the content and your chosen methodology respond to their needs and make it likely that they can participate actively in the session and engage easily enough with the material?

The Deposit of Faith

47. Scripture and Tradition are central to the life of the Church and to catechesis. The apostles entrusted to the whole Church the message of salvation, the 'sacred deposit' of faith which is contained in Scripture and Tradition. '"Sacred Tradition and Sacred Scripture make up a single sacred deposit of the Word of God" (*DV* 10), in which, as in a mirror, the pilgrim Church contemplates God, the source of all her riches.'[6]

Education in faith should always, therefore, be built on 'an authentic introduction to *lectio divina*, that is, a reading of the Sacred Scriptures done in accordance to the Spirit who dwells in the

[4] *CIC* can. 769.
[5] *GDC* 149.
[6] *CCC* 97.

Church'.[7] The study of Scripture requires not only an historical exegesis, using serious historical research methods, but also a theological exegesis that reflects on the spirit in which the text was written and on how it has come to be understood in the Church.[8] As Pope Benedict has pointed out: 'every text must be read and interpreted keeping in mind the unity of the whole of Scripture, the living tradition of the Church and the light of faith.'[9]

The living Tradition of the Church, all that the apostles received from Christ and have handed on through the bishops, their successors, comprises everything Christians need to live in holiness and increase their faith. 'The Church, in its doctrines, life and worship perpetuates and transmits to every generation all that it itself is and believes.'[10] Tradition makes progress in the Church with the help of the Holy Spirit, in whom there is growth in insight into the realities and words being maintained, practised and professed.

The People of God, assisted by the Holy Spirit and guided by the Magisterium of the Church, welcomes and reflects upon the deposit of faith, gifted to us in Scripture and Tradition, guarding it and witnessing to it faithfully. Authentic interpretation of the deposit of faith has been entrusted to the living teaching office of the Church alone, that is, to the successor of Peter, the Bishop of Rome, and to the bishops in communion with him.[11] To this Magisterium belongs also the task of defining dogmas, the formulations of the truths contained in divine Revelation.[12]

Scripture, Tradition and the Magisterium are so closely united with one another that one cannot stand without the other:[13] 'Tradition, Scripture and the Magisterium, all three of which are closely connected, are "each according to its own way", the principal sources of catechesis.'[14]

A Hierarchy of Truths

48. The Church has always sought to provide a coherent synthesis of the Christian faith, based on its understanding that there exists a 'hierarchy of truths'[15] handed down to us from God. To confirm such a hierarchy of truths, as both the *General Catechetical Directory* (1971) and the *General Directory for Catechesis* (1997) do, is not to suggest that some truths are less important to

[7] *GDC* 127.
[8] See Benedict XVI, *Address of His Holiness Benedict XVI during the 14th General Congregation of the Synod of Bishops*, 14 October 2008.
[9] Benedict XVI, *Angelus*, St Peter's Square, 26 October 2008.
[10] *DV* 8.
[11] See *DV* 10.
[12] See *CCC* 85-90, 100.
[13] See *CCC* 95.
[14] *GDC* 96; see also *DV* 10c.
[15] See *UR* 11.

Christian faith, but 'that some truths are based on others as of priority and are illuminated by them'.[16] The Gospel message should be presented wholly. Nothing essential should be left aside. Some elements will be presented early in the process, while others flow from these fundamental points and can be presented at a later stage. What is essential is that each person is helped to live their faith fully, with the support of the Christian community:

> Catechesis is an *education in the faith* of children, young people and adults, which includes especially the teaching of Christian doctrine imparted, generally speaking, in an organic and systematic way, with a view to initiating the hearers into the fullness of Christian life.[17]

What priority, then, should be given? In the first instance, Christian faith is always organised around the mystery of the Holy Trinity, in a christocentric perspective. The history of salvation is told through the same lens, recounting all that God has done, revealed fully in Jesus Christ. The Hebrew Scriptures, the Old Testament, is understood as a preparation for the New Testament, in which God speaks through his Son, Jesus. He in turn establishes the time of the Church, in which we are invited to live as his disciples under the guidance of the Holy Spirit:

> The history of salvation, recounting the 'marvels of God' (mirabilia Dei), what He has done, continues to do and will do in the future for us, is organised in reference to Jesus Christ, the 'centre of salvation history'. The preparation for the Gospel in the Old Testament, the fullness of Revelation in Jesus Christ, and the time of the Church, provide the structure of all salvation history of which creation and eschatology are its beginning and end.[18]

In the Church's presentation of the Gospel message, priority is given to the essential elements of the faith, taught constantly down through the centuries. All of Christian life is encapsulated here:

● The Apostles' Creed reveals how the Church in her time has always presented the Christian mystery in a vital synthesis, summarising all of the Church's doctrine around profession of faith in Father, Son and Holy Spirit.

● The Sacraments are the gift of Christ to regenerate the whole of life. Each sacrament has its own particular place, but the Eucharist is the high point of communion with God in Jesus Christ, and with one another in the Church.

● Building on the Ten Commandments, which express the implications of belonging to God in covenant,[19] the double commandment of love of God and love of neighbour provides the hierarchy of moral values that Jesus Christ himself established.[20] The way of Jesus Christ is summed up in the

[16] *GCD* 43; *GDC* 114.
[17] *CT* 18; see also *CCC* 5.
[18] *GDC* 115.
[19] See *CCC* 2062.
[20] See *GDC* 115.

Beatitudes and lived according to the Christian virtues of faith, hope and love, the foundations of Christian moral activity.[21]

- The Our Father focuses the heart and mind on the essence of the whole Gospel. It summarises the immense riches of prayer contained in Scripture and in all the Church's life.[22]

The *Catechism of the Catholic Church*

49. The Church, then, has always used short documents, such as New Testament texts, creeds and liturgical prayers, to state the faith. Over recent centuries, catechisms have also been used in the Church as universal or local texts, giving a comprehensive treatment of the faith. The *Catechism of the Catholic Church* (CCC), first published by Pope John Paul II in 1992[23] and finalised in 1997, provides us in our time with a comprehensive account of all that the Catholic Church teaches. It is 'a statement of the Church's faith and of Catholic doctrine, attested to or illuminated by Sacred Scripture, the Apostolic Tradition and the Church's Magisterium'.[24] It refers us to the deposit of faith as believed, celebrated, lived and prayed:

- Profession of Faith (the Creed)
- Celebrating the Christian Mystery (the Sacraments)
- Life in Christ (the Beatitudes and Ten Commandments)
- Prayer in the Christian Life (the Lord's Prayer)

Structured around these four established pillars, the Catechism is presented as a doctrinal point of reference for the six fundamental tasks of catechesis and for the preparation of local catechisms. It does so without predetermining the composition or organisation of the one or the other: 'The best structure for catechesis must be one which is suitable to the particular concrete circumstances and cannot be established for the whole Church by a common catechism.'[25] A Compendium to accompany the Catechism, providing in concise form all the essential elements of the Church's faith, was approved by Pope Benedict XVI in 2005 and published in English in 2006.[26]

[21] See CCC 1812-1813.
[22] See GDC 115.
[23] See *Catechism of the Catholic Church* (Dublin: Veritas, 1994).
[24] *FD* 4a.
[25] J. Ratzinger, 'Il Catechismo della Chiesa Cattolica e l'ottismo dei redenti', J. Ratzinger and C. Schönborn, *Brief Introduction to the Catechism of the Catholic Church* (Rome: 1994), pp. 26-7.
[26] See *Compendium of the Catechism of the Catholic Church* (Dublin: Veritas, 2006).

50. This National Directory for Catechesis is designed to assist us in considering how to engage with lifelong education in faith within our local and national context. It is not possible or even desirable here to repeat or even to try to summarise all that is presented in the universal Catechism. It is useful, however, to outline briefly the key concepts treated of fully in the Catechism, as a reminder to all of the teaching that sustains the fundamental tasks of catechesis and gives life to faith development efforts of one kind or another. The Catechism, when studied and unpacked, can invigorate all those involved in faith development processes, giving them new momentum. Catechetical programmes for adults as well as children, for home as well as parish, depend for their direction on the universal *Catechism of the Catholic Church* in the first place, on the *General Directory for Catechesis*, and now on this *National Directory for Catechesis in Ireland*, always seeking to remain faithful to the teaching of the Church and the people who are the Church. Initiatives in new evangelisation and in theological reflection should also base all their efforts in the Catechism and Directories. Religious education in schools should keep these sources in mind for Catholic students and for those interested in knowing more about the Catholic faith.

**STUDY GROUP: REFLECT TOGETHER ON THE
*CATECHISM OF THE CATHOLIC CHURCH***

Consider setting up a group to look at the Catechism over a period of time. Think of it like a book club taking a night to discuss a particular section read beforehand:

- Do you have the *Catechism of the Catholic Church* [CCC] or the *Compendium of the Catechism of the Catholic Church* in your home?
- Do you read it?
- Which sections appeal to you?
- What does it mean to you in your life?
- Have you marked particular phrases, quotes, paragraphs that help you in your faith?
- Which particular sections have taught you something new?
- What methodology is helpful in the group?
- In what way do you think you could bring what you have learned to others?
- In what ways could the Catechism be misused?

The Profession of Faith:
The Apostles' Creed

51. There would be no common faith if we had no common language of faith. The words and phrases we hold in common make it possible for us to speak of what we believe. 'As a mother who teaches her children to speak and so to understand and communicate, the Church, our Mother, teaches us the language of faith in order to introduce us to the understanding and the life of faith.'[27] It is only when lived that faith fully makes sense and gives us new life.

In the Creed, we profess our belief in the central teachings of the Church, handed down to us by the gift of God. The Creed, in its three-part structure, proclaims the nature of our relationship with God. 'We believe in no one but God: the Father, the Son and the Holy Spirit.'[28] The mystery of relationship with the Trinity is at the heart of Christian life. It is in this very relationship that we come to know God, the creator of heaven and earth, the Living God, revealed to us by Jesus as our compassionate and merciful Father. In the embrace of the Father, we come to know the goodness of our created nature, we become aware of the corruption of sin, and we acknowledge our need for salvation, forgiveness and love without end in God.

52. In the Creed, the wonder of the Incarnation is attested to. God has given of himself completely, taking on our human nature in Jesus Christ. The Paschal Mystery of Christ's passion, death and resurrection, as the ultimate response to the human need for salvation, is affirmed, revealing the full extent of God's love for us and the possibility of our living, with all our sins forgiven, a new life in loving service of God and of one another. Our understanding of the human person is transformed in the light of the Incarnation. Human life is brought to fulfilment in the Redemption offered by the Cross and Resurrection. With Mary, the model of discipleship and Christian mission, we say yes to Christ. In him we are newly expressed and newly created, given dignity beyond compare.[29]

[27] CCC 171.
[28] CCC 171.
[29] See *RH* 8-10.

The Creed confirms, too, our belief that it is through the Holy Spirit that we are enabled to live in the love of Jesus Christ. We do not stand alone. Under the guidance of the Spirit, we become together the Church, proclaiming in Christ the communion of saints, the forgiveness of sins, the resurrection of the body and life everlasting. The Church, by the power of the Spirit, witnesses to Christ for the life of the world:

> The Church's fundamental function in every age and particularly in ours is to direct man's gaze, to point the awareness and experience of the whole of humanity towards the mystery of God, to help all men to be familiar with the profundity of the Redemption taking place in Christ Jesus.[30]

Belief is a gift and a responsibility. In the Church, our faith grows and matures and bears fruit. It may decay if we do not live life fully, drawing nourishment from the soil within which we have been planted. It can wither if we do not water it in prayer. But faith can grow strong through trials and become robust in doing good. The Creed vocalises our complete trust in God, who will fulfil every one of our needs:

The Apostles' Creed[31]

I believe in God, the Father almighty,
creator of heaven and earth.

I believe in Jesus Christ, his only Son, our Lord.
He was conceived by the power of the Holy Spirit
and born of the Virgin Mary.
He suffered under Pontius Pilate,
was crucified, died, and was buried.
He descended to the dead.
On the third day he rose again.
He ascended into heaven
and is seated at the right hand of the Father.
He will come again to judge the living and the dead.

I believe in the Holy Spirit,
the holy catholic Church, the communion of saints,
the forgiveness of sins, the resurrection of the body,
and life everlasting. Amen.

[30] *RH* 10.
[31] See *CCC* 197.

> ## PAUSE FOR REFLECTION: I BELIEVE; WE BELIEVE
>
> Faith is a personal act – the free response of the human person to the initiative of God who reveals himself. But faith is not an isolated act. No one can believe alone, just as no one can live alone. You have not given yourself faith as you have not given yourself life. The believer has received faith from others and should hand it on to others. Our love for Jesus and for our neighbour impels us to speak to others about our faith. Each believer is thus a link in the great chain of believers. I cannot believe without being carried by the faith of others, and by my faith I help support others in the faith.
>
> CCC 166.

The Celebration of Christian Mystery: The Sacraments

53. The Church is not an end in herself, but, as Vatican II says, a 'sacrament'; that is, a sign and instrument of innermost union with God and of unity among all people.[32] The seven sacraments of the Church, the sacred signs of Jesus Christ, might be described as 'gateways' through which Christ continues to make his entrance into this world. His presence and action in the world is not confined to these sacraments, but through them we are 'united with Christ'. The whole cosmos continues to be a revelation of God's power and love, the more so as we grow in human knowledge and consciousness. The sacraments, however, touching all the stages and all the important moments of Christian life, celebrate life with Christ. They are signs perceptible by the senses, more exactly sign-actions, made up of words and gestures, that effect what they symbolise.[33] The sacraments are rooted in the life of Jesus Christ. In his healings and miracles, we find a kind of 'prototype' of his sacraments.[34] Through the sacraments, we receive the gift of grace – that is to say, the very life of God. They have a past and a present, but they also point us to the future: they are a 'foretaste' of heaven.[35]

Sacraments of Initiation

54. Although in the Acts of the Apostles there are cases of very quick initiation into the Christian life, as the Church settled into its role in human history the preparation for Baptism often took up to three years. The catechumens in the Early Church, on their journey toward Baptism, received instruction, usually from the bishop himself. They learned the Creed, received the Lord's Prayer, and were examined on the manner of their life and their knowledge of the faith (the 'scrutinies'). Finally, usually at the Easter Vigil, they were initiated into the Church through Baptism and Confirmation, and received the Eucharist for the first time.[36] Since Vatican II, the

[32] See *LG* 1.
[33] See CCC 1084.
[34] See CCC 547.
[35] See CCC 1130.
[36] See C. Schönborn, *Living the Catechism of the Catholic Church: Volume 2, The Sacraments* (San Francisco: Ignatius Press, 2001), pp. 57-8.

Church has restored this process of preparation and re-established a *Rite of Christian Initiation of Adults* following the model of the Early Church.[37] Very often, however, people who received these three sacraments as children, still today, do not realise that they form a unity.

Baptism is the entrance to life in the Spirit and the basis of the whole Christian way of life.[38] It is 'the foundation of communion among all Christians'.[39] Immersion in water represents plunging into the death and burial of Christ; cleansing, 'the washing of regeneration'; and new creation, resurrection with Christ to new life.[40] The adult who is baptised after completing the RCIA process, becomes one with Jesus Christ, is freed from original sin and from personal sin, and is recognised as a child of God. He or she is incorporated into Christ and into his Church, and receives the gifts of the Holy Spirit. 'A baptised person belongs forever to Christ.'[41]

Infant Baptism has become a sign in the Church, almost from the beginning, that God loves us first. God's love is undeserved. We do not win it for ourselves in life. The child who is baptised becomes, too, a participant in the divine life of the Trinity and is drawn into communion with all Christians. Any Christian person will not want to withhold Baptism from their child.[42] Yet infant Baptism clearly brings with it responsibilities, on the part of parents and godparents, with the help of grandparents, the wider family and the local Christian community. Christian parents accept the responsibility of bringing their child to Christ through a religious and prayerful upbringing. They seek to encourage her or him to grow personally in the faith they have been gifted with at Baptism and to become fully members of their family, the Church.

Confirmation is the sacrament of growth in the Holy Spirit. Both Baptism and Confirmation bestow the gifts of the Holy Spirit, but the relationship between them has sometimes been compared to the relationship between Easter, when the risen Lord greeted the disciples with peace and breathed the Holy Spirit on them, and Pentecost, when they became aware of the power of the Holy Spirit, strengthening them to become his witnesses.[43] In the Church, the appropriate age for Confirmation is a continuing debate.[44] Whenever it takes place, catechesis for Confirmation should 'awaken a sense of belonging to the Church'.[45] It should strengthen one's bond with one's bishop and with the whole Christian community.

The Eucharist, 'the Sacrament of sacraments',[46] is the 'source and summit of Christian life.'[47] It is the sacrament of our innermost union with God.[48] Instituted by Jesus Christ at the Last Supper through the blessing and sharing out of bread and wine, the celebration of the Eucharist makes sacramentally present Christ's total sacrifice of himself, for us, on Good Friday

[37] See *RCIA*.
[38] See *CCC* 1213.
[39] *CCC* 1271.
[40] See *CCC* 1214-1228.
[41] *Compendium of the Catechism of the Catholic Church* 263.
[42] See *CCC* 1250.
[43] See C. Schönborn, *Living the Catechism of the Catholic Church: Volume 2, The Sacraments*, p. 75.
[44] See *SCar* 17-19.
[45] *CCC* 1309.
[46] *CCC* 1211.
[47] *LG* 11
[48] See *CCC* 1322-1336.

at Calvary. The bread and wine become the body and blood of Christ. At the altar, we are united with him in his cross and resurrection. The People of God gathered together, participating in the Eucharist through Christ, with him and in him, offer everything they are, too, to God for the good of all humankind:

> In the bread and wine that we bring to the altar, all creation is taken up by Christ the Redeemer to be transformed and presented to the Father. In this way we also bring to the altar, all the pain and suffering of the world, in the certainty that everything has value in God's eyes.[49]

From the altar we receive the Body of Christ, broken, crucified, risen and really present. In his victory over sin and death, we become what we have received: the Body of Christ, the Church, the community of unselfish service, of profound and active love formed, living and progressing under the Spirit. Our lives take on new meaning. The Eucharist offers us intimate communion with Jesus Christ and committed communion with one another, a tender but radically life-changing embrace. This 'profound encounter with the Lord Jesus'[50] touches us deep within. It transforms our being in his love. And in us he reaches out, in ways often unknown, to offer healing and hope to our wider community and society as a whole: 'By its nature the Eucharist is the sacrament of peace.'[51]

PRAYERFUL MEDITATION: *SANCTI VENITE*

Draw near and take the body of the Lord,
And drink with faith the blood outpoured.

Offered was he for greatest and for least,
Himself the Victim, and himself the Priest.

He that all his saints in this world rules and shields
To all believers life eternal yields.

He feeds the hungry with the bread of heaven
And living streams to those who thirst are given.

Approach you then with faithful hearts sincere,
And take the pledges of salvation here.

Ireland, seventh century.

Sacraments of Healing

55. Jesus gifted the disciples with peace and joy, sending them as the Father had sent him, to bring forgiveness into the world (John 20:19-23). The Church should be a sign and instrument of that forgiveness and reconciliation. The sacrament of **Penance and Reconciliation** celebrates Christ's forgiveness of us and his healing of our hearts and minds. By confessing, we take responsibility for

[49] *SCar* 47.
[50] *SCar* 50.
[51] *SCar* 49.

our sin, recognising it for what it is. Our sorrow for what we have done, or what we failed to do, leads to contrition, absolution, penance and renewed hope. We can act differently, and pledge ourselves so to do. We open ourselves in Jesus Christ to reconciliation with God and with one another.[52]

The Anointing of the Sick is meant for those living with serious illness, as well as for those who are close to death. Jesus sent his disciples out to care for the sick, and by so doing to participate in his ministry of compassion and healing. From the beginning, Christians have put care for the sick high on their agenda, knowing that in this they are serving Christ himself. Those who receive this sacrament are strengthened by the Holy Spirit; given the grace to unite their own suffering with that of Christ; forgiven their sins; and brought to understand that they can contribute 'to the good of all'. The sick person 'is in a certain way... consecrated' to work for the salvation of all.[53]

PAUSE FOR THOUGHT:
HEALING THROUGH THE SACRAMENTS

Through the sacraments, Christ himself touches, strengthens, heals us. The sacraments are, so to speak, the earthly hands of the heavenly, risen Lord. What he touches is healed.

Christ does not heal by simply taking away the symptoms of the illness. His healing goes into the depths. As he said to the paralytic: 'My son, your sins are forgiven' (Mark 2:5). Christ heals the whole man. His healing begins at the root of all that is unhealthy: the sin that separates us from God, the source of life (CCC 1421). That is why the healing element of the forgiveness of sins is part of every sacrament. We are really healthy only when we are reconciled with God, united with Christ, and filled with the Holy Spirit. Then pain and sickness can have a positive 'salutary' effect. How mild are the troubles of this world, when we have the Holy Spirit!, says the Curé of Ars.

The more we recognise in faith the Church herself as the sacrament of God's love, the more the healing dimension of the sacraments will open itself up to us. She is healing fellowship, loving Mother, who dispenses the 'medicine' of Christ to us.

C. Schönborn, *Living the Catechism of the Catholic Church: Volume 2, The Sacraments*, p. 104.

---

[52] See CCC 1440-1460.

[53] See CCC 1499-1525.

Sacraments at the Service of Communion

56. In a sense, all the sacraments have a healing effect and are at the service of communion. Holy Orders and Marriage do, however, confer a particular mission in the Church and serve to build up the 'People of God' through service of others.[54]

Three forms of ordained ministry have been handed down at the service of Christ and his people: bishop, priest and deacon. **Holy Orders** is the sacrament through which the mission entrusted by Jesus to his apostles is continued in the Church until the end of time. It is the sacrament of apostolic ministry.[55] In the New Covenant, there is but one priest, Jesus Christ. The whole People of God is, however, priestly, each participating in what is called the common or baptismal priesthood according to his or her vocation in Christ.[56] Within the Church, some men are called, through ministerial priesthood, to make present and visible, 'without diminishing the uniqueness of Christ's priesthood',[57] the presence of Christ as Head and Spouse of

his Body, the Church. The ministerial priesthood, differing in essence by its being at the service of the common priesthood, is 'a means by which Christ unceasingly builds up and leads his Church'.[58] And so the priest turns toward God the Father, lifting up all he is and all that the faithful have to offer, in Christ. He speaks and acts before the People of God 'in the person of Christ', offering them the very Body and Blood of Jesus sacrificed for them. Through priests, despite their human frailty, Jesus continues to teach, sanctify and build up the community of the faithful. Through them, the Church continues to experience the loving kindness and forgiveness of Christ and to respond to that love in worship, praise and thanksgiving.

In the Bible, there is no stronger image for the covenant between God and God's people than married love. The mutual love of man and woman is an image of the absolute and unfailing love with which God loves us.[59] In the sacrament of Marriage, the promise

[54] CCC 1534.
[55] See CCC 1536.
[56] See CCC 1546.
[57] CCC 1545.
[58] CCC 1547.
[59] See CCC 1604.

made by a man and a woman to be faithful to each other, all their days, and their openness to the children they may receive, establishes between them a partnership of the whole of life, 'an unbreakable union of their two lives'.[60] Christian marriage reflects the New Covenant between Christ and the Church, the Bride for whom he gave his life.[61] As a commitment to love and to life, Christian marriage, blessed by God, builds up the ecclesial community and is deserving of its full support. Christian marriage is a true sacrament, signifying and communicating grace, echoing the faithful love of God.

Life in Christ:
The Beatitudes and Commandments

57. God created man and woman in God's own image.[62] God created us as rational beings, giving us the dignity of persons who can initiate and control our own actions.[63] The freedom we have is not so that we can choose indiscriminately between good and evil, but so that we can of our own accord choose what is good and what corresponds to the truth.[64] By means of an informed conscience, we recognise what God expects of us. If we ignore the voice of conscience within our hearts, we do ourselves violence and act against our own happiness. The education of conscience is the task of a lifetime.[65]

The Beatitudes

58. The Christian understands the desire for happiness as coming from God. This hope is in our hearts in order to draw us to God. When Jesus went out onto the hills above the Sea of Galilee to proclaim the Beatitudes, he explained the essence of all his teaching. Those who are open to new hope, those who are poor, humble, afflicted, pure in heart, can all find happiness in God. They are blessed, and so are we, in recognising God's love for us. In the Beatitudes, Jesus strikes at the deepest level our desire for happiness, a longing that cannot be fully and finally satisfied here in this earthly life, but only in the realisation of the kingdom of heaven:

[60] CCC 1605.
[61] See CCC 1616-1617.
[62] See Gen 1:26.
[63] See CCC 1730.
[64] See Aid to the Church in Need, in collaboration with the Congregation for the Clergy, *I Believe: A Little Catholic Catechism* (Königstein im Taunus: Aid to the Church in Need, 2004), p. 148.
[65] See CCC 1776-1789.

Blessed are the poor in spirit, for theirs is the kingdom of heaven.
Blessed are those who mourn, for they will be comforted.
Blessed are the meek, for they will inherit the earth.
Blessed are those who hunger and thirst for righteousness, for they will be filled.
Blessed are the merciful, for they will receive mercy.
Blessed are the pure in heart, for they will see God.
Blessed are the peacemakers, for they will be called children of God.
Blessed are those who are persecuted for righteousness sake, for theirs is the kingdom of heaven.
Blessed are you when people revile you and persecute you and utter all kinds of evil against you falsely on my account.
Rejoice and be glad, for your reward is great in heaven.
(Matthew 5:3-12)[66]

[66] See CCC 1716.

MEDITATION:
BE BLESSED IN THE LORD

Come to Galilee and be blessed.
Come, see, and be blessed.
Hear him calling, and be blessed.
Stay with the Lord, and be blessed.
Take root in his land, and be blessed.
Walk along the lakeshore, and be blessed.
Bathe your feet in the water, and be blessed.
Listen to his words, and be blessed.
'Be merciful and be blessed.'
'Be a peacemaker and be blessed.'
Marvel at the crowds that follow him, and be blessed.
'Feed them yourselves', and be blessed.
'But I have only five loaves and two fish': Be blessed.
Watch the sunrise together, and be blessed.
Know the darkness and the light, and be blessed.
Say 'I love you, Lord', and be blessed.
Say 'You know I love you', and be blessed.
Throw out your nets, and be blessed.
Confront your fears, and be blessed.
Cross over to the other side, and be blessed.
Face into the storm, and be blessed.
Accept your weakness, and be blessed.
Acknowledge your sin, and be blessed.
Ask for healing, and be blessed.
Come to the water of life, and be blessed.
Drink deep of the Lord, and be blessed.
Walk with him on Tabor, and be blessed.
Know yourself beloved, and be blessed.
Live in the Lord, and be blessed.
Give him space to hold you, and be blessed.
Breathe in his Spirit, and be blessed.
Let go of past pain, and be blessed.
Celebrate your joy, and be blessed.
Sing out your praises, and be blessed.
Stay a while in this place, and be blessed.
Know too when it is time to move on, and be blessed.
Take his love with you, and be blessed.
Set your face for Jerusalem, and be blessed.

G. Byrne, Mount of Beatitudes, Galilee, 2004.

The New Commandment of Love

59. When Jesus was asked if, from among all the laws and precepts of the Old Testament, there was one commandment that was more important than the others, that might sum them up, he replied that you must love the Lord your God with all your heart, with all your soul, and with all your mind, and you must love your neighbour as yourself. His New Law rests on this twofold commandment, which Jesus describes as the basis and fulfilment of all others. Our joy should be to live in the love of God as Jesus has done and to love one another as he has loved us.[67] This is our programme for life. The new commandment of love, lived in the spirit of the Beatitudes, constitutes the *magna carta* of the Christian life.[68] Love, as Pope Benedict points out, is lived by the Christian, freely, as a response to God's gift of love. Love is much more than a law imposed upon us: 'Since God has first loved us (cf. 1 John 4:10), love is no longer a mere 'command'; it is the response to the gift of love with which God draws near to us.'[69]

STARTING POINT: COMMITMENT OUT OF LOVE

The new law is called a *law of love* because it makes us act out of love infused with the Holy Spirit, rather than out of fear; a *law of grace,* because it confers the strength of grace to act, by means of faith and the sacraments; a *law of freedom,* because it sets us free from the ritual and juridical observances of the Old Law, inclines us to act spontaneously by the prompting of charity and, finally, lets us pass from the condition of a servant who 'does not know what his master is doing' to that of friend of Christ...

CCC 1972.

PRAYERFUL REFLECTION: HIS FRIEND IS MY FRIEND

In God and with God, I love even the person whom I do not like or even know. This can only take place on the basis of an intimate encounter with God, an encounter which has become a communion of will, even affecting my feelings. Then I learn to look on this other person not simply with my eyes and my feelings, but from the perspective of Jesus Christ. His friend is my friend... Seeing with the eyes of Christ, I can give to others much more than their outward necessities; I can give them the look of love which they crave... No longer is it a question, then, of a 'commandment' imposed from without and calling for the impossible, but rather of a freely bestowed experience of love from within, a love which by its very nature must then be shared with others. Love grows through love. Love is 'divine' because it comes from God and unites us to God...

DCE 18.

[67] See Jn 15:9-12.
[68] See *GDC* 115.
[69] *DCE* 1.

The Ten Commandments

60. The Ten Commandments are presented in the *Catechism of the Catholic Church* as a framework upon which to build a Christian life. They are written in the heart of humankind, meeting with recognition in many religions, precisely because they reflect what is right and true. They are understood to be an obligation on all men and women, always and everywhere:[70]

1. I am the Lord your God: you shall not have strange gods before me.
2. You shall not take the name of the Lord your God in vain.
3. Remember to keep holy the Lord's day.
4. Honour your father and your mother.
5. You shall not kill.
6. You shall not commit adultery.
7. You shall not steal.
8. You shall not bear false witness against your neighbour.
9. You shall not covet your neighbour's wife.
10. You shall not covet your neighbour's goods.[71]

The Decalogue ('the ten words'), revealed by God to Moses, proclaims God's law. It confirms the implications of belonging to God.[72] To keep the Commandments means to cling to God with our whole heart, living in covenant, living in communion with God.

The Ten Commandments are an invitation to true freedom: living in God's love according to the law that God has written into our hearts. They are an invitation to grow, to live life fully in open and honest relationship with God, and with one another, in a way that is respectful of the world and all it contains. The New Law of Christ, the Law of the Gospel, 'fulfils, refines, surpasses and leads the Old Law to its perfection'.[73] It does not abolish the Ten Commandments, but reveals their full potential, seeking to reform our hearts, teaching us to live in justice, peace and love, and orienting us towards the Kingdom of God. Jesus wishes all humanity to become like God, who is Love itself. In the Beatitudes, as well as in the Our Father and in Matthew 25, for instance, Jesus spells out how being a follower of his means taking the Ten Commandments and making of them a positive law of love: calling God 'Our Father'; helping make God's kingdom come; doing God's will; feeding those who are hungry or thirsty; providing for the homeless; visiting those who are sick or in prison.[74]

[70] See *CCC* 2072.
[71] This is the traditional catechetical formula. See CCC 2051 ff; Ex 20:2-17; Deut 5:6-21.
[72] See *CCC* 2062.
[73] *CCC* 1967.
[74] See C. Maloney, F. O'Connell and B. O'Reilly, *Alive-O 7*, Teacher's Book (Dublin: Veritas, 2003), pp. 82-83.

GROUP REFLECTION:
THE BEATITUDES GO FURTHER

A life lived according to the Ten Commandments is good; it is a way to true life. Christ though wants more. The Beatitudes go further; the Sermon on the Mount demands more – not only to refrain from killing, but to love one's enemies (CCC 2054). When we follow him, he himself becomes the guideline of our conduct; he lives and loves in us (CCC 2074).

C. Schönborn, *Living the Catechism of the Catholic Church: Volume 3, Life in Christ* (San Francisco: Ignatius Press, 2001), p. 90.

Prayer in the Christian Life: The Lord's Prayer

PAUSE FOR REFLECTION: WHAT IS PRAYER?

Life cannot be reduced to activity, to efficiency. It is also contemplation, friendship, relaxation, celebration. In prayer man places himself explicitly in a state of dependence on God and in the radiance of his Love. He gives thanks for the gifts received and prepares to receive those which he is requesting. At a still deeper level, the Christian places his entire being in a filial communion with God, through Jesus. In so doing he expresses the fundamental attitude of faith, hope and charity in ways which vary according to the situation, the joys, the sorrows – both personal and shared in the community.

Aid to the Church in Need, *I Believe: A Little Catholic Catechism*, p. 175.

61. Throughout the Scriptures, we observe an unceasing dialogue between God and human beings. In their one-to-one conversation with God, the prophets draw strength for their mission. The Psalms express all human sentiments, nourishing the prayer of believers, whether as individual or communal prayer. Jesus often retires to a quiet place to pray, to give thanks and to offer entreaty to the Father, in the power of the Spirit.

Christian prayer has several different forms of expression: adoration, praise, thanksgiving, petition, lament and intercession. It can be entered into in a variety of fashions: vocal prayer expressed outwardly in words, meditation or quiet reflection frequently starting from the Word of God, and contemplation, described by St Teresa of Avila as 'nothing else than a close sharing between friends; it means taking time frequently to be alone with him who we know loves us'.[75]

[75] St Teresa of Jesus, *The Book of Her Life* 8.5, *The Collected Works of St Teresa of Avila*, trans. K. Kavanagh and O. Rodriguez (Washington, DC: Institute of Carmelite Studies, 1976), Vol 1, p. 67; see also CCC 2709.

The pattern of all Christian prayer and the prayer that unites all Christians is the Lord's Prayer, the prayer Jesus taught his disciples. It is a summary of the whole Gospel[76] and holds within it a synopsis of all that is meant by Christian prayer. Its first proclamation is summarised by St Matthew in the Sermon on the Mount,[77] where it is placed at the centre of Jesus' teaching. 'The Sermon on the Mount is teaching for life, the *Our Father* is a prayer; but in both the one and the other the Spirit of the Lord gives new form to our desires, those inner movements that animate our lives. Jesus teaches us this new life by his words; he teaches us to ask for it by our prayer.'[78] In the Irish tradition, the Lord's Prayer is simply known as 'An Phaidir' – *The* Prayer.

An Phaidir
Ár nAthair atá ar neamh,
Go naofar d'ainm,
Go dtaga do ríocht,
Go ndéantar do thoil ar an talamh
Mar a dhéantar ar neamh.
Ár n-arán laethúil tabhair dúinn inniu,
Agus maith dúinn ár bhfiacha,
Mar a mhaithimidne dár bhféichiúna féin,
Agus ná lig sinn i gcathú,
Ach saor sinn ó olc.

The Lord's Prayer
Our Father, who art in heaven,
Hallowed be thy name.
Thy kingdom come,
Thy will be done on earth as it is in heaven.
Give us this day our daily bread,
And forgive us our trespasses
As we forgive those who trespass against us,
And lead us not into temptation,
But deliver us from evil.[79]

[76] See CCC 2761.
[77] See Mt 5-7; see also Lk 11:2-4.
[78] CCC 2764.
[79] Mt 6:9-13. See CCC 2759-2865.

And from the earliest days of the Church, the Lord's Prayer has been concluded with a hymn of praise by the assembled community:[80]

> For the kingdom,
> the power and the glory are yours,
> now and for ever. Amen.

PERSONAL REFLECTION:
IT IS THE HEART THAT PRAYS

According to Scripture it is the *heart* that prays... The heart is the dwelling-place where I am, where I live; according to the Semitic or biblical expression, the heart is the place 'to which I withdraw'. The heart is our hidden centre, beyond the grasp of our reason and of others; only the Spirit of God can fathom the human heart and know it fully. The heart is the place of decision, deeper than our psychic drives. It is the place of truth, where we choose life or death. It is the place of encounter, because as image of God we live in relation: it is the place of covenant.

CCC 2563.

SCRIPTURE:
THE PEACE OF GOD BE WITH YOU

Have no anxiety about anything, but in everything by prayer and supplication with thanksgiving let your requests be made known to God. And the peace of God, which surpasses all understanding, will keep your hearts and your minds in Christ Jesus.

Finally brethren, whatever is true, whatever is honourable, whatever is just, whatever is pure, whatever is lovely, whatever is gracious, if there is any excellence, if there is anything worthy of praise, think about these things...and the God of peace will be with you.

(Philippians 4:6-9)

---

[80] See CCC 2760.

Ecumenical Outreach

62. The very brief introduction to the foundations of Catholic faith outlined in this chapter immediately points up the need to address, under the guidance of the Holy Spirit, a Christianity that is divided and continues to be less than it could be: 'Because of the divisions among Christians, the fullness of universality, which is proper to the Church governed by the Successor of Peter and the Bishops in communion with him, is not fully realised in history.'[81] Building up the Church and educating for community living, the fifth fundamental task of catechesis, requires an energetic and ongoing ecumenical evangelisation to establish the fullest possible unity among Christians.

The restoration of Christian unity was one of the principal concerns of the Second Vatican Council.[82] Since then, great strides have been made, although there remains the hope of fuller and more comprehensive agreements, leading to unity of faith, sacraments and community living.[83] Recognising that 'the desire to recover the unity of all Christians is a gift of Christ and a call of the Holy Spirit',[84] we place all our hope 'in the prayer of Christ for the Church, in the love of the Father for us, and in the power of the Holy Spirit.'[85] Ecumenical conversation, at all levels of life, should be encouraged locally and nationally, with genuine and respectful unity among Christians as its prize: 'Catechesis, therefore, is always called to assume an "ecumenical dimension" everywhere.'[86] Every opportunity should be availed of to work collaboratively, where possible, with other Christians in exploring issues of faith:

> To believe in Christ means to desire unity; to desire unity means to desire the Church; to desire the Church means to desire the communion of grace which corresponds to the Father's plan from all eternity. Such is the meaning of Christ's prayer: *'Ut unum sint'* [that they may all be one (Jn 17:21)].[87]

The witness offered at the beginning of the new millennium, as the Holy Year Door at the Basilica of St Paul-Outside-the-Walls was opened together by the Pope, the Archbishop of Canterbury and Orthodox Metropolitan Athanasius, provided an image for the twenty-first century, a teaching and learning moment, a sign of the possible unity keenly sought after by so many. In his homily on

[81] Congregation for the Doctrine of the Faith, *Responses to Some Questions Regarding Certain Aspects of the Doctrine of the Church*, 29 June 2007.
[82] See UR 1.
[83] CCC 820; see also UR 1.
[84] See UUS 1995; see also Pontifical Council for the Promotion of Christian Unity, *Directory for the Application of Principles and Norms on Ecumenism*, 1993.
[85] UR 24.
[86] GDC 197.
[87] UUS 9.

that day, Pope John Paul, speaking of unity as a demand of the Christian conscience, confirmed its great significance in the proclamation of the Good News:

> In this basilica built in honour of Paul, remembering the words with which the Apostle today has challenged our faith and our hope, *'by one Spirit we were all baptised into one body'*, let us ask Christ to forgive everything in the Church's history which has compromised his plan of unity. Let us confidently ask him, *the door of life, the door of salvation, the door of peace*, to support our steps, to make the progress already achieved long-lasting, to grant us the support of his Spirit, so that our commitment will be ever more authentic and effective... The future of evangelisation, the proclamation of the Gospel to the men and women of our time, greatly depends on this.[88]

THE ONGOING PROCESS OF DYNAMIC UNION WITH CHRIST

Although the Catholic Church has the fullness of the means of salvation, 'nevertheless the divisions among Christians prevent the Church from effecting the fullness of catholicity proper to her in those of her children who, though joined to her by baptism, are yet separated from full communion with her'. The fullness of the Catholic Church, therefore, already exists, but still has to grow in the brothers who are not yet in full communion with it and also in its own members who are sinners 'until it happily arrives at the fullness of eternal glory in the heavenly Jerusalem'. This progress is fully rooted in the ongoing process of dynamic union with Christ: 'Union with Christ is also union with all those to whom he gives himself. I cannot possess Christ just for myself; I can belong to him only in union with all those who have become, or will become, his own. Communion draws me out of myself towards him, and thus also towards unity with all Christians.'

Congregation for the Doctrine of the Faith,
Commentary on the Document: Responses to Some Questions Regarding Certain Aspects of the Doctrine of the Church, 29 June 2007.

The Challenge of Inculturation

63. The Church by her very nature, united with Christ, crucified and risen, her ever-present Origin, continually seeks to bring the Good News of God's love into all the strata of human life, offering new 'criteria of judgement, determining values, points of interest, lines of thought, sources of inspiration and models of life'.[89] We recognise the Church, broken as she is, but living in the power of

[88] John Paul II, *Homily at St Paul-Outside-the-Walls, Opening of the Holy Door: Week of Christian Prayer for Unity*, 18 Jan 2000.
[89] *EN* 19.

the Holy Spirit, as a people wherein humankind can 'see' Christ and so come to discover humanity's true home in the heart of God, our merciful and caring Father. Through the Church, the culture of the Resurrection takes root in human history.

Catechesis guides the Christian into a deep, personal, lived faith and the accompanying interior change and conversion it calls for. Such change, if it is real, leads us to the desire to transform humanity from within and make it new: 'Now I am making the whole of creation new' (Revelation 21:5). Catechesis cannot be limited, then, to the level of personal ethics. In putting on Christ,[90] we let him enter more deeply into our whole lives, bringing him into our world, our relationships, family, workplace and wherever we go. We are invited by Christ to recognise the needs of the world around us and to engage, by our very presence and way of life, in an evangelisation of its culture. At the same time, we recognise that we are shaped by the culture within which we live. We seek new ways to express within our culture what we believe and value in Jesus Christ. Inculturation, then, is a two-way process, 'the unceasing interplay of the Gospel and of man's concrete life, both personal and social',[91] by which the Gospel is woven into the variety of human cultures and authentic cultural values are integrated into Christian life.[92] Inculturation is entered into willingly and attentively. The truth of life today and the truth we come to know in the Gospel disclose each other, inform each other, build upon each other.

64. In this context, the reflection on Christian faith that we have engaged with in this chapter leads us to dialogue with the ever-changing Irish context, reviewed in Chapter 1. St Patrick and other early missionaries who came to Ireland explained the Gospel in terms that the local people of the time could understand. They also used what was good in the culture to bring the Gospel message to its full potential for the Church as it developed in Celtic Ireland. So today, we need new ways of engaging with the variety of cultural influences, indigenous as well as newly arrived, that make modern

[90] See Col 1:26ff; Eph 3:4-9; Rom 46:25-27.
[91] *EN* 29.
[92] See *EA* 59.

Ireland such a rich tapestry. We must be prepared not only to acknowledge and live the refreshing and challenging message of the Gospel, but also to engage with our cultural reality, learning from it, thoughtfully and not uncritically, new ways of expressing our knowledge and understanding in Christ.

Christians, of course, acknowledge that God reached out in a particular way to a particular culture in Jesus Christ. The Gospel message cannot be isolated from the culture in which it was first inserted or from the cultures within which it has been expressed down the centuries.[93] On the other hand, the members of the Church in Ireland today must discover new ways of presenting Jesus Christ with confidence for our time and people. We must attempt to find the language, and live the message, in the public space as well as in our families, parishes and other Christian communities, in such a way that we can hear Christ anew, follow him with enthusiasm, and introduce him personally to those who are searching. 'We can say of catechesis, as well as of evangelisation in general, that it is called to bring the power of the Gospel into the very heart of culture and cultures.'[94]

STARTING POINT: IN COMMUNION WITH CULTURE

The Church has been sent to all ages and nations and, therefore, is not tied exclusively and indissolubly to any race or nation, to any one particular way of life, or to any customary practices, ancient or modern. The Church is faithful to its traditions and is at the same time conscious of its universal mission; it can, then, enter into communion with different forms of culture, thereby enriching both itself and the cultures themselves.

GS 58.

[93] See *CT 53*.
[94] *CT 53*

> **TO DO:**
> **ENGAGE IN THE DIALOGUE THAT IS**
> **INCULTURATION**
>
> Consider what action is necessary to address the challenge of inculturation, and how this might best be achieved. The *General Directory for Catechesis* suggests that the local Church should:
>
> ● encourage what in the culture is compatible with the Gospel message and also help people identify what in the culture is incompatible with it;
>
> ● engage in the necessary dialogue between the Gospel and the relevant culture, recognising that the Gospel possesses power to regenerate and change that culture;
>
> ● develop an intimate knowledge of the culture within which to present the Gospel;
>
> ● develop a respect for and an adult response to the language that is proper to the message of the Gospel – in particular biblical language, the historical-traditional language of the Church and doctrinal language.
>
> See *GDC* 203-208.

Inter-religious Dialogue

65. More than ever before in Ireland, the desire to live Christ in the world brings us into conversation with people who have not met Jesus and do not know the power of his love. Participating in the life and mission of the Church, we are drawn into an appreciation and respect for other people's search for and closeness to God. The Holy Spirit, active in the Church, sows the seeds of the Word where the Spirit wills: 'Indeed, it is always the Spirit who is at work, both when he gives life to the Church and impels her to proclaim Christ, and when he implants and develops his gifts in all individuals and peoples, guiding the Church to discover these gifts, to foster them and to receive them through dialogue.'[95] We are invited, then, into authentic inter-religious dialogue. We seek to learn more and more about the ways God works in the world, receiving from and giving to those of other religions. We engage also with those who do not have a religious commitment that, through inter-cultural dialogue, we may learn together something of the truth that seeks to transform us all.

66. We are reminded by the Second Vatican Council of the honour due to our 'elder brothers and sisters', the Jewish people,[96] through whom we have received so much. Since God does not take back the gifts bestowed or the choices made,[97] we recognise the common

[95] *RM* 29.
[96] See John Paul II, *Visit to Rome Synagogue*, 1986.
[97] See *NA* 4.

spiritual inheritance we hold with the Jewish people. The Church deplores anti-Semitism and happily encourages mutual understanding and appreciation among members of the Jewish and Christian faithful:

> The Church believes that Christ who is our peace has through his cross reconciled Jews and Gentiles and made them one in himself (see Ephesians 2:14-16).[98]

Among the many prophetic actions of Pope John Paul II in building up proper relations with the Jewish people were his visits to the synagogue in Rome in 1986 and to the Holy Land in 2000, where he honoured the victims of the Holocaust at Yad Vashem, and placed a Prayer of Repentance in the Western Wall. Pope Benedict XVI has also sought to build strong ties with the Jewish people, visiting three synagogues in a relatively short time period – Cologne (2005), New York (2008) and Rome (2010). Such emblematic moments encourage us as we seek to build together on the strong spiritual ties that bind the Christian and the Jewish peoples so closely together.

The diversity of people now living in Ireland, noted in Chapter 1, has in a very short time seen us welcome many Muslim people into Irish society, as they take up the invitation to work and live in this country. The Church has a profound respect for Muslims and holds out the hand of friendship to them, believing, as Pope Benedict has said, that 'Jews, Christians and Muslims are called to develop the bonds that unite us'.[99] Vatican II recognised that in worshipping God, who is one, merciful and almighty, the Creator of heaven and earth, Muslim believers strive to submit themselves unreservedly to the decrees of God.[100] The Church urges all Christians and Muslims 'that a sincere effort be made to achieve mutual understanding; for the benefit of all men, let them together preserve and promote peace, liberty, social justice and moral values'.[101]

[98] *NA* 4; see also Commission for Religious Relations with the Jews, *On the Correct Way to Present the Jews and Judaism in Preaching and Catechesis in the Roman Catholic Church*, 1985.
[99] Benedict XVI, *Address to the Members of the Foundation for Interreligious and Intercultural Research and Dialogue*, 1 February, 2007.
[100] See *NA* 3
[101] *NA* 3.

BUILDING TOGETHER
A WORLD OF PEACE AND FRATERNITY

Continuing, then, the work undertaken by my predecessor, Pope John Paul II, I sincerely pray that the relations of trust which have developed between Christians and Muslims over several years, will not only continue, but will develop further in a spirit of sincere and respectful dialogue, based on ever more authentic reciprocal knowledge which, with joy, recognises the religious values that we have in common and, with loyalty, respects the differences.

Inter-religious and inter-cultural dialogue is necessary for building together this world of peace and fraternity ardently desired by all people of good will... I am profoundly convinced that in the current world situation it is imperative that Christians and Muslims engage with one another in order to address the numerous challenges that present themselves to humanity, especially those concerning the defence and promotion of the dignity of the human person and the rights ensuing from that dignity.'

Benedict XVI, *Address to the Ambassadors of Countries with a Muslim Majority and the Representatives of Muslim Communities in Italy*, 25 September 2006.

People committed to a great variety of other non-Christian religions have, also, come to live in Ireland in recent years. The religions embraced by these people vary greatly. Vatican II signalled the Church's strong conviction that God's providence, evident goodness and saving designs, by the work of the Holy Spirit, extend to all humanity and to all religions that seek in their own way to calm the human heart through a programme of life based on doctrine, moral precepts and sacred rites:

> The Catholic Church rejects nothing of what is true and holy about these religions. She has a high regard for the manner of life and conduct, the precepts and doctrines which, although differing in many ways from her own teaching, nevertheless, often reflect a ray of that truth which enlightens all men.[102]

67. At the beginning of the twenty-first century, it has become clear that inter-religious and intercultural dialogues can only be entered into fully and with ease when those seeking to dialogue reverence their own beliefs and customs as well as those of others. We do not enter into dialogue with empty hands but bring with us all the riches of the truth that God has revealed to us. The Church, aware of the great hope she has received in Christ, continues always to make him known. The Christian 'can and must say that Jesus Christ has a significance and a value for the human race and its history, which are unique and singular, proper to him alone,

[102] *NA* 2.

exclusive, universal, and absolute. Jesus is the Word of God made man for the salvation of all.'[103] Dialogue does not dispense from proclaiming the Word. Although closely connected, dialogue and proclamation have their own place.[104] Recognising and respecting the riches associated with another person's religious commitment, Christians witness graciously to the truth of God's love for us in Jesus Christ, crucified and risen, whom we have come to know and love personally, through the generosity of the Holy Spirit.

In our increasingly diverse cultural and religious reality, it is important that all those who are involved in leadership roles in the local Church are encouraged and fully equipped to engage in open and respectful dialogue with people of different religious traditions. Indeed, catechesis and all faith development processes, taking place at the parish or school level, within ecclesial movements, small Christian communities and Catholic organisations, always in an environment that is genuinely supportive of the participant's own Christian faith, can usefully embrace learning about a variety of religions and their truth claims. We should all be able to honour people of different religious convictions, and reverence their commitment, without in any way succumbing to relativism:

> This requires Catholic communities ... to appreciate their own identity even more, prove their loyalty to Christ, know the content of their faith well, rediscover their missionary calling and thus commit themselves to bear witness for Jesus the Lord and his gospel. This is the necessary prerequisite for the correct attitude of sincere dialogue, open and respectful of all but at the same time neither naïve nor ill-equipped.[105]

> Let Christians, while witnessing to their own faith and way of life, acknowledge, preserve and encourage the spiritual and moral truths found among non-Christians, also their social life and culture.[106]

[103] *DI* 15.
[104] See *RM* 55a; Pontifical Council for Inter-Religious Dialogue, *Dialogue and Proclamation: Reflection and Orientations on Inter-religious Dialogue and the Proclamation of the Gospel of Jesus Christ* (Rome: 1991).
[105] *EMCC* 60.
[106] *NA* 2.

FOR REFLECTION AND PRAYER:
THE SPIRIT'S GIFT OF DISCERNMENT

The Holy Spirit is at work in the whole course of pastoral life from beginning to end. When we speak of the power of the Spirit we may usually think more of the strength the Holy Spirit gives for determined, energetic and constant action. But according to Christian belief, we owe to the Holy Spirit also the proper preparation and first beginning of any valuable work in the Kingdom of God, be it in the action of an individual Christian or of a Christian community. Spirit-filled work supposes the guidance of the Spirit already in the stage of discernment which precedes the action and leads to it.

In a time of cultural and religious pluralism and transition, and in a time of much uncertainty and confusion, also within the Christian community, the Spirit's gift of discernment is even more needed than in the era of a monolithic Christian society.

J. Hofinger, *Pastoral Life in the Power of the Spirit*
(New York: Alba House, 1982), p. 207.

SECTION C
SHARING THE
GOOD NEWS

CHAPTER 4

Adult Faith Development

68. Every presentation of the Gospel is an invitation to be evangelised. It is an invitation made to all, young and not so young, without exception. Adult Christians reflect constantly on the Gospel. They do so, not alone but as part of their local Christian community. They are content when others are intrigued by Christ and enter into dialogue about the relevance of his teaching for life and for our world today.

This dialogue is an essential element in the life of the adult Christian, as she or he seeks to respond to the wisdom and power of God the Father, through Jesus Christ, in the Holy Spirit: 'All the baptised, because they are called by God to maturity of faith, need and have therefore a right to adequate catechesis.'[1]

Bringing the faith of the baptised to full growth necessitates continuing faith development through all of life. Such ongoing education in faith is designed to deepen or sometimes to recover a person's commitment to their faith. Lifelong physical and psychological development, heightened at transition moments in life, requires that all faith education be age- and need-appropriate: 'Adults cannot be content with primary school religious knowledge. Doubts and difficulties about faith nearly always come from misunderstanding or lack of adult knowledge about our religion.'[2]

Adults who possess a mature faith serve as an example to others and should see themselves as a resource for catechesis and other forms of faith development among children, adolescents and other adults. They should be prepared to investigate how they can become involved collaboratively at the heart of the faith community, working together as lay people, religious and priests, each according to his or her role and gifts.

Since Vatican II, a new type of collaboration between lay people and clergy has happily come about in the Church. The

[1] *GDC* 167.
[2] *HFH*, p. 37.

spirit of readiness in which great numbers of lay people have offered themselves for the service of the Church must be counted among the best benefits of the Council. In this, there is a new experience of the fact that we are all the Church.[3]

All members of the Church should, therefore, be prepared to participate occasionally in ongoing education and training to further their own faith development and in order to minister more effectively, one to the other. Those in positions of pastoral leadership should never tire of engaging with their personal conversion and renewal for their own sake, for the sake of others and for the sake of the Kingdom of God: 'a kingdom of truth and life, a kingdom of holiness and grace, a kingdom of justice, love and peace.'[4]

The Catechesis of Adults

69. In seeking to build up the Kingdom of God, it is no wonder, then, that 'the *Magisterium of the Church*, imbued with the spirit of renewal of the Second Vatican Council (cf. *CD* 14; *AG* 14), has constantly affirmed with authority, clarity and insistence, the centrality and importance of the catechesis of adults.'[5]

STARTING POINT:
THE CHIEF FORM OF CATECHESIS

Catechesis for adults, since it deals with persons who are capable of an adherence that is fully responsible, must be considered the chief form of catechesis. All the other forms, which are indeed necessary, are in some way oriented to it.

GDC 20; see also CT 43.

Initiation of Adults into the Catholic Church
The catechesis of adults is the chief form and model for all catechesis and for faith development at every level in the Church. Adult conversion to Christ remains the essential action around which formation in faith takes place. In the Early Church, adults were initiated after a period of formation in the community, focused around catechetical instruction given by the local bishop. As highlighted in Chapter 2, the *Rite of Christian Initiation of Adults*, renewed in the years following Vatican II, has re-established a process of adult catechesis and liturgical celebration leading up to reception of the sacraments of initiation, Baptism, Confirmation and the Eucharist. In recent years, the Church in Ireland has witnessed a growing demand for adult initiation, and a deepening awareness of the *Rite of Christian Initiation of Adults*. Adult initiation should be seen as an event in the life of the parish

[3] *The Extraordinary Synod of Bishops* 6, 1985.
[4] Preface of Christ the King.
[5] ACCC 4.

community, as well as a special moment in the individual's journey. The parish, with the aid of the diocese, welcomes and supports the person in coming to know, understand and live the Christian way of life. Each parish or group of parishes should be able to facilitate the RCIA process locally in conjunction with the diocese.

Adult Faith Development

70. In our time, when lay faithful are being entrusted with particular tasks in their faith community, it is all the more clear that a fully educated adult faith, inspired by the Holy Spirit, contributes significantly to the continued growth of the Church.

STARTING POINT: NEW VITALITY

We are entering a period of new vitality for the Church, in which adult Catholic laity will play a pivotal leadership role in fulfilling the Christian mission of evangelising and transforming society. For adults to fulfil their roles in this new era of the Church, their faith formation must be lifelong, just as they must continue to learn to keep up with the changing world.

National Conference of Catholic Bishops of the United States of America,
Our Hearts Were Burning Within Us
(Washington, DC: USCCB Publishing, 1999) 29.

Ongoing adult catechesis, new evangelisation and theological reflection are essential in the work of building up a vibrant, informed and confident Church. This is more than an individual undertaking, but belongs properly to the local Christian community, drawing the adult Christian into fuller communion and enriching the community in the process. 'Adult education in religion is one of the urgent religious needs in Ireland in our time. An educated world needs an educated faith.'[6]

The *General Directory for Catechesis* acknowledges that any engagement with adults 'must take serious account of their experience, of their conditioning and the challenges they have encountered in life'.[7] Discussion, as to how adults perceive themselves living, responding and growing in faith, and the effect they see this might have in their life, should be at the heart of any process that seeks to help adults to develop their Christian faith. The Gospel is offered

[6] *HFH*, p. 37.
[7] *GDC* 172.

to young and old, to men and women, to those with economic resources and to those who are impoverished, to perpetrators of violence and to its victims, to those who know Jesus Christ and to those who do not, to those who participate in the Church's rituals and to those who come occasionally, to those who are rooted in the Christian heritage of Ireland, of whichever denomination, and to those who bring new things to us from other lands. Because their questions, as well as their needs, are many and varied, different categories of adult should be recognised:

- Adults of other faiths or none who seek Baptism and, therefore, faith formation in the form of the catechumenate, according to the *Rite of Christian Initiation of Adults.*
- Adults who have experienced basic faith formation and sacramental initiation but require ongoing faith development.
- Adults whose basic formation may have been incomplete, and who may not participate any longer in the sacramental life of the Church.
- Those of other denominations who wish to enter into full communion with the Catholic Church.[8]

There are many and wonderful opportunities for engaging as adults with the Good News. Proper education and training can release this energy within the Christian community. The encouragement of those who are interested and enthusiastic can bring new life to the whole community. The parish priest, as stated in the Code of Canon Law, bears responsibility for catechesis in the parish and for ensuring the authentic presentation of faith to adults. 'By virtue of his office, the parish priest is bound to ensure the catechetical formation of adults, young people and children.'[9] With the help of the Parish Pastoral Council, 'a leadership group through which priests and people work together as partners in fulfilling the mission of Christ in their own place',[10] he establishes parish policies and procedures in this area of pastoral outreach.

71. Each parish or group of parishes should have a qualified member of staff designated as **Faith Development Coordinator**. Depending on the size of parish, it may be that a number of parishes working together, or in the first instance a deanery, takes the initiative in establishing such a position. This experienced and professionally qualified person, a priest, religious or lay pastoral worker, coordinates, under the direction of the parish priest, a comprehensive approach to faith development in the parish, initiating and supporting adult faith development as well as that for children and young people. The diocese, as always, should be involved in supporting such projects, providing a designated diocesan **Adult Faith Development Adviser**, available to encourage, resource and provide a variety of training possibilities for parish personnel.

[8] See *GDC* 172.
[9] *CIC* can. 776; see also *CIC* cann. 519, 528.1, 773, 777.
[10] Irish Catholic Bishops' Conference, Commission for Pastoral Renewal and Adult Faith Development, *Parish Pastoral Councils: A Framework for Developing Diocesan Norms and Parish Guidelines* (Dublin: Veritas, 2007), p. 18.

The Faith Development Coordinator seeks to reach out to adults, at whatever stage of evangelisation may be considered appropriate. He or she identifies a variety of needs, both of parishioners themselves and of those who might, for the first time, like to know something of Christ. He or she supports elements in parish life that can help initiate faith and foster growth in faith. The Faith Development Coordinator works with the parish priest and parish staff, and in collaboration with neighbouring parishes, in providing a diverse range of quality programming for adult education in faith.

Occasionally there will be need for catechists of adults, who provide a fundamental service as part of any RCIA process, accompanying catechumens as they delve further into the life of Christian faith. By reflecting on their own Christian lives, volunteer catechists can witness to other adults interested in coming to know the Christian way of life more fully. Whether priests, religious or lay people, they must be people of adult faith, capable of supporting and leading other adults as they seek to deepen their faith.[11] Such catechists, under the direction of the Parish Priest and Faith Development Coordinator, need to receive appropriate education and training for the task they undertake. Their training must take into account 'the particular circumstances of the local Church, the people's needs, the catechist's skills and abilities, and the resources available'.[12]

**PARISH PASTORAL COUNCIL:
SUPPORTING ADULT FAITH DEVELOPMENT**

Together with the Parish Priest and the Faith Development Coordinator, establish parish structures for the instigation or rejuvenation of adult faith development initiatives. In conjunction with other local parishes, clarify the most pressing adult faith education needs and the best method of provision within the local situation.

A Supportive Environment for Adult Faith Development
72. Adult catechesis should always begin by taking into account the nature and experience of the participants. It should reflect their needs and address their issues, valuing their personal,

[11] See ACCC 71; *Ministering to Adult Learners*, p. 17.
[12] ACCC 77.

spiritual and cultural resources. All adult faith development initiatives should acknowledge difference among participants. They should also support those who minister in the parish, as they fulfil by the graciousness of God their pastoral and catechetical roles within the community.

The role of the parish faith community in creating a supportive environment should be recognised and promoted. The faith community should welcome those who are newly arrived in the parish. It should prioritise the ongoing pastoral care of adults, seeking to facilitate their full liturgical participation (*leitourgia*) and providing opportunities for them, not only to grow in knowledge of their faith (*kerygma*), but, also, to offer service within the community at a whole series of levels (*koinonia/diakonia*).[13] In fact, adult faith development should be thoroughly embedded in the practical activities of the parish community, including the celebration of the liturgy and the work of justice, building upon existing points of contact between adults and the life of the Church.

TO DO: TASKS OF ADULT CATECHESIS

- Promote formation and development of a mature faith life in the Risen Christ.
- Encourage a correct assessment of the socio-cultural changes within society in the light of faith.
- Support clarification of current moral and religious questions.
- Highlight the relationship between faith and life, pointing to the value of the social teaching of the Church.
- Develop the rational foundations of faith to facilitate an accurate understanding of the Gospel and of Church teaching.
- Encourage adults to participate in and assume responsibility for the Church's mission to evangelise, giving Christian witness in society.

GDC 175.

---

[13] See *GDC 174.*

A great variety of situations and circumstances can be grounds upon which adult faith can usefully be further investigated: participation in the RCIA itself; catechesis adapted to the liturgical year or special events in the life of the Church and of society; preparation for sacramental celebrations such as Marriage and the initiation of children; critical moments like the sickness and/or death of a loved one; significant experiences, for example, adult children leaving home; daily concerns, such as promoting social justice, inclusion of those who have been marginalised, and ecological sustainability; and ongoing formation for those preparing for or involved in lay collaborative ministry.[14]

73. Without doubt, the Sunday parish liturgy provides a core focus for liturgical catechesis and ongoing faith development, based upon the three-year lectionary cycle. The full potential of the Sunday liturgy in this regard will only be realised when priests and parish teams work closely on the basis that the liturgy is, indeed, the summit toward which all the activity of the Church is directed, and fount from which all her power flows.[15] 'The Sunday celebration of the Lord's Day and his Eucharist is at the heart of the Church's life.'[16] Greater planning and resources are needed to ensure that what many parishes are implementing for the Family Mass liturgy can be provided for all liturgical celebrations so that they can be celebrated to a high liturgical standard according to the liturgical norms of the Church. Many adults, once invited, and given proper instruction and encouragement, are willing to become involved in specific roles for the good of the worshipping community. Their confidence in what they have to offer grows once they understand what is required, what is useful and what enhances the liturgy.

Priests and parish pastoral councils may become aware of people who have already furthered their own faith development, especially through participation in the academic study of theology and the development of pastoral skills in formal, accredited courses.

[14] See *GDC* 176.
[15] See *SC* 10.
[16] *CCC* 2177.

Together they can devise ways of best putting the knowledge and skills they have gained at the service of the local Christian community. The parish, invoking the wisdom of the Holy Spirit, may also be able to encourage other members of its own community to take up study or to avail of practical workshops and bring the fruits of their learning back to the parish. The possibilities are endless, at diocesan as well as parish level, when people are confirmed in their conviction that they, too, have something to offer the local Church.

PARISH DISCUSSION: MODELS OF ADULT FAITH DEVELOPMENT TO BE CONSIDERED AND ACTED UPON AS AGREED AT LOCAL LEVEL

- *Rite of Christian Initiation of Adults*
- Support programmes for family members of those being initiated into the faith
- Ongoing family catechesis
- Spiritual preparation of those planning to get married
- Ongoing engagement with the sacramental life of the Church
- Liturgical formation
- Building up the local Christian community
- Training and ongoing support for members of Catholic-school boards of management
- Participation as parents in parish–school support for Christian initiation of children
- Education in Scripture, Theology and Church History
- Reflection on justice and peace issues leading to Catholic action
- Participation in liturgy and liturgical music initiatives
- Retreats, spiritual direction, prayer-group support

Sensitivity to Adult Ways of Learning

74. At all stages of preparation, initiation, ongoing oversight and review, adult Christians should be involved in recognising their own faith needs, and devising education and action programmes that are both relevant and feasible. Finding ways of involving adult parishioners in preparatory reflection can, in itself, be a challenging first step. It is vital, however, that efforts are made to differentiate between the varying needs of people and to plan accordingly. For some adults, introductory material may be sufficient, while others may be interested in a deeper theological discussion. Initiation, ongoing catechesis or a renewed evangelisation may be considered apt, depending on the individual and circumstance. Continuing reflection on the process, therefore, and on the needs of participants, can greatly increase understanding and help people make allowances for one another.

A developed sense of inter-personal and communication skills is central to the success of any adult faith programme. Awareness of how adults learn is essential. Personal involvement and active participation are indispensable.

As well as the exposition of material by an expert speaker (which should build on the adult need for self-direction, their experience as a learning resource, their interest in real-life tasks and their focus on achieving their full potential),[17] group work, study circles, one-to-one discussion and action research can all be employed depending on circumstances and needs, but always with the guidance of catechetically trained personnel. Busy adults, especially parents, can often find the setting aside of time for such activities difficult to prioritise. Arrangements entered into should respect the commitment of all involved. Assessment and evaluation are necessary components of any such initiative and should be built into the programme. Organisers should strive to keep in contact with adults who have completed courses, to learn from them and provide them with opportunities to participate in new initiatives.

Within dioceses, parishes, ecclesial movements, groups and organisations, a high priority should be given to providing resources to ensure the ongoing faith development of adult members. Those involved in organising adult programmes should be assured at an early stage that the financial and other resources necessary to operate the programmes are effectively in place. Advertising and promotion should be given attention, so that people will become easily aware of what is being offered.

75. Information technology and other new and varied methods of communication should also be utilised. For adults, with a premium on their time, distance learning can be helpful. Email and chat-rooms, as well as digital video files and pod-casting, make for easy exchange of ideas and straightforward contact with education leaders. It is good to keep in mind, however, that informed and up-to-date material, personal interaction at some level and an appreciation of community are essential, if such programmes are envisaged as an ecclesial endeavour that hopes, in the Spirit, to build up the local Church as well as the individual.

[17] See M. Knowles, *The Modern Practice of Adult Education* (New York: Association, 1971).

LEADERSHIP DISCUSSION: RESPECTING THE
FREEDOM AND AUTONOMY OF ADULTS

Above all one must begin by accepting adults where they are…
it is essential to keep in mind the specific adults with whom
you are working, their cultural background, human and
religious needs, their expectations, faith experiences, and their
potential…

Of fundamental importance is the *dialogical approach* which,
while recognising that all are called to the obedience of faith
(Rm 1:5), respects the basic freedom and autonomy of adults
and encourages them to engage in an open and cordial
dialogue. In this way, they can make known their needs and
can participate, as they should, as subjects or agents in their
own catechesis and in that of others.[2]

ACCC 56-57.

Adult religious education should not isolate itself or be isolated
from other local adult education initiatives.
Collaboration with other forms of adult education, with
the community, with local/county libraries and with
third-level institutions should be seen as particularly
valuable without distracting from the particular
discipline that is catechetics. Literature, history, the
creative arts, art history, music, science, stewardship of
the earth's resources, and archaeology, are among the
many fields of study that will have something valuable
to contribute to an adult discussion of faith today. It is
also of great importance that all efforts to renew and
deepen the faith of Catholic communities, should be
ecumenically aware, encouraging appropriate
engagement and interaction with members of other
Christian communities, as highlighted in Chapter 3.
Dialogue with people of other religions and with the
dominant cultural influences of our time, can also
ensure that our faith is lived in open conversation with what is
believed by others.

PAUSE FOR REFLECTION: THE ENCOUNTER
BETWEEN FAITH, CULTURE AND SCIENCE

'The catechesis of adults will be surer of success when it opens
to the encounter between faith, culture and science, in which
an attempt is made to integrate them with one another while
respecting the specific identity of each' (John Paul II,
'Discourse to the members of COINCAT', *L'Osservatore
Romano*, 30 October 1988, p. 4).

Hence, whatever knowledge and methodologies allow a more
adequate reading of historical, social and religious phenomena,
both in their negative and positive aspects, have a right to a place
in adult catechesis. With their help, catechesis will be able to
provide a more enlightened Christian interpretation of reality.

ACCC 51.

Young Adults

76. Opportunities should be provided for young adults, specifically,
to be introduced to, or grow in, personal faith and spirituality. This
is a time in their lives when other important personal choices are
being made. In modern living, young adults are often exposed to
values that are at odds with those of their Christian heritage.
Opportunities must be provided, therefore, to encourage them to
celebrate and live their Christianity, and come to know its fullest
meaning in their lives and the significance of its contribution to the
cultural world within which they live.

Young adult ministry is often confused with youth ministry.
Although they may be connected, and can be creatively catered for
together, an approach that recognises the different and particular
needs of young adults and adolescents is ideal. Young adult
ministry is directed toward adults, and its language and activities
should be for adults, even when this is in a leadership role with
youth. People in their twenties and thirties have other obligations
and often put in long hours of study or work. It is important, then,
to listen to them and to respond to their adult needs.

Evangelisation is at the heart of any pastoral ministry that reaches
out to young adults. It is clear that in Ireland today, while women
and men in their twenties and thirties are the largest section of the
Catholic population, they are frequently its least active part. It is
necessary, today, to present the vision and tradition of Catholic
faith imaginatively, and in so doing invite young adults, even those
who have received sacramental initiation, to experience a deep
sense of personal lived faith. The *Rite of Christian Initiation of
Adults* should be kept in mind, as many young adults may be

coming to know the love of Jesus and to experience the question of faith commitment for the first time. Many may have experienced a largely secular education. New evangelisation initiatives should be considered key for those who have been baptised but have not yet come to own their own faith. All those who have recently left school (18-25 year olds) should be supported by the Christian community and helped to belong. They should be assisted to find a place for reflection, dialogue and responsibility in the Church.

77. Third-level students, among others, as they engage in in-depth study and reflection in specific areas of human life, should be encouraged to recognise the contribution of Christian thought and love in the world, and contemplate its meaning not only for themselves but for their relationship with others. The value of third-level education should be strongly affirmed, contributing as it does to the development of the individual, the local community and to the good of society generally. A consumerist or business model is not adequate. A variety of teaching and learning approaches, based on the range of human needs, interests and abilities, should be promoted. In this way the third-level sector can contribute the vital and fruitful input it should have in building a

better, more wholly functioning, moral, just and more equitable society into the future.

In this context, the future of theology as a science in itself, and of denominational theology in particular, is worthy of specific mention. The place of this discipline within our third-level structure is of the greatest importance, not least because of the diversity of peoples, values and beliefs now present in our society. It is precisely at this present moment that all those who contribute to an open and respectful academic study of religion, theology, philosophy, religious education, pastoral care and spiritual development should be supported. In this way we can contribute to 'a deeper realisation of the harmony between faith and science'[18] and to the fullest possible understanding of human life and human relationships. The Universities, facilitated by the State, can serve society well by providing both space and resources for teaching, study and research in these disciplines. Lecturers and other staff members of the University Faculties and Colleges of Education, working in

[18] GE 10.

theology and associated fields of study, should have full confidence in the academic contribution they can make, knowing that their disciplines are respected and supported for what they have to offer young people and the future of Ireland. Doctoral-level research in these disciplines is crucial for the development of new and profound attitudes in society essential to life lived at its fullest. An holistic understanding of education is as important to defend at third level as it is at other levels.

The ongoing faith development of third-level students is also of the greatest importance. Third-level chaplains can offer an excellent service in the general pastoral care of university students. The provision of catechetical and ongoing faith development processes and programmes for Catholic students should also be encouraged. Social solidarity projects, good liturgical celebration, moments of prayer and opportunities to learn how to pray, meetings where faith can be robustly explored, including the engagement of notable guest speakers and the provision of lecture series in College, are all useful mechanisms for helping young adults to uncover the riches of life in Jesus Christ:

> You know well that only through Christ's gaze can we discover the ultimate truth about the human person, the truth about ourselves... Never cease to seek him, therefore, and in his eyes you will discover an attractive reflection of the goodness and beauty that he himself has poured into your hearts with the gift of his Spirit. May this mysterious reflection of his love be the light that always guides you on your way.[19]

Third-level students can, with the help of others, come to a deep understanding of their place and mission in Church, connecting back to their home parish at the weekend with a greater sense of the contribution they can make and the responsibility that is theirs. Many will only begin at this stage of their lives to understand the life-giving nature of Christ's love for them and the wisdom of the Catholic faith: 'Catechising young adults often means assisting them to move from the faith they learned as children to personal appropriation of the faith as adults.'[20]

78. Four goals for effective outreach to young adults have been identified by the National Conference of Catholic Bishops of the United States of America:

- Connecting young adults with Jesus Christ.
- Connecting young adults with the Church.
- Connecting young adults with the mission of the Church in the world.
- Connecting young adults with a peer community.[21]

[19] John Paul II, *Advent Mass for the Students of the Roman State Universities*, 14 December 2004.
[20] J. C. Cusick and K. F. DeVries, *The Basic Guide to Young Adult Ministry* (New York: Orbis Books, 2001), p. 5.
[21] USA, National Conference of Catholic Bishops, *Sons and Daughters of the Light: A Pastoral Plan for Ministry to Young Adults* (Washington, DC: United States Catholic Conference, 1997), 28-41.

We, too, need to evangelise young adults by inviting them to become active at local level, in the parish, in the diocese and in groups that contribute to proclaiming the Word, worshipping the Lord, serving our neighbour and building up the community. As young adults are maturing and making choices in life, an invitation to belong again, to make a commitment to the Christian community, to contribute to the well-being of others and to find new ways of bringing good news to their own contemporaries and to younger people, should be encouraged. It is only when young adults are connected with Church that their generosity and energy will become available in the parish community.

Faith development programmes for young adults, organised at parish, group of parishes or deanery level, are an essential part of the life of a faith community. Whether organised formally or informally, such programmes should acknowledge the often crucial life decisions young adults have to make at this time in their lives. Scripture groups, prayer groups and Small Christian Communities give young adults an opportunity to explore together their understanding of faith and how it might inspire their decisions. Local courses in Christian philosophy and theology can touch into some of the most important questions on their minds. Psychological and sociological matters dealt with in the light of faith, and questions concerning the moral life in our world today, can fascinate and support the young adult. The opportunity to reflect on human experience can often, by the work of the Holy Spirit, bring out a deep appreciation of gifts and possibilities, as well as of the need for justice and solidarity.

PARISH INITIATIVE: YOUNG ADULT FORUM

Establish a Young Adult Forum in association with the Parish Pastoral Council, suitable to local needs, conditions and possibilities, at which proposals can be discussed, researched and acted upon, such as:

- Young Adult Faith Development Group
- Liturgical Music Ministry
- Young Adult Prayer and Adoration Groups
- Visitation of parish sick and elderly
- Support for parish Youth Initiatives
- Overseeing of Monthly Parish Newsletter
- Creation and ongoing development of Parish Website
- Support for Catholic justice projects worldwide

The local Faith Development Coordinator should give particular attention to initiatives that reach out to young adults. It is to be hoped that they will become the backbone of the parish in the future. They need education and training as well as everyday support in embracing a thoughtful Christian way of life. Diocesan structures to support this form of catechesis should be given high priority.

79. It is essential that modern forms of communication and social networking are engaged with in inviting young adults to look more deeply at the spiritual and moral questions raised in their life. Such questions are questions for society, too. This age-group are themselves best placed to uncover and develop new ways of speaking to their contemporaries and to the culture they are building into the future. They are aware of the contexts and ways in which young people meet, interact and 'chat' today. They are at ease with current means of mass communication, such as the Internet and local and regional  radio. Familiarity with the worldwide web means that their horizons are never limited to their own locality. Projects that encourage young adults to investigate for themselves, using the Internet, for instance, and Distance Learning modules, can be very productive. Facilitated by parish, university chaplaincy, chaplaincy to the armed forces, or diocese, for example, young adults can be encouraged to make a significant contribution to the up-building and evangelisation of the local Christian community.

In recent times, World Youth Day, celebrated every two or three years in a different part of the world, has created a hugely positive experience for young adults. It has opened them to an understanding of the Church as a worldwide movement, celebrating joy, love, care for the world and its peoples, justice and peace, walking in the footsteps of Jesus Christ. World Youth Day has become a sign of the Holy Spirit at work, where there is openness and generosity. At the time of writing, this has become the single largest youth ministry event for young adults and youth in the Irish Church. It has become an occasion of witness within the Church and to the world at large as to what is possible when young adults are touched by faith in Jesus Christ.[22]

[22] See *www.wyd.ie*

STARTING POINT:
WORLD YOUTH DAY, 'OWNING UP TO GOD'

I keep quiet about my faith at home... It's been incredible to
come to something like this where you can be more open than
ever with others. You don't have to talk to them, you just
know everyone has something in common, a connection in the
heart.

Imelda McGrath, quoted by Derek Scally, 'Owning Up to God',
The Irish Times, 20 August 2005.

Marriage Preparation and Support

80. Marriage preparation, ongoing marriage education and
relationship counselling are all elements of marriage support that

have the potential to contribute in a
significant manner to the faith
development of couples. ACCORD,
the Catholic Marriage Care Service,
has a particular mandate within the
Catholic Church in Ireland to
provide support for the vocation of
marriage in our faith community.
Its national and diocesan services
are widespread and easily
accessed.[23]

Marriage preparation courses offer
couples an opportunity, in our time-
hungry world, to explore aspects of
the marriage relationship with each
other in company with other
couples preparing to celebrate the
sacrament of Marriage. Issues such
as communication, commitment,
conflict, fertility and children can
usefully be discussed, alongside an
understanding of the sacrament of
Marriage, commitment to love of
God and love of neighbour,
spiritual support and responsibility
within the Christian community,
growth in prayer and the sharing of faith with the next generation.
Such courses, in addition to preparing for the wedding day, help
prepare the couple, too, for life-long sacramental commitment.
They can contribute to the individual's self-development, to the
couple's understanding of themselves as a couple, to their ongoing
faith development, and to the commitment they can make to their

[23] See *www.accord.ie*

local parish community. Inter-church and inter-religious marriage preparation is a significant part of ACCORD's work.[24]

> ## QUESTIONS FOR COUPLES TO SHARE: GOD AND MARRIAGE
>
> In what ways do you want God to be part of your married life in the years ahead? In what ways do you want as a couple to be part of the Church community as a support for your marriage and family life and also because of what you can bring to it?
>
> ACCORD Catholic Marriage Care Service,
> *Marriage: A Journey, Not a Destination*
> (Maynooth: ACCORD Catholic Marriage Care Service, 2003), p. 34.

81. ACCORD's recently developed Marriage Enrichment courses have an important contribution to make, helping married couples to work on strengthening their marriage relationship. Early initiatives in this area indicate their value both to couples and to their families.[25] Personal Enrichment courses also provide worthwhile opportunities for self-development, leading to enhancement of personal and marriage relationships. Couples can be encouraged to discuss the spiritual and moral matters associated with married life and with fidelity to the teaching of the Church in this regard.[26] People often need support in engaging with these significant issues. They can be helped to make good decisions based on Christian principles, with the Holy Spirit as their guide.

The other side of ACCORD's work is its marriage counselling service. The purpose of marriage counselling is to help couples resolve conflict and difficulties in their relationships and to help empower them to live more rewarding lives. The counsellor creates a space for the person and for the couple. Nothing is imposed, but all are aware that the service offered is undertaken within an atmosphere that is supportive of marriage. Openness to God and to discovering a personal call to deeper faith within the Church, has the potential to help people to rediscover meaning for themselves and for their marriage. Such marriage counselling support is not only healthy; it can be transformative.

[24] See *www.accord.ie/ marriage_preparation_ programme/interchurch _marriage_preparation/*
[25] See *www.accord.ie/ marriage_enrichment/*
[26] See John Paul II, *Familiaris consortio*, and Paul VI, *Humanae vitae*.

REFLECTION:
ATTENTIVE LISTENING, SPEAKING AND LOOKING

It may come as a relief to learn that changing one's partner is
all that is involved in improving a marriage but, since everyone
is a partner, it also involves changing one's self... The precise
way in which counselling triggers these changes seems to lie in
the provision of a safe, accepting space where emotions
generated in distressed relationships – including
disappointment, loneliness, anger, sadness, hate, etc. – can be
given expression and where hearing, and being heard, by the
other, one sees and experiences the partner in a different
light... Perhaps the space of counselling itself can model the
possibilities of intimacy through the simple acts of attentive
listening, speaking and looking. In this intimate space, hope
can be restored, healing can begin and love can grow again.

Kieran McKeown et al., *Unhappy Marriages: Does Counselling Help?*
(Maynooth: ACCORD Catholic Marriage Care Service, 2002), pp. 32-3.

Parenthood and Family Ministry

82. The primary place of encounter with God for most adults, and
children, is family life. For Christians, the family is the first
experience of Church: 'The home should be the first church which

children know, and
in which they are
reminded about
God and helped to
pray by what they
see around them.'[27]
It is within family,
'the domestic
Church',[28] that we
first live our
Christianity, that
we identify what
Christian life
consists in, that we
learn beliefs and
values, and grow
in prayer. When we
speak of family,
based upon the
love of husband
and wife,[29] we are
not talking about something idealised or unreal. Families come
with all kinds of problematic questions: loneliness, separation, self-
interest, addiction, abuse of one kind or another, as well as love,

[27] *HFH*, p. 8.
[28] *LG* 11; see also *FC*
21; *CCC* 2204.
[29] See *CCC* 2202.

support, play, care and loyalty. They can carry positive and negative connotations, depending on a person's family story. Family is the reality within which we speak of faith integrated with life as it is lived.

The family is the primary context within which Christian formation takes place. 'The family in fact constitutes a community of love and solidarity, which is uniquely suited to teach and transmit cultural, ethical, social, spiritual and religious values, essential for the development and well-being of its own members and of society.'[30] Family life demonstrates that learning and growing is a lifelong process. As we live through the different stages of family life, we never stop learning. As we endeavour to pass on our faith to children and grandchildren, we learn in new ways too.[31] When we say that parents are 'the first and best teachers of their children in faith',[32] this is not said as a vague aspiration. Nor should it be seen as a burden. It is a truth that needs to be given special attention and supported within our parish communities:

> To hand on to your children the faith you received from your parents is your first duty and your greatest privilege as parents. The home should be the first school of religion, as it must be the first school of prayer.[33]

Parents, guardians and grandparents learn that family moments are, in themselves, sacred. Family rituals build up a sense of family as community.[34] Small ways in which parents teach their children, loving them, caring for them, providing for them, are already contributing to the children's growth. Giving children a sense of what it means to experience trust, generosity, tenderness and hope is, in itself, a gift. Indeed, it is pre-evangelisation. Helping them to know that they, too, can be gentle, forgiving, pure in heart, compassionate and bringers of peace, is to proclaim the Good News of Jesus Christ in a profound way. To pray with our children about life in all its realities is sacred. For parents to play with their children day by day is sacred too.

[30] CSDC 238; Holy See, Charter of the Rights of the Family 3 (Vatican City: Vatican Polyglot Press, 1983), p. 9.
[31] For a variety of articles on different issues arising for parents in sharing their faith with their younger family members, see 'Parenting'. Available from www.catholic ireland.net
[32] See blessing at the end of the Rite of Baptism for Children.
[33] John Paul II, Limerick, 1979.
[34] See T. Gunning, The Little Book of Christian Rituals in the Home (Dublin: Veritas, 2007).

PLAN OF ACTION:
HOMES THAT ARE FILLED WITH LOVE

Dear parents, the greatest need your children have is that you should take time to spend with them, that you should take time to talk to them, that you should make time to listen to them. You may ask what all this has to do with religion... There is no more vivid sign that God is alive, and that God loves, than Christian homes which are filled with love... Homes that are filled with supposed 'religion', but are empty of love, will simply turn young people off religion and turn them away from God. Dear parents, your children need your love even more than they need the food you give them, and very much more than they need money. Try to bring up your children in such a way that they will remember their childhood days as days filled with God and filled with love.

HFH, pp. 19-20.

83. Family Ministry in many dioceses in Ireland seeks to support families in their vocation as domestic churches.[35] It is crucial that language is found and initiatives conceived of which help parents to develop a sense of the home as a sacred place. Religious education in schools and catechetical programmes in the parish can give children and young people the language within which to talk about and reflect on the spiritual and religious realities lived at home. It is in the home, however, that they will first make sense of, or question and respond to, the religious, spiritual and moral values with which they are presented.

There can be no doubt that good adult faith development, focused on adult forms of learning, and aware of family and inter-generational needs, is essential to help parents and others make the most of family as the source and high point of faith-filled love. Equally in schools, discussion of what is meant by a Catholic 'ecclesiology of the domestic church' could usefully be provided within Religious Education. Certainly within Catholic schools, it should be fundamental to the ethos overseen by the Board of Management and lived and celebrated in the school. Colleges of Education, in helping trainee teachers understand and reach out to faith communities, should provide up-to-date study of ecclesiology, including its significance for family as well as for parish, for Catholic schools and for ecumenical, inter-religious and inter-cultural dialogues.

All catechetical and other faith development initiatives taken in association with the parish should have a family element woven into the approach. Those helping with sacramental initiation in parishes and schools, for example, rather than focusing simply on preparation for receiving the particular sacrament, should

[35] See for example *www.parishandfamily.ie*

emphasise the occasion as part of the person's growth into deeper participation in family, parish and Church. Adult faith education, too, should always encourage participants to consider the benefits of what they are reflecting on for their families, for their relationships and for their lives. Opportunities to help parents be more aware of the religious education and formation programmes in schools and the process involved should be encouraged. Their understanding of such programmes and their willingness to participate with their young people in discussing religion and undertaking recommended activities together is of great benefit to young people as they negotiate the meaning of life.

PARISH PASTORAL COUNCIL: FAMILY MINISTRY?

Connect with your diocesan Family Ministry Office, local school Boards of Management and with other local Parish Pastoral Councils in order to provide support for parents, guardians and families in the faith formation and development of children.

Family Ministry, as well as seeking to facilitate faith development within the family, will always find itself reaching out to families who are struggling in one way or another. Families who have members with special needs often appreciate any effort that may be made to support them in the community. Where there is a breakdown in family life, helping the family to maintain a sense of family community, even where people are no longer living together, can make a useful contribution. Outreach to families suffering from deprivation, and often disconnected from the Church as well as from society generally, is a major concern for Catholic parishes, organisations and groups. The Christian community defines itself by how well it supports families in need.

84. It has been noted in Family Ministry circles that men can often become cut off from spiritual exploration and religious practice. Male spirituality can seem underdeveloped. Unless the man is a priest, deacon or religious, it can, it seems, be difficult to find ways of expressing his natural spirituality and his significant religious needs. Many men find themselves offering their time and expertise in organising sporting events for young people. What services, then, might they be asked to provide within the parish community that would draw them into active participation and help them to develop a sense of their spiritual selves? Attention to this question in the coming years would surely be worthwhile for individuals, families and Church organisations. Efforts to bring some men together locally to discuss their role in the faith community might be helpful. If space is created within which to name and reflect on the true spiritual needs and concerns of men today, a way forward

might be found that leads to concrete action being taken for and by men within the local Church. The spiritual and religious dimension of life is as essential for men today as it is for women. The active participation of men is of paramount importance for the development of parish communities and for the Church as a whole.

The Single Life

85. The vocation to the single life is worth particular mention in regard to adult catechesis. In fact, the single life in modern society warrants renewed attention. Some people today choose to remain single. They see this vocation as the most appropriate for them, taking up the opportunity to dedicate themselves in a variety of ways to the service of others. There are many, too, who may not feel they chose a single life, but who have learned to live that vocation actively and positively. Some have found themselves single parents. Others, having followed a call to marriage, have for a variety of reasons come to live the single life again. Among those who have been married but have separated, some take on the responsibility of caring for their children, for the most part, alone. Many, of course, by God's providence, find themselves, at a particular point in their life, widows or widowers, and perhaps having raised a family, living a newfound vocation to the single life.

Like everyone, single people need support in the Christian life. They should be considered and ministered to as the people they are. Their experience of life is recognised and acknowledged within the Christian community. Their particular faith journey needs to be sustained within that faith community, and opportunities provided for enrichment and growth. While the vocations to married life, to the priesthood and to religious life are often highlighted and reflected on in parish, the vocation to single life deserves fuller attention. Specific moments and carefully conceived programmes should be developed with single people, giving them an opportunity to know that they are appreciated and happily provided for within the Christian community. Having met Jesus and his Church, no one should ever feel alone. God, our loving Father, has invited us all into the community of joy that, together in the Holy Spirit, can experience the salvation won for us by Christ Jesus our Lord. Single people can minister to others in a rich variety of ways. It is often perceived to be the case, and sometimes is true, that single people have time and a certain freedom. They frequently commit themselves, generously and beyond the call of duty, to parishes, schools and other organisations. Without imposing on them, the parish in particular should invite some of its single people to be trained in catechesis and in the ongoing faith development of adults. Without their special efforts, many programmes and initiatives would be very much the poorer. In their drawing close to

Jesus, they, too, contribute to the plan God has formed long ago: 'By living with the mind of Christ, Christians hasten the coming of the Reign of God.'[36]

Bishops, Priests, Deacons and Religious

86. Bishops and priests, as well as religious men and women, have continuously put themselves at the service of the Catholic community in Ireland and beyond. Their's is a vocation to an exclusive loving commitment to God and neighbour in Christ, expressed within the Christian community according to a variety of recognised charisms. The celebration of the liturgy and sacraments, the building up of the parish and school community, the intellectual study of the faith and personal witness to its meaning in life, are the everyday interest and concern of these pastoral leaders and ministers. They have played a particularly significant role in catechesis down to the present day. With the restoration of the permanent diaconate, deacons 'called to proclaim the Gospel and to preach the word, to instruct the people of God through the homily and through catechesis'[37] also contribute to evangelisation within the parish community and beyond. Just as all these people speak to others of faith, encouraging them day by day, they, too, have a continuing need to be ministered to and to have opportunities for ongoing faith development in their own lives.

In addressing the formation of priests, Pope John Paul clarified four areas that need constant and ongoing attention: human formation, spiritual formation, intellectual formation and pastoral formation.[38] While these areas are the focus of training for ministry, they also form the basis of the continuing education that is a necessary part of every priest's and deacon's life and of the life of women and men religious. None should presume that they have come to a moment where there is no longer a requirement to investigate and reflect on current concerns in all four of these areas. Nor should priests and religious ever draw back from the challenge to love that is at the very heart of the Gospel and at the heart of human dignity and fulfilment:

[36] CCC 2046.
[37] Irish Catholic Bishops' Conference, *The Permanent Diaconate: National Directory and Norms for Ireland* (Dublin: Veritas, 2006), 18.
[38] *PDV* 43-59.

Man cannot live without love. He remains a being that is incomprehensible for himself, his life is meaningless, if love is not revealed to him, if he does not encounter love, if he does not experience it and make it his own, if he does not participate intimately in it.[39]

87. In our world today, faced with unbelief, with globalising and secularising worldviews, with lack of willingness to commit, and difficulties of one kind or another within Church life, those who have taken religious vows may find themselves reflecting deeply on their changing role in Irish society. On the other hand, they have a certain confidence that they have something particular to say from their experience of life, something to offer others from

their encounter with Christ. But where to begin? Many of those who minister as priests and religious in the Church received their training in times that envisaged them as the only pastoral leaders available to people in parishes, schools and hospitals. Today, Christ's lay faithful, led by the Spirit of love and generosity, are increasingly being invited to collaborate and become co-responsible with their ordained ministers in the pastoral ministry they exercise in the service of the People of God.

In Catholic parishes, movements and organisations, collaborative teamwork is to be chosen decisively and encouraged wholeheartedly. The Second Vatican Council, and the times that have followed in its aftermath, have offered a renewed vision of lay people in the Church. Their role as disciples of Christ, by virtue of their baptismal calling, is essential in building up the faith community. The lay faithful are being entrusted with various responsibilities, both at parish and diocesan level, in Catholic schools, hospitals and organisations. The advent of parish pastoral workers, and specifically of Faith Development Coordinators, together with the great variety of volunteer services offered by lay people, is particularly welcome. Formation for this work of collaboration with their priests is of great importance so that they may fulfil their responsibilities and apostolates both completely and with the mind of the Church. Priests and religious, too, must prepare themselves for ongoing change. It is necessary that they be offered formation in the proper understanding of the participation of the lay faithful in the exercise of the sacred

[39] *RH* 274.

ministry. They should be ready, also, to support the provision of adequate education and skills training for those lay people who are willing and deemed suitable to be invited to co-responsibility with the ordained in the exercise of the Church's ministry.

CO-RESPONSIBLE LAY PEOPLE

It is necessary to improve pastoral structures in such a way that the co-responsibility of all the members of the People of God in their entirety is gradually promoted, with respect for vocations and for the respective roles of the consecrated and of lay people.

This demands a change in mindset, particularly concerning lay people. They must no longer be viewed as 'collaborators' of the clergy but truly recognized as 'co-responsible', for the Church's being and action, thereby fostering the consolidation of a mature and committed laity. This common awareness of being Church of all the baptized in no way diminishes the responsibility of parish priests. It is precisely your task, dear parish priests, to nurture the spiritual and apostolic growth of those who are already committed to working hard in the parishes. They form the core of the community that will act as a leaven for the others.

Benedict XVI, *Pastoral Convention of the Diocese of Rome*, 26 May 2009.

88. A variety of models can be suggested for the continuing education of clergy and religious. Priests in a diocese will need to meet regularly, together with their bishop, to discuss the implementation of a Diocesan Plan, drawn up with other diocesan interest-groups. The Diocesan Priests' Council should be encouraged to keep the faith development of priests high on its agenda. Appointments, ongoing formation of priests and support for priests who may be in difficulty, should all be given particular attention in every diocese. Diocesan clergy and religious priests working in parishes should be supported and resourced, in identifying and engaging with personal and ministerial education. At national level, provision for the development of a national understanding among priests, as well as support mechanisms and a plan of action for renewal, deserves the fullest attention of bishops, priests, religious and laity.

SIGNIFICANT AREAS FOR THE CONTINUING FAITH
DEVELOPMENT OF BISHOPS, PRIESTS, DEACONS
AND RELIGIOUS

● Ongoing personal and community education.
● Continuing spiritual renewal and development of personal prayer life with the help of a spiritual director.
● Renewed study of theological development and trends.
● In-depth study of current Papal teachings.
● Personal participation in adult faith development programmes with lay people.
● Formation in the collaboration of the lay faithful in the exercise of sacred ministry.
● Support in knowing how to participate in positive change and to empower others.
● Ongoing training in liturgical celebration, including homiletics, the ordering and use of sacred space, familiarity with liturgical music, drawing others into participation, and understanding significant opportunities for liturgical catechesis.
● Implementing the objectives set out in this *National Directory for Catechesis*.

Religious congregations, generally, it must be said, have come to provide good support for members of their communities in assessing their particular gifts and helping to put those gifts to use in the world of today, in accord with the charism of the order. This, too, is work that should never be taken for granted. Personal renewal can lead to a rekindling of energy and commitment within the religious community and within the local Church.

Co-operation between clergy and religious communities within a parish and within a deanery is essential and can work for the good of all. Often, the most useful enrichment of faith takes place when clergy, religious and lay people gather together to reflect, pray, participate in discussion and learn from one another. Listening to how others experience the Church can be enlightening and rewarding. It may be that over the coming years, diocesan assemblies will be organised, where priests, religious and lay people can discuss, after a period of preparation, ways in which the diocese can be more proactive in catechising its own people and reaching out to others. The continuing faith development of adults, including priests, deacons and religious, should be given priority in such discussions.

When it comes to looking at the specific content of adult faith development programmes, there is often a desire to get back to simpler times, to ask the right question and know the right answer. We need, today, as pointed out in Chapter 1, to allow for the complexity of life in Ireland. The anguish that people experience, including priests, religious and bishops, and the sometimes unsatisfactory human limits of the answers we can give, must be acknowledged. Parents are only too aware of how inadequate they can feel at times in their role. Bishops, priests and religious may need to stay with the difficult questions that arise for them, too, in their ministry. They need to grapple with the challenges presented by faith, hope and love. To be a leader in faith is to recognise that all of us share the same questions about our world, about life, about God's goodness and about our ability to respond to God's love; it is to be one who encourages others to live truthfully and dynamically in that love.

Adults of Mature Years

89. The elderly are a gift of God to the Church and to society. In faith development, they have the same rights and responsibilities as all Christians, and should never be seen as passive objects in any sense. 'It is not a question of doing something for older people, but of accepting them in a realistic way as partners in shared projects – at the level of thought, dialogue and action.'[40] Where possible, they should participate fully in the catechetical journey of the local faith community. Care should be taken by that community to ensure that those of advanced years, often after a lifetime of service to the Church, to their local parish and to its schools, do not feel isolated or left alone. Their personal and family circumstances, as well as health and well-being, will always be the concern of a caring and present community:

> If the elderly are in situations where they experience suffering and dependence, not only do they need health care services and appropriates assistance, but — and above all — they need to be treated with love.[41]

The elderly seek and need to participate in ongoing faith development appropriate to their stage in life. In the light of Christ, many significant issues for this age-group take on new significance: embracing the present, confronting limitations, reflecting on death itself, reconciliation and forgiveness, expanding the circle of one's love and compassion. As the *General Directory for Catechesis* points out, for those with a rich and solid faith, an attitude of thanksgiving and hopeful expectation can be cultivated. For those whose Christian practice has, over time, been weakened, new evangelisation can provide light and a new religious experience. For those who reach old age 'profoundly wounded in body and soul', catechetical outreach can help develop an attitude of prayer, forgiveness and inner peace. The Directory calls for 'a catechesis of hope' looking forward joyfully to finally meeting with God.[42]

A dialogue between the generations also suggests itself, both within the family and within the Christian community. The elderly, engaged and inspired by the Holy Spirit, are a source of great wisdom and insight for the young. They can provide the service of handing on to the young their experience of life lived in faith. They can learn too in conversation with young people. By staying in contact with developments among the younger generations, and in society generally, they continually open themselves up to new ways of looking at life, engaging with it and with the people they encounter day by day. Grandparents, in consultation with parents, can have a gentle but strong role in encouraging the faith life of the young. Sometimes, too, they can find themselves in the position of guardian, with an even more significant role to play. One way or

[40] John Paul II, *Message to the Second World Assembly on Ageing*, Madrid, 3 April 2002.
[41] *CSDC* 222.
[42] See *GDC* 187.

another, children and young people will often see and take to heart what the older generation says and does in a way that can be surprising and very uplifting:

> The elderly constitute an important school of life, capable of transmitting values and traditions, and of fostering the growth of younger generations, who thus learn to seek not only their own good but also that of others.[43]

90. Active retirement groups can be a very positive and encouraging development within a parish community. Many people of mature years are highly skilled, have time available and are very happy to put their expertise at the disposal of the Church and voluntary groups. They are often people who form the backbone of parish communities, being present regularly at the daily liturgy and available for organisational duties. They know that 'to experience Church means to personally meet the living Christ in it'.[44] They may have great expertise and experience in management, finance, business, education and in other areas, but have often had little opportunity to take part in up-to-date discussion of their faith. Active retirement groups of one kind or another can be significant in themselves. For those who have connected or reconnected with the regular life of the parish, the opportunity to be part of a theological reflection group, appropriately facilitated by the Faith Development Coordinator or other qualified person, can be a wonderful experience. By listening, reflecting and praying together, a retired group can become active in the  Christian community, building up the parish in practical ways, and bringing the results of their action with Jesus Christ back to their group for further thought and prayer. They can find ways, too, of including older people, who remain at home, in their company. Such active retirement groups can contribute together, not only to their own spiritual uplifting, but also to the life of the whole community.

[43] *CSDC* 222.
[44] *ETCS* 40.

CHAPTER 5

Sharing our Faith with the Young

91. The 'primary and natural responsibility'[1] for children's education belongs to their parents/guardians. 'Parents, and those who take their place, have both the obligation and the right to educate their children.'[2] They have a vital part to play within the educating community. So, too, parents/guardians take on the principal role in the faith formation of their children, introducing them to Jesus and preparing them for the sacraments of initiation, Baptism, Confirmation and the Eucharist. It is true that many parents today feel the need for support in this role, having become unfamiliar with what it asks of them, or even alienated from the institutional Church. However, they do not have to take this duty on alone; they do so with their wider family and within their parish community. They are supported by the priests of the parish, by other parents/guardians and by those who participate in the planning and programming of parish catechesis. The local Catholic school, a constitutive part of the parish, contributes generously to the children's faith development, seeking 'to inculcate in pupils the qualities of personal integrity and moral courage which are marks of an authentic Christian personality'.[3] Sharing faith with the young is the work of the whole Christian community, a responsibility it is happy to undertake and to invest its energy in. Adult Catholics recognise that in this conversation, children, too, can be an inspiration to them, opening adults to fresh ways of seeing life, love and relationships, with one another and with God and, thereby, coming to understand their own faith anew.

The Baptism of Children

92. Parents/guardians who, recognising the significance of faith in their own lives, offer their children Baptism, accept gladly the responsibility of bringing them up in the faith. This is put to them at the beginning of the celebration of the sacrament: 'You have asked to have your child baptised. In doing so, you are accepting

[1] *CSTTM* 20.
[2] *CIC* can. 793.
[3] Irish Catholic Bishops' Conference, *Vision '08: A Vision for Catholic Education in Ireland* (Maynooth, 2008), p. 5.

the responsibility of training him/her in the practice of the faith. It will be your duty to bring him/her up to keep God's commandments as Christ has taught us, by loving God and our neighbour. Do you clearly understand what you are undertaking to do.' And they respond: 'We do.'[4] They pledge themselves to become 'their own children's catechists',[5] to prepare them appropriately to receive the other sacraments of initiation, and to help them to interpret the meaning of the Gospel in their day-to-day lives.

Choosing to have your child baptised is, therefore, a very significant decision, not to be taken lightly. A full conversation should take place between the parents/guardians, the wider family and with parish leaders. The integrity of the sacrament must be respected, while the desire of the parents/guardians to baptise their child should also be encouraged. This requires careful discussion before a decision to baptise is finalised. A Baptism Team in the parish or group of parishes, working in conjunction with the priests, trained and under the direction of the Faith Development Coordinator, should be prepared to enter into catechesis with parents/guardians concerning the meaning and responsibilities associated with the sacrament. Accessible literature should be available to guide parents/guardians in what is involved in having their child baptised. Support systems need to be put in place and a catechist from the Baptism Team chosen to accompany the parents/guardians once they have made the decision to baptise their child.

Godparents and grandparents should be encouraged in their role of supporting the parents in the faith formation of their children. Family and parish support for parents/guardians, godparents and grandparents as they foster the human and spiritual growth of their child is essential. The decision to baptise, taken in a reflective manner and guided by the Holy Spirit, is to be celebrated and recognised within the local Christian community to which the family, and now the newly baptised child, belong.

GROUP REFLECTION: A CHILD OF GOD

Through Baptism an infant is welcomed into a community that claims as its own the simple beauty of the Christmas story and the dramatic realities of Holy Week. Through Baptism the community celebrates a baby as a child of a loving God, someone whose family ties extend to heaven. Thus infant Baptism signifies the crucial roles that the family, the Church community and the Christian story play in developing, within children, the Christian view of life.

Joseph Stoutzenberger, *Celebrating Sacraments*
(Winona: St Mary's Press, 2000), p. 149.

---

[4] *Rite of Baptism for Children.*
[5] *HFH*, p. 10.

This faith-filled occasion presupposes the promise of all those participating in it that they will do everything in their power to help the young person to come to know and deepen the gift of Christian life that they have been given: 'The child demands full respect and help in its spiritual and human growth... Those who have given life to children and have enriched them with the gift of Baptism have the duty continually to nourish it.'[6]

Presenting the Gospel to Children

Nurturing the Faith of Children

93. Children who have been baptised should first be offered the life of faith, as we have seen, within their family and in their parish. Before looking at the great contribution being made by Catholic primary schools, it is important to consider how parents and the wider parish community can fully grasp their role and responsibilities. The social and cultural reality in Ireland today, discussed in Chapter 1, and the drift away from regular participation in the Sunday liturgy, means that there can be difficulties in this regard. Parents/guardians are, once again, invited to take on the primary role of educating their children in the faith. They should not feel isolated in this but should turn to their parish community for support:

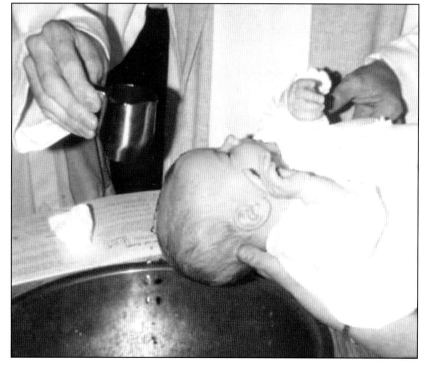

'Whether or not students attend Catholic schools, the parish has the responsibility of integrating all Catholic students into the life of the Church.'[7] The various stages of their initiation will require catechesis, both at home and in the parish, as well as the religious education and preparation for the sacraments that takes place in school and will be highlighted later in this chapter. Family Ministry, organised in the parish and in the diocese, can develop useful strategies for helping families to engage actively in family catechesis.

[6] GDC 177.
[7] Irish Catholic Bishops' Conference, *Guidelines for the Faith Formation and Development of Catholic Students* (Dublin: Veritas, 1999), p. 12.

> ## FAMILY REFLECTION: PARENT AND CHILDREN, LEARNING TO PRAY TOGETHER
>
> The frantic pace at which we live our lives has led many to look for quiet spaces and opportunities for reflection... Our Catholic tradition is full of rich opportunities for developing our relationship with God; for example through the sacraments, especially the Eucharist, and Christian meditation, novenas and places of pilgrimage. In order to be able to help their children to pray, parents need to pay attention to their own prayer lives. Thankfully, in recent times, it has become easier and easier to find books, magazines, websites and other resources which are designed to help sustain and develop our prayer. All of these are ways of quietening down, of making space for a vital connection with God who loves us.
>
> Irish Catholic Bishops' Conference, *Nurturing Our Children's Faith*
> (Dublin: Veritas, 2006), p. 2.
> Available from *www.catechetics.ie/educationinfaithsunday*

Parish programmes, under the direction of the Faith Development Coordinator, can address faith formation in a variety of ways, depending on the circumstances and needs of the children attending. Fun activities, such as games, videos, drama, singing, parish picnics and entertainment days, can play a role too. It should be remembered that children can teach one another much, as they journey together in faith: 'To teach children to share with one another in a concrete way is an important step in forming a Christian conscience. It expresses and develops the missionary spirit.'[8]

94. Each young person is unique and will develop at his or her own pace. Parents/guardians and parish personnel need to be aware of the general characteristics of children's development, while addressing the particular needs of the young people in their care. **Infancy and Early Childhood**, up to the age of six, is recognised as a most important stage in the child's development. With this age-group, care and education are closely intertwined and must be met in a unified way, with care being the dominant requirement up to three years of age, and education becoming more significant from three years onwards.[9] High-quality early participation in family faith activities is important, laying the foundations for all future catechesis and further faith development. '*Education in the faith* by the parents should begin in the child's earliest years. This already happens when family members help one another to grow in faith by the witness of a Christian life in keeping with the Gospel. Family catechesis precedes, accompanies and enriches other forms of instruction in the faith.'[10] With the younger schoolgoing age-group, a pre-evangelisation style is often appropriate, focused on providing a

[8] John Paul II, *To the Children of Bahia*, Brazil, 20 October 1991.
[9] Republic of Ireland, Department of Education and Science, *Ready to Learn: White Paper on Early Childhood Education*, 1.1, 2003. Available at *www.education.ie*
[10] CCC 2226.

basis for a life of faith: 'a sense of trust, of freedom, of self-giving, of invocation and of joyful participation.'[11]

95. **Middle Childhood,** as a stage of development, generally involves children finding their place in the groups and communities to which they belong. Children at this stage also begin to develop basic reasoning abilities, and they identify and understand laws and rules. At this stage, a child's faith journey is focused on participating and belonging. It is fitting, therefore, that the child's initiation into the faith to which they belong, and within which they are beginning to participate, should be emphasised at this point.

Over the centuries, a practice has developed in the Catholic Church whereby First Holy Communion is received a number of years before the child has celebrated Confirmation. A clearly defined process of sacramental preparation for First Holy Communion and for the sacrament of Penance and Reconciliation (which always precedes First Holy Communion) should be in place in all parishes, along with the programme that takes place in the Catholic parish school.[12] The focus at certain Sunday liturgical celebrations, and perhaps through a *Faith Friends* initiative, will be on reception of the Eucharist, but good-quality preparation for First Penance and Reconciliation is also necessary and vitally important. Such a parish programme will

help all involved to see the parish as their faith community; the faith community within which the child is being initiated and encouraged to belong. It will be of particular assistance to parents/guardians who are preparing their children for the sacraments, but whose children do not attend a Catholic school. The parish programme should be agreed with parents/guardians in the expectation that, having made the decision to go ahead with this stage of their child's initiation, they are happy to participate in the preparation programme. A volunteer First Communion Team, working with the priest and Faith Development Coordinator, should incorporate a group of committed parents/guardians each year, who will become part of the team and ensure that parents/guardians generally are involved in the programme.

[11] *GDC* 178.
[12] See C. Ryan, *Reconciliation and Eucharist: Alive-O Adapted for Use in the Home and Parish* (Dublin: Veritas, 2003); J. Maloney, *Let's Celebrate in the Name of the Lord: First Communion and First Penance* (Dublin: Veritas, 2004).

It is very appropriate that the children's parish preparation prior to First Communion should be coordinated through participation at the parish celebration of Sunday Mass. In recent years, programmes have been set in motion in many parishes, using a particular Mass, often one Sunday a month, as a time suitable for engaging all involved in the process.[13] This takes place within the sponsoring community of faith. As the focus is on celebrating and participating fully in communion with God and with the parish community in Jesus Christ, this is particularly fitting. Suggestions for prayer and discussion at home are a key element. Parents are given the confidence to engage fully in the process, both at home and in parish. Such programmes have the added value of helping the parish faith community to become more aware and involved in the sacramental initiation of the children. Their Christian initiation can be catechising not only for the individual child but for his or her family and for the entire Christian community, drawn together into the Father's love.

PARISH PROMISES:
SUPPORT, HELP AND PRAYER FOR OUR CHILDREN

Now we ask the community of faith to journey with these families as their children prepare to become full members of the Church. As members of the family of God it is our responsibility to support, help and pray for these children. They are a reminder that through our Baptism we are all children of God.

Do This in Memory 2, p. 20.

---

96. **Pre-adolescence** is characterised by a reduced dependence upon family and by the growth of peer influence. While concrete thinking still predominates, the faith journey may be characterised by searching and questioning, as elements of uncertainty may arise. The realities of this age-group, the *General Directory for Catechesis* asserts, while particularly significant in the developed world, are often not sufficiently recognised or paid adequate attention: 'sufficient account is not taken of the difficulties, of the needs and of the human and spiritual resources of pre-adolescents, to the extent of defining them as a *negated age-group*.'[14] Particular attention should, therefore, be given in coming years to understanding and responding to the needs of this 'forgotten' age-group.

In Ireland, as elsewhere, Confirmation has traditionally been celebrated at pre-adolescence, as the child begins to move toward a more independent way of living. Home and parish catechesis in preparation for Confirmation are as significant as the programme that takes place in Catholic schools. A parish-based element of preparation for Confirmation can best be conceived of as a number of evenings where parents/guardians and children participate together in reflection and activity. Connection with Sunday Mass

[13] See, for example, M. Mahon and M. Delaney, *Do This in Memory: A Parish-Based Preparation Programme for First Eucharist* (Dublin: Veritas, 2004, 2005 and 2006).
[14] GDC 181.

celebrations can also be made. This process, organised with the Faith Development Coordinator, can be offered by a parish volunteer Confirmation Team, working with parents/guardians. The focus should be on bringing the child to understand the gifts of the Holy Spirit at work in their lives.[15]

The sacrament of Confirmation, then, is to be celebrated as a sacrament of initiation, not of final commitment. It is not a time for celebrating maturity in the faith. It is a moment in the young child's journey toward fuller participation in the Church, under the power and with the support of the Holy Spirit. The pastoral approach is one in which the community of faith welcomes fully the children being confirmed, inviting them to begin now to walk with Jesus and learn how to become a good, honest and enthusiastic follower of his, living life in his compassionate love, guided by his Spirit. The young person is only beginning on the road and should be encouraged to understand that they have much to learn yet about God's love for them, and how to live their life in that love, loving others as Jesus does. The Confirmation Team should also consider a post-Confirmation programme[16] to help young people realise that they are now at the start of their journey toward adult faith, supported by their parish community.

97. To encourage parents/guardians, parishes and schools to collaborate in their respective roles in the Christian initiation of their children, the Parish Priest, with the Parish Pastoral Council, working perhaps in cooperation with a number of local parishes, should put in place, as mentioned in Chapter 4, a professionally qualified and adequately resourced **Faith Development Coordinator**. Ideally, this person is supported by parish volunteer groups such as a Baptism Team, Confirmation Team and First Communion Team. Each of these may be organised between a group of parishes, according to local needs and resources. The Faith Development Coordinator, at the invitation of the priest and working with him, initiates and oversees parish faith formation initiatives. He or she works closely with parents/guardians and in conjunction with school personnel to establish supportive activities at home and in parish to complement the work ongoing in school for the religious education, formation and Christian initiation of young people.

[15] See M. Mahon, *You Shall Be My Witnesses* (Dublin: Veritas, 2009); *Confirming Our Children: A Programme of Parish Liturgies in Preparation for Confirmation* (Dublin: Veritas, 2003 and 2004).
[16] The planning for such programmes could follow the model laid out in *Alive-O 7* (Dublin: Veritas, 2003), pp. 223-53.

PARISH PASTORAL COUNCIL REVIEW:
PARISH SACRAMENTAL PREPARATION

Review in association with Diocesan Faith Development Services and other parishes locally, the provision for preparation in the parish of those going forward for each of the sacraments of initiation, Baptism, Confirmation and the Eucharist, and for the first celebration of the sacrament of Reconciliation.

In particular, parents/guardians of children for Baptism, Confirmation, First Communion and First Penance and Reconciliation should be facilitated in the parish with ongoing catechetical training and support. This should not be seen as an imposition on parents/guardians, but as a help in sharing their faith with their children.

It should be considered the norm, then, that children are initiated into the sacraments within their own faith community and in their own parish or local church. For First Communion, this should, by preference, take place at the Sunday liturgy. Where there are a large number of children, a strategy should be arranged with parents/guardians whereby First Communion could take place at any one of a number of Masses, over a particular weekend or over a number of Sundays, during the month of May.

The local bishop will often visit a parish to celebrate the sacrament of Confirmation with its young people, their parents, sponsors, family and friends. On this day, the link between the local Christian community and the bishop, as well as the diocese, is made visible. Through him or his representative, we know ourselves to be incorporated into the universal and apostolic Church. If a bishop chooses to celebrate Confirmation at Pentecost, he participates at one location, and all are united with him through their priests, his co-workers, in other parishes. Whatever local customs apply, both Confirmation and First Communion should be reclaimed as parish events, whereby the child completes initiation into his or her faith community.

ADULT DISCUSSION:
CELEBRATING THE SACRAMENTS

Discuss ways for adult family, relations, neighbours and friends to support the children as they are initiated in the faith and celebrate reception of the sacraments, other than by offering financial gifts.

[17] See Sacred Congregation for Divine Worship, *Directory on Children's Masses* (London: CTS, 1974).

98. Family Mass has become a popular form of ministry to families in a parish.[17] In Ireland today, as indicated in Chapter 2, children

and young people need to know they belong to their faith community: 'Young members of the Church need to feel and believe that they have a valuable contribution to make to the local parish community.'[18] Family Mass, under the direction of the parish priest as the custodian of the sacred liturgy, has the added benefit of lifting the Sunday celebration for all those who attend. Very often, this type of celebration will become a form of

ministry to the rest of the parish, as well as to young families. It is better celebrated as a Family Mass, not a Children's Mass. All members of the family and all age-groups have a role to play. Although a children's choir may be one focus of the celebration, everything should not be left to children, with adults becoming spectators rather than participants. In some parishes, parents/guardians of young children have also formed a choir with other adults, leading the congregational singing at the Family Mass once a month. A group of parents/guardians, trained over time in good liturgy, should act as leaders, stimulating others to organise lectors, processions, liturgical art, special events, after-Mass community gatherings, etc. The Family Mass Team, working together with the parish's other faith development teams, can become a real focus for renewal in the parish.

TO DO: FAMILY MASS INITIATIVE

Investigate good pastoral practice with regard to Family Masses:

- Ongoing training of coordinators
- Participation of all age-groups
- Facilitation of children's choir
- Development of parents'/adult choir
- Establishing groups of supportive parents/guardians, for example, to train readers, to provide community tea/coffee occasionally after Mass, to support youth initiatives
- Co-operation with those involved in parish sacramental preparation of children
- Coordination with priests of the parish
- Interaction with Family Mass groups in other parishes

[18] Northern Ireland, Council for Catholic Maintained Schools, *Life to the Full: A Vision of Catholic Education*, p. 34.

In the particular case where children are without religious support at home, have not been baptised or have not completed their journey of initiation, it is the responsibility of the Christian community to address the situation. It can do this, the *General Directory for Catechesis* suggests, 'by providing generous, competent and realistic support, seeking dialogue with the families, proposing adequate forms of education and providing catechesis which is proportionate to the concrete possibilities and needs of these children.'[19]

Children's Religious Education in School

99. Primary schools seek to launch children on their lifelong journey with an education that honours them personally and helps them to develop and use their affective, active and cognitive

learning capacities. Heart, hands and head all have a role to play in how we learn and what we learn. Religious education for children necessitates such a synthesis between heart, hands and head. At the same time, it contributes to ensuring that the education children receive is holistic, experiential and life-enhancing.

Religious Education takes place in primary schools in Ireland within circumstances supported by Education Acts in both jurisdictions.[20] A *Core Syllabus for Religious Education in Northern Ireland,* drawn up by the four major churches – Church of Ireland, Presbyterian, Methodist and Roman Catholic – and negotiated with the Department of Education, Northern Ireland, became compulsory in 1996. The *Revised Core Syllabus for Religious Education,* again prepared by the four main churches, was published by the Department in June 2007.[21] This syllabus is continuous from primary through post-primary school education. It sets out Religious Education subject matter for Key Stages 1-4. It provides a common core for the teaching of Religious Education, which schools are free to build on in a way that suits the needs of their pupils and the ethos of the school. The *Code of Practice, Northern Ireland (1998),* which guides special education, emphasises the value of children's spiritual development, stating that 'every child attending either a mainstream or special school must receive religious education and attend collective worship, unless this would be against the wishes of the parents or the pupil's statement indicates otherwise'.[22]

In the Republic of Ireland, primary school religious education, focused on the formation of children within their faith community,

[19] *GDC* 180.
[20] See Government of Ireland, *Education Act, 1998* (Dublin: The Stationery Office, 1998); for Northern Ireland see the *Education Reform Act, 1988* and the *Education Reform (Northern Ireland) Order, 1989.*
[21] *Revised Core Syllabus for Religious Education.* Available from *www.deni.gov.uk.*
[22] *Code of Practice, Northern Ireland (1998),* p. 47.

is understood as coming within the remit of the various faith communities. These, in turn, provide both syllabuses and programmes for religious education and formation in their schools. The *Education Act, 1998* confirms the requirement that schools 'promote the moral, spiritual, social and personal development of students...in consultation with their parents, having regard for the characteristic spirit of the school'.[23] The spiritual and moral aspects of education have been confirmed as fundamental to education and to fostering maturity in all young people. In fact, the National Council for Curriculum and Assessment, in its general definition of education, calls for education in all schools to 'contribute to the development of all aspects of the individual, including aesthetic, creative, critical, emotional, intellectual, moral, physical, political, social and spiritual development'.[24]

My Shepherd is the Lord

The Introduction to the revised *Primary School Curriculum* for the Irish Republic acknowledges and values the contribution of religious education as one of the curriculum areas in primary schools: 'In seeking to develop the full potential of the individual, the curriculum takes into account the child's affective, spiritual, moral and religious needs.'[25] Religious education and formation has always been considered in Ireland to be of the utmost importance for this age-group.[26] The Irish State continues this tradition by recognising the role of Christian denominations and other faith traditions in designing curricula for religious education in the schools they manage and in supervising its teaching and implementation.[27] As an outreach of the local parish, Catholic primary schools seek to encourage the young people belonging to the parish, or other local parishes, to grow and develop in their faith.

100. Catholic primary schools in the Republic and in Northern Ireland are required to follow a religious education and formation programme that fosters and deepens children's Catholic faith. Any new syllabus/curriculum, and programmes arising from it, will continue to follow this approach. Efforts to involve children in a creative mix of affective, active and cognitive learning, suited to their age and development, as well as to the varying levels of family participation in faith-based activities, are to be welcomed. Previous models, highlighted in different ways down through the centuries, should be integrated: the doctrinal approach (learning the teaching of the Church); the kerygmatic approach (focused on coming to know and love Jesus Christ); and the anthropological approach (taking into account the circumstances and experience of the learner). The positive effects of a more recent 'pastoral' model

[23] Government of Ireland, *Education Act, 1998*, 9 (d); for background see K. Williams, *Faith and the Nation: Religion, Culture and Schooling in Ireland* (Dublin: Dominican Publications, 2005).

[24] National Council for Curriculum and Assessment, *A Programme for Reform: Curriculum and Assessment Policy Towards the New Century*, 1993, p. 26.

[25] Ireland, Department of Education and Science, *Primary School Curriculum: Introduction* (Dublin: The Stationery Office, 1999), p. 58.

[26] See *Rules for National Schools Under the Department of Education* (Dublin: The Stationery Office, 1965), Rule 68.

[27] See Ireland, Department of Education and Science, *Primary School Curriculum: Introduction*, p. 58.

[28] In recent years the *Children of God* series, and its re-presentation *Alive-O*, has provided schools with such a programme. The *Alive-O* series has, in fact, led to significant interdenominational and crossborder discussion, which has provided a new coherence in what is offered in a wide range of Catholic and other schools, based on an underlying affirmation of the value of supporting and nurturing the Christian faith of children. An Irish-language edition, *Beo go Deo*, is available, as is a Scottish edition. The Church of Ireland Education Board, together with the Methodist and Presbyterian Boards of Education, has developed the *Follow Me* series based on *Alive-O*.

[29] See J. W. Berryman, 'Faith Development and the Language of Faith', D. E. Ratcliff (ed.), *Handbook of Children's Religious Education* (Birmingham, Alabama: Religious Education Press, 1992), p. 41.

[30] Irish Catholic Bishops' Conference, *Vision '08*, p. 7.

[31] J. W. Fowler, *Stages of Faith: The Psychology of Human Development and the Quest for Meaning* (San Francisco: Harper & Row, 1981), p. 149.

[32] Catholic Primary School Management Association, *Management Board Members' Handbook* (Dublin: Veritas, 2007), p. 7.

are also becoming evident: a deeper awareness of the connections between home, parish and school; a vision of the parish community as a catechetical community; recognition of the ongoing need for the spiritual care of all educators, parents/guardians, teachers, parish ministers; and greater sharing of ideas, responsibilities and resources at diocesan and parish levels. As well as pupil texts, a significant teacher's manual, videos, posters, workbooks and material for use at home and in the parish are all to be considered helpful. The six fundamental tasks of catechesis, identified in the *General Directory for Catechesis*, and discussed in Chapter 2 above, should be at the centre of the programme: promoting knowledge of the faith; liturgical education; moral formation; teaching to pray; education for community life (including the ecumenical dimension); and missionary initiation (including inter-religious dialogue).[28]

In the religious education of children, co-operation between home, parish and school is essential in encouraging young children in coming to know who they are and to whom they belong. There is common agreement that the dominant faith development issues during childhood are belonging and being cherished.[29] 'It is communities which educate… Education enables us to enter into the community's experience and knowledge, its history and culture, its values and faith.'[30] In later childhood, the child 'begins to take on for him- or herself the stories, beliefs and observances that symbolise belonging to his or her community'.[31] All school-based education, and every school whatever its ethos, should respect and support the faith of the children under their care.

101. All primary schools fall under the obligation, identified by the Departments of Education, North and South, to contribute to the moral, spiritual and religious development of the child. The religious education and formation that takes place in the primary school does so within the particular ethos or defined characteristic spirit of that school. Such ethos is evident in the belief system, values, spirit and attitudes that are encouraged across the whole school. Ethos is not simply an aspiration; it is a reality, whether carefully defined or not, that shapes behaviour, decision-making and style of relationship within the education community and beyond.

Every school belongs within a community. Parents and the community share their traditions and values with their young people through their school. The Catholic primary school is identifiable by its Catholic ethos. It 'models and transmits a philosophy of life inspired by belief in God and in the life, death and resurrection of Jesus Christ'.[32] The whole school is rooted in and moved by the Gospel values of respect for life, love, solidarity, truth and justice. The Catholic school promotes the dignity, self-esteem and full development of each person, made in

God's image and uniquely loved by God. It welcomes, is respectful of, and engages with, people of all beliefs.[33] The Catholic primary school defines itself in relation to the local Christian community, of which it is an essential part. It builds on 'the foundation of love and faith which parents nurture at home'.[34] Catholic primary schools in the Irish Republic operate under the *Schedule*, agreed with the Minister for Education, reproduced below.

AGREED SCHEDULE FOR
A CATHOLIC PRIMARY SCHOOL
IN THE REPUBLIC OF IRELAND

A Roman Catholic school (which is established in connection with the Minister) aims at promoting the full and harmonious development of the person of the pupil: intellectual, physical, cultural, moral and spiritual, including living relationship with God and other people. The school models and promotes a philosophy of life inspired by belief in God and in the life, death and resurrection of Jesus Christ. The Catholic school provides Religious Education for the pupils in accordance with the doctrines, practices and tradition of the Roman Catholic Church and promotes the formation of the pupils in the Catholic Faith.

Catholic Primary School Managers' Association,
'Deeds of Variation for Catholic Primary Schools',
CPSMA Members' Handbook, p. 19.
Available from *www. cpsma.ie/publications*

The contribution of the Board of Management, principal, teachers and other staff in witnessing to the Catholic ethos of a school, cannot be overestimated. The Board of Management ensures a spirit of partnership with the patron and trustees, parents and children, school staff and the parish community.[35] Religious education is provided for Catholic pupils in accordance with the doctrine and tradition of the Catholic Church, seeking always to confirm and deepen their experience of lived Christian faith. Prayer is a feature of the school day and celebrations of the sacraments are a regular part of the school community's life. Interaction during the Religion period should be respectful and supportive of students of other religions, too. The Catholic school promotes tolerance, respect and inclusiveness. Its educational perspective is Catholic and ecumenical by nature and open to inter-religious and inter-cultural dialogues. It promotes 'the formation of young people in the construction of a world based on dialogue and the search for community ... on the mutual acceptance of differences rather than on their opposition'.[36] All students should be encouraged to have a good knowledge of the Catholic faith and its traditions, and also of other faith

[33] See the Northern Commission for Catholic Education, *Catholic Education: The Vision* (Belfast, 2006), p. 3.
[34] Northern Ireland, Council for Catholic Maintained Schools, *The Catholic School* (1992).
[35] See Mater Dei Institute of Education and Catholic Primary School Management Association, *Wellsprings: Workshop Participants Booklet* (Dublin: Veritas, 2008), pp. 13-15. Also available from *http://wellsprings.mater dei.ie*
[36] ETCS 53.

communities. On the other hand, no pupil need receive, or be present at, any religious education of which her or his parents or guardians disapprove. Timetabling should be arranged to allow easy withdrawal.[37] In today's world, with so much movement of peoples, Catholic schools should have great clarity about this issue:

> Catholic schools must not renounce their own characteristics and Christian-oriented educational programmes when immigrants' children of another religion are accepted. Parents wishing to enrol their children should be clearly informed of this. At the same time no pupil must be compelled to take part in a Catholic liturgy or to perform actions contrary to his or her religious convictions.[38]

The Catholic primary school, usually under the patronage of a bishop and attached to a parish, works closely with the local Catholic faith community, and in particular with the priest and the local Faith Development Coordinator, who visit the school regularly in a supportive role. The connection between school and parish is in this way acknowledged and reinforced day by day. A spirit of mutual respect is promoted within the school community, recognising the dignity and value of every human person.[39] Where parents/guardians of children, other than Catholic children, attending the school, wish to provide suitable faith education for their children, the school principal will be happy to encourage them in this regard.[40]

[37] See *Rules for National Schools Under the Department of Education*, Rule 69.
[38] EMCC 62.
[39] See Catholic Primary School Management Association, *Management Board Members' Handbook*, p. 8.
[40] See Irish Catholic Bishops' Conference, *Catholic Primary Schools: A Policy for Provision into the Future* (Dublin: Veritas, 2007), 4.3.

THE CATHOLIC SCHOOL IN IRELAND

- Catholic education is inspired by Jesus Christ. It is person-centred, seeking to develop the full potential of each person.
- Catholic education proposes a sacramental view of reality, helping pupils to see God 'in the bits and pieces of everyday life'.
- Catholic education takes place in open, happy, stimulating and mutually respectful communities.
- Catholic education values intellectual and practical reason, promoting dialogue and understanding between faith, tradition, culture and heritage.
- Catholic education values tolerance and inclusiveness. Catholic schools welcome pupils of other traditions, faiths and none, seeing diversity as offering opportunities for deeper understanding among people holding diverse convictions.
- Catholic education seeks to enable pupils to act with integrity and justice, in pursuit of the common good in an imperfect world, and to act as stewards of creation.

Irish Catholic Bishops' Conference,
Vision '08: A Vision for Catholic Education in Ireland –
Executive Summary.

TO DO: CATHOLIC SCHOOL COMMUNITY REVIEW

Board of Management, principal, staff and parents engage in regular review of how the school community lives up to its Catholic ethos. Consider:

- Description of ethos
- Mission Statement
- Connection with local parish(es)
- RE Policy
- Pastoral Care
- SPHE and RSE Policy
- Provision for liturgy and reflective space
- In-service in these areas
- Parents' Council

102. As well as contributing to the religious education of children, the Catholic primary school, as an outreach of the local Catholic parish, plays a very significant role in the Christian initiation of Catholic children as they grow into fuller participation in their local Christian community. The Catholic school, in conjunction with its parish, and other local parishes, helps prepare its Catholic pupils for the reception of the sacraments of initiation. This takes

place at the behest of the parents/guardians, with their co-operation and in partnership with their parish community.

In general, teachers in the Catholic primary-school sector participate willingly and generously in the faith formation of Catholic pupils.[41] Complaints arise from time to time that primary

teachers experience themselves as isolated in the sacramental preparation of children, being left to cater for this alone, without the input of parents/guardians, and sometimes with the minimum of interest from the parish too.[42] Such misconstruction, or even abandoning, of roles should not be allowed to develop. Where it is observed, it should be corrected. The school and its teachers support parents/guardians and their parish in the Christian initiation of children, not the other way round.

The diocese, as part of its Faith Development Services, provides support for schools in both the religious education and the preparation for sacramental initiation of Catholic pupils. It does this through its Primary Diocesan Adviser(s) for Religious Education, who visits schools, supporting school principals and providing in-service and resources for teachers and chaplains. These advisers often make themselves available also to support parish programmes for parents/guardians and their children as they prepare to receive the sacraments. The diocesan Education Office, a further element within the Faith Development Services of the diocese, facilitates the management and smooth running of the Catholic schools, under the patronage of the local bishop.

In Catholic primary schools, it is the role of the school **Principal** on behalf of the Board of Management to facilitate a consistent and coordinated approach to religious education, appropriate to the school's ethos, and to oversee the school's contribution to the Christian initiation of its Catholic pupils. Those training for principalship in a Catholic school today and those already in position need to be offered in-depth and continuing formation on what is meant by Catholic leadership in the complex world in which we live. It is appropriate that a teacher with specific training be given a post of responsibility as **Religious Education Coordinator**. Their role is to coordinate the religious education activities of the other teachers within the school, not to relieve them of their responsibilities, and in particular to support and resource teachers whose pupils are preparing for reception of the

[41] See Irish National Teachers' Organisation, *Teaching Religion in the Primary School*, (Dublin: INTO Publications, 2003) pp. 43-55.
[42] See Irish National Teachers' Organisation, *Teaching Religion in the Primary School*, pp. 54-5.

sacraments of initiation. The Principal and/or the Religious Education Coordinator should be in ongoing communication with the local Faith Development Coordinator and visiting priest, so that parish, home and school preparation is linked and cooperative. Trainee teachers who wish to work in Catholic schools will have participated in modules at College that will help them to become aware of and engage with religious education and formation, Catholic teaching, the Catholic school, Catholic sacramental initiation, and appropriate means of supporting the faith of Catholic pupils. As part of their training, student teachers should also be encouraged to participate in faith development initiates suitable for their own spiritual needs, as suggested in Chapter 4. School boards of management should seek to support and facilitate individuals and groups of teachers in taking initiatives designed to help them to engage with their own ongoing faith development.

A practical difficulty arises when the Catholic pupils in a school come from a variety of parishes. The parishes, along with the parents/guardians, should take a leading role in preparing for the celebration of the sacraments, and they should expect the children from the parish to be initiated normally within their own parish community. Parents and parish personnel should ensure that children already feel they belong to their parish, and know the other children, so that it is natural for them to celebrate their First Communion within their own parish community and in their own parish church.

103. The Catholic Church accepts, given the pluralism of religious belief that exists in Ireland today, that there should be choice and diversity within the national education system: 'In new areas of population it is incumbent upon the State to plan for the provision of school sites and to ensure, in consultation with the various patron bodies, that there is a plurality of school provision reflecting the wishes of the parents in the area.'[43] It may also be desirable for the Catholic Church to enter into new patronage arrangements, providing such arrangements uphold the rights of

[43] Irish Catholic Bishops' Conference, *Catholic Primary Schools: A Policy for Provision into the Future*, 5.1.

Catholic parents/guardians, in relation to the religious education and formation of their children within the school curriculum.[44]

Parents/guardians of Catholic children attending schools other than Catholic schools must, as is always the case, take responsibility for the catechetical formation of their children and give particular attention, with the support of their parish, to the preparation of their young people for the sacraments of initiation.[45] As well as the catechesis they give at home, they are asked to ensure that they provide for their children's participation in a full sacramental preparation programme, before putting their children forward for sacramental initiation in their parish.

Together with parents/guardians, the local parish will take responsibility for the pastoral care of students in a Catholic special-needs school in the parish. Even though students will attend such a school from a wide catchment area, the parish, with the support of parents/guardians and teachers, will seek to include the students whenever possible in parish activities. Preparation for the sacraments by children with special educational needs who do not attend Catholic schools will require particular and individual attention.

Presenting the Gospel to Adolescents

Nourishing the Faith of Adolescents

104. The *General Directory for Catechesis* affirms that young people are to be embraced as active participants in their own religious development, bringing the message of Christ out into the world: 'young people cannot be considered only objects of catechesis, but also active subjects and protagonists of evangelisation and artisans of social renewal.'[46]

[44] See Irish Catholic Bishops' Conference, *Catholic Primary Schools: A Policy for Provision into the Future*, 5.2.
[45] See *CIC* cann. 773, 776, 777, 798, 804.
[46] GDC 183.

Adolescence, the stage between childhood and adulthood, is characterised by physical change and a search for identity. Of its nature, this transition time will involve a degree of uncertainty. Rapid social change is also central to what is happening in the life of the adolescent. The need to become independent and self-affirming, before taking on adult responsibilities, is crucial. A certain dependency upon peers, heavy pressure from the consumer society, and the magnetism of modern forms of media, computerisation and communications technology, have all to be negotiated. These influences impact heavily upon the life of the adolescent, demanding their constant attention. Critical reflection and questioning often emerges at this stage in the young person's growth toward maturity. While this is a necessary growth process, sometimes, in the short term at least, it seems to be at the expense of religious and other commitments. Indeed, many observe a growing cultural phenomenon among young people of rejecting, to a greater or lesser degree, institutional affiliation of one kind or another: dismissal of parental and other adult advice, behavioural problems at school, early school leaving, disassociation from parish and from participation in religious ritual, and a seeming lack of connection with meaningful support services when succumbing to alcohol and drug use and when feeling suicidal. Understood positively, however, adolescence can be seen as an important opportunity for the young person to search out meaning in life and develop a sense of their true personal identity. It is only when the young person knows who they are and what is important for them that they can truly move toward a more intimate understanding of relation with others and, indeed, with God.

GROUP DISCUSSION: UNDERSTANDING THE RELIGIOUS QUESTIONING OF YOUNG PEOPLE

The religious questioning of young people today needs to be better understood. Many of them are asking about the value of science and technology when everything could end in a nuclear holocaust; they look at how modern civilisation floods the world with material goods, beautiful and useful as they may be, and wonder whether the purpose of life is really to possess many 'things' or whether there may not be something far more valuable; they are deeply disturbed by the injustice which divides the free and rich from the poor and oppressed.

RDECS 20.

Ongoing faith development for this age-group is a constant challenge. It needs to use appropriate language that will speak to adolescents and the realities that face them, highlighting the relevance of their religious faith in life, even as they are searching. Family and parish catechesis for adolescents, and efforts to support and inform their faith at school, should attempt to help them to integrate their faith with their responsibilities and with the events of their everyday lives. An authentic and honest approach to faith, acknowledging the opportunities and possibilities open to most young people today, may well be viewed not only as real but also as refreshing, challenging and genuinely forward-looking.

DISCUSSING FAITH: A TWO-WAY PROCESS

Answering teenagers' questions and meeting their arguments
can be demanding. But it will 'stretch' and strengthen our own
faith... Discussing religion with teenagers is by no means a
one-way process. We learn as much from them as we teach
them. Adults can become disillusioned, and 'settle for'
mediocrity in the name of realism. It can be good for us to be
challenged by young people. Many teenagers demand sincerity
in religion. They can be generous, idealistic... They have a
keen sense of justice. They want to make the world a better
place. They want to bring Christianity into life, into society. All
this can challenge us adults into trying harder to be Christian
ourselves.

HFH, pp. 31-2.

105. The *General Directory for Catechesis* observes that adolescent
catechesis often demands a pre-catechetical missionary dimension,
bringing the young people alive to the importance of faith before
engaging with them in a more formally catechetical deepening of
faith. This is particularly significant in our time. 'A necessary
"adaptation of catechesis to young people" is urged, in order to
translate into their terms "the message of Jesus with patience and
wisdom and without betrayal".'[47]

Research published in 2000 helps us to focus on what might be
useful for young people in Ireland today, in finding positive
meaning through affiliation to a Christian community.[48] The
authors propose that intervention on three levels is indicated:

- **Pre-evangelisation:** Opening up the sensibilities and
  imagination of young people who are uninformed or
  alienated in order to allow them to experience God in a
  meaningful way in their lives.
- **Evangelisation:** For those who have a basic openness to
  religious learning, a direct approach is suggested, both at the
  informational and formational levels, seeking to help young
  people develop an affiliation and commitment to God,
  Church and neighbour.
- **Support:** For those who have already made a commitment to
  the world of religion, personal mentoring is suggested,
  especially at times of transition, in order to help young
  people develop their relationship with God in a more
  personal way.

[47] *GDC* 185; see also
CT 40.
[48] See D. Tuohy and P.
Cairns, *Youth 2K:
Threat or Promise to a
Religious Culture*
(Dublin: Marino
Institute of Education,
2000).

Four issues are suggested as crucial:

1. **Language:** developing appropriate symbols that speak to the culture and concerns of young people, inspiring as well as explaining.
2. **Participation:** strategies that promote participation, acceptance and a deep experience of community.
3. **Space:** providing opportunities for reflection rather than focusing entirely at the level of activity.
4. **Process:** awareness of and support for young people in the transitions they make, into secondary education, through puberty, choosing a career, leaving home, etc.

PROGRAMME PLANNING: SKILLS CENTRAL TO ADOLESCENT SPIRITUAL GROWTH

Religious faith skills include:

- How to recognise God's presence
- How to live life with Christ
- How to pray
- How to share faith experiences
- How to apply the Bible to one's own life
- How to use the religious imagination
- How to participate in communal worship

Moral living skills include:

- How to recognise the face of Christ in others
- How to recognise and respond to others in need
- How to build and maintain healthy relationships (and terminate unhealthy ones)
- How to handle sexual and social pressure
- How to obtain second chances
- How to avoid alcohol and drug abuse
- How to handle violence
- How to analyse society's values and issues
- How to distinguish between right and wrong

Emotional awareness skills include:

- How to respond to Christ, present as he promised
- How to stay hopeful
- How to handle anger
- How to handle fear
- How to initiate and accept reconciliation
- How to practise problem-solving
- How to express affection
- How to handle rejection

Adapted from M. Carotta, *Sometimes We Dance, Sometimes We Wrestle: Embracing the Spiritual Growth of Adolescents* (Orlando, Florida: Harcourt Religion, 2002), p. 57.

It is of the utmost importance that adolescents are helped to see the local Church as a living and vibrant community that cares for them and will support them. The development of post-Confirmation programmes that encourage young people, already initiated into membership of the Church, to consider personally and take responsibility for their own faith development, as mentioned above, would be very constructive. Support for this personal faith journey should be offered in the home, within the parish community and at school.

Catholic parents/guardians can and should make it their special care to be informed about the types of catechesis and religious education available to their young people in the parish and in schools. At home, they can encourage in-depth conversation, appropriate to the age and needs of adolescents, listening to the young people's concerns and challenging them lovingly. Such conversation can be helpful for the adolescent and also for their parents/guardians and family.

106. The parish should bear in mind the wider pastoral context of the adolescent and seek, in co-operation with parents/guardians, to provide a space within the parish community where young people feel welcome. Adolescents, today, are often crying out for a place in which they can be themselves, be at ease with others, and feel acknowledged and supported for who they are, rather than feel continually overburdened, pressured and suffocated. Good liturgy, particularly appropriate music, may create the right ambience for worship. The parish should seek to respond, too, to the need adolescents have to find space for reflection and prayer. Group activities, particularly those associated with justice, service and helping those most in need, can also be constructive. An element of good fun, being together and working for others, can be very beneficial in helping young people come to terms with themselves and with others. Pilgrimage too, and perhaps especially preparation for and participation in World Youth Day, can provide an extraordinary catechetical moment. Youth groups, folk groups, prayer groups, clubs and sports associations, linked with parish,

can give young people a supportive peer group in which to grow, while at the same time highlighting their parish community's care for them. The availability of the Faith Development Coordinator and of youth ministers can be an invaluable asset for young people themselves and for involving them in parish. Parish youth ministry is supported by the diocesan youth ministry team.[49] Professional child and youth safety procedures should always be in place. Often, those who have enjoyed youth initiatives of one kind or another, will remain on into young adulthood and become leaders within the group. Personal accompaniment and spiritual direction can be made available for those adolescents and young adults who would like to investigate their faith life somewhat more thoroughly.

FOUR GOALS OF YOUTH MINISTRY

- Goal One To help young people grow, both in a personal sense and a spiritual sense.
- Goal Two To give young people the opportunity to experience and be disciples of Jesus Christ in their lives.
- Goal Three To inspire and facilitate young people to take an active role in the Catholic community.
- Goal Four To encourage the Catholic community to continually put aside any prejudices about young people and to recognise and empower their talents and energy.

Irish Catholic Bishops' Conference,
Called Together. Making the Difference:
A Framework Document for Youth Ministry in Ireland, pp. 22-23.

Young people at Transition Year and senior cycle level in school should be invited to consider committing themselves at a series of levels to service within the Christian community and beyond. This, rather than at sacramental initiation, is an appropriate time to speak, in parish and in school, of commitment and maturity in faith. Young people, before finishing school, should be invited to experience in parish what it means to be an active, committed, Spirit-filled Christian, alive to how faith in Jesus can transform their way of life as adults. A variety of service tasks, already highlighted above in Chapter 2, could be acknowledged and encouraged by an awards system: community building, sharing and witnessing to their faith, service of those in need, and liturgical participation and ministry.[50] Young people have so much to offer, to share with one another, with their community, and especially with people in need of care and attention. They carry within them, too, as a gift from God, seeds which, if properly cultivated, will help them to live through challenges they may have to face. These challenges can seem sometimes to be too much for their parents/guardians and others who, at the same time, help prepare them to live in times yet to come.

[49] See Irish Catholic Bishops' Conference, *Called Together. Making the Difference: A Framework Document for Youth Ministry in Ireland* (Dublin: Veritas 2009), p. 44.

[50] For examples of what can be achieved see Diocese of Derry, John Paul II Award. Available from *www.thepopejohnpaul iiaward.com*

TO DO: PARISH YOUTH INITIATIVES

Research and consider a variety of youth initiatives that might be acted upon by the Youth Ministry Team in your faith community:

● Youth pilgrimages
● Diocesan Youth Services helping others in need
● Youth groups
● Liturgical music group
● Faith development group
● Prayer group
● Justice group
● Faith Friends to assist sacramental initiation of younger children
● Connection with parishes in other parts of the world
● Walks, runs and fasts for those in need

Religious Education of Adolescents

107. In Northern Ireland, the *Core Syllabus for Religious Education*, agreed between the four main churches and approved

by the Department of Education, Northern Ireland, continues into second level, covering Key Stage 3, from First to Third Year.[51] Students can go on to study Religious Education for GCSE and A-level examinations. They do this following the Syllabus laid down by the

[51] Veritas has provided *Fully Alive* for this age-group in Northern Ireland, a three-year programme building on the *Alive-O* primary school series.

Northern Ireland Education Board or one of the other United Kingdom boards. The Catholic Church confirms that Religious Education is an essential part of the school week for all Catholic students, whether or not those students are participating in State examinations in Religious Education. Generally speaking, in

Northern Ireland, the syllabuses used focus on the Christian tradition, allowing the students to study within the context of their own religious tradition. They should be supported with suitable resources and textbooks.

In the Republic's post-primary sector, State examinations in the subject Religious Education have been introduced, on an optional basis, in recent years. The Catholic community acknowledges the efforts of the Department of Education, in the Irish Republic, to put in place a Religious Education programme in second-level schools that is appropriate for all students, whether they have a particular religious commitment or not. In a Catholic school, knowledge, understanding, skills and attitudes associated with the Catholic faith will always be given priority. The Junior Certificate and Leaving Certificate Religious Education syllabuses, as well as the Leaving Certificate Applied Religious Education modules and the Curriculum Framework for Senior Cycle Religious Education (catering for those not taking examinations), while limited, should be viewed as useful tools for the religious education and faith formation of Catholic students, opening them to critically significant questions and to the profound in daily life.

All these programmes of study are taught within the defined ethos or characteristic spirit of the school. The young person's religious experience is welcomed and supported. Young people are helped to know and belong to their religious tradition and to know about other religious faiths. It is significant that, according to the aims of these syllabuses, teachers should not simply give information, but should seek to contribute to the spiritual and moral development of the students within their religious tradition.[52] As is pointed out in the Bishops' guidelines for junior cycle and senior cycle Religious Education, the religious education of Catholic students in second-level schools should always seek to support and inform their faith. The Bishops' guidelines offer suggestions for ensuring and enabling the syllabuses to be delivered as Catholic religious education.[53] These syllabuses can continue the work of introducing young Catholics to the concepts and language of community, faith, worship, morality, prayer and service. They encourage and support them in reflecting on their own experience and commitment to the Catholic religious tradition and invite them to encounter and engage with other religious traditions in Ireland and elsewhere.[54] These syllabuses invite all students to dialogue with the Christian tradition in Ireland and with its denominational expressions, acknowledging the unique role of Christianity in Irish life and culture.[55] Those of no faith are encouraged to develop spiritual and moral foundations upon which to engage with the world, its religions and particular faith communities.[56]

[52] See Ireland, Department of Education and Science, *Junior Certificate Religious Education Syllabus* (Dublin: The Stationery Office, 2000), p. 5; *Leaving Certificate Religious Education Syllabus* (Dublin: The Stationery Office, 2003), p. 5.

[53] See Irish Catholic Bishops' Conference, *Guidelines for the Faith Formation and Development of Catholic Students* (Dublin: Veritas, 1999); Irish Catholic Bishops' Conference, *Guidelines for the Faith Formation and Development of Catholic Students at Senior Cycle* (Dublin: Veritas, 2006).

[54] See *Junior Certificate Religious Education Syllabus*, p. 4.

[55] See *Junior Certificate Religious Education Syllabus*, p. 4.

[56] See *Junior Certificate Religious Education Syllabus*, p. 4.

Towards a Policy on RE
in Post-Primary Schools

The Irish Catholic Bishops' Conference

From the Christian community's perspective, religious education and faith formation, though distinct, are always connected. All good religious education, limited as it most certainly will be, prepares the human heart to encounter the profound, putting the student and teacher in dialogue with ultimate questions.[57] Religious education opens individual students and teachers to the possibility of being more fully in touch with their own faith life. Such awareness may help them to take their religious understanding to new levels, not just of study but of commitment and responsibility. The study of religion in class can be both intellectually challenging and personally stimulating.[58]

108. All second-level schools, encouraging critical thinking across the Curriculum among adolescents and recognising the multi-faceted world they inhabit, should give significant time and space to support young people in developing the spiritual and moral dimension of their lives. Two hours of Religious Education, that is, three class periods, is the accepted minimum for all classes at second level, a time allocation that the Irish Catholic Bishops join in affirming as the least amount of time that can be considered appropriate. Anything less is clearly insufficient. These class periods should be taken by qualified religious educators, whether or not the class group is sitting a State-certified Religious Education examination.[59]

The Catholic Bishops of Ireland have provided a document, *Towards a Policy on RE in Post-Primary Schools*,[60] seeking to help schools plan for the religious education of Catholic students in the classroom. Each diocese provides a Post-Primary Diocesan Adviser for Religious Education, as part of its Faith Development Services. The diocesan adviser will arrange to visit schools to discuss with the principal, religious educators and coordinator of chaplaincy services, the particular needs of the Catholic pupils in the school with regard to Religious Education and faith support, as highlighted in Chapter 2. Religious Education should never be content simply to study religions as a phenomenon in society. It should always acknowledge the faith experience of students and help them to delve deeper into the meaning of religious commitment in their lives: 'We must be ready to repeat the basic essentials over and over again, so long as the need is present. We need to integrate what has been learned, and respond to the

[57] See G. Byrne, *Religious Education Renewed: An Overview of Developments in Post-Primary Religious Education* (Dublin: Veritas, 2005), p. 20.
[58] See P. M. Devitt, *Willingly to School: Religious Education as an Examination Subject*, Into the Classroom Series 1 (Dublin: Veritas, 2000), p. 55.
[59] See Irish Catholic Bishops' Conference, *Guidelines for the Faith Formation and Development of Catholic Students*.
[60] See Irish Catholic Bishops' Conference, *Towards a Policy on RE in Post-Primary Schools* (Dublin: Veritas, 2003).

questions which come from the restless and critical minds of the young.'[61]

All students, Catholic or otherwise, should be able to attend second-level Religious Education classes which follow the Department syllabuses, investigating the spiritual and moral questions central to human living. The Catholic school will facilitate this without in any way diminishing the primary support it gives to the faith of Catholic pupils, or by adopting a relativist ethic. Vatican II states clearly that young people 'should be open to dialogue with others and willingly devote themselves to the promotion of the common good'.[62] The Catholic school seeks to 'develop in the school community an atmosphere animated by a spirit of liberty and charity based on the Gospel'.[63] Openness to faith, to spiritual and religious commitment and to moral living, is fundamental to the whole-school approach to education adopted in a Catholic school. It takes up its responsibility to develop the whole person through a process of integrating faith and life and culture.[64] Every effort is made to help Catholic students to grow into a mature, personally owned and cherished faith, which can support them all their life, in times of difficulty as well as in times of joy.

109. Catholic students, whatever school they attend, should expect their faith to be respected and supported at school. The catechetical input provided at home and in the parish should be enhanced by post-primary schools in a manner appropriate within the school context. The commitment over the years, within the second-level Catholic school sector, of religious congregations, patrons and trustees, boards of management, principals, teachers, religious educators, coordinators of chaplaincy services, ancillary staff, parent committees and many others, has been a constant reminder of the value so many people place on Catholic education and of the efforts they are willing to make, often at great cost to themselves, to support the faith life and general well-being of the young. Today, renewed understandings of trusteeship are being developed and Catholic trusteeship groupings are being established. Qualified lay people, supported by these groupings, associated with the religious congregations that founded Catholic schools under the inspiration of pioneers such as Nano Nagle, Edmund Rice, Mary Aikenhead, Catherine McAuley and Teresa Ball, are leading this work into the future.[65] It is essential that those who take on the role of Principal in Catholic second-level schools are fully supported through the provision of initial and ongoing professional education that highlights an understanding of and capacity for leadership in a Catholic school. It is to be hoped that this Directory, in drawing all interested parties into discussion, will contribute to building upon the efforts of those who have, through their dedication and energy, passed on to us an education system that is highly prized.

[61] RDECS 23.
[62] GE 1.
[63] GE 8.
[64] See CS 37.
[65] See Irish Catholic Bishops' Conference, Vision '08, p. 6. A national Catholic Education Service was established in 2008.

> STARTING POINT:
> KNOWLEDGE, VALUES AND TRUTHS
>
> In the Catholic school's educational project there is no separation between time for learning and time for formation, between acquiring notions and growing in wisdom. The various school subjects do not present only knowledge to be attained, but also values to be acquired and truths to be discovered. All of which demands an atmosphere characterised by the search for truth, in which competent, convinced and coherent educators, teachers of learning and of life, may be a reflection, albeit imperfect but still vivid, of the one Teacher. In this perspective, in the Christian educational project all subjects collaborate, each with its own specific content, to the formation of mature personalities.
>
> *CSTTM* 14.

110. The opportunities available through senior cycle Religious Education are worthy of particular consideration. The Transition Year programme in schools in the Irish Republic allows students to become involved in projects associated with religion and with religious living. The flexibility of the programme means that decisions can be made at local level, using the resources of the parish community to support student learning in this area. Social outreach activities, through agencies such as Trócaire and Concern, fundraising for charities, living the Gospel in daily life, connection with parish and diocese, and career choices of a vocational and service nature, can all be investigated during Transition Year. Preparation for and debriefing of these activities can be as valuable as the assignments themselves. The Leaving Certificate Religious Education Syllabus and the Curriculum Framework for Senior Cycle Religious Education in schools in the Republic, can also be adapted imaginatively to encourage active religious commitment. The Veritas programme for the former highlights faith seeking understanding,[66] while its programme for the non-examination Curriculum Framework emphasises faith seeking to come to life in action.[67] An optional award system, encouraging young people to investigate for themselves what active Christianity and service in the Church might mean, could be focused, as mentioned in the previous section, on community-building (*koinonia*), liturgical service (*leitourgia*), care for those in need (*diakonia*), and witnessing to Christian faith (*kergyma/martyria*). The six fundamental tasks of catechesis could be revisited in this regard. Learning by doing and reflecting on the experience can impact strongly on young people. This scheme, based on observing and learning certain skills and completing a number of associated tasks, could be awarded within the parish community on behalf of the local bishop, usually by the young person's parish priest. While teachers would be invited to oversee the classroom element associated with such an award scheme, they

[66] See M. de Barra (ed.), *Faith Seeking Understanding* series (Dublin: Veritas, 2004-2006).

[67] See T. Gunning, *The Inner Place: Senior Cycle Religious Education* (Dublin: Veritas, 2006) and *Into The Deep: Senior Cycle Religious Education* (Dublin: Veritas, 2007).

will be supported in this by their Diocesan Adviser for Religious Education, by local parishes, and by hospitals, nursing homes, clubs and groups willing to become involved. This Church-based initiative could also be a support for those studying for Religious Education examinations, who could also be assisted in completing tasks within the parish context.

111. An emphasis on vocational discernment, on Christian action in society and on missionary responsibility in the world, is to be considered very appropriate at this stage in a young person's faith development. Indeed, efforts in many second-level schools in recent years to connect with schools and parishes in Third World countries have been very praiseworthy. Such projects seek to raise funds for significant life-changing projects, and, where possible, for students and teachers to visit such initiatives. They have opened the eyes of many young people, creating wonderful opportunities for solidarity with and care for the more vulnerable people of our world. These projects have also served to alert young people to issues associated with global sustainability and to the repeated exploitation of  the natural resources of developing countries, to the detriment of their people and of the natural balance of creation. Often, Catholic schools have linked up with members of their founding congregation at work in Africa, Asia and South America, and begun to understand more clearly the charism of the order, and the vitality of its members, their efforts to provide healthcare and education, to promote better living conditions for the poor and to encourage self-help, as they continue to work for the salvation of the world, and its peoples, in Jesus Christ. Connections with Christian community projects in other European countries and with the Universal Church should also be borne in mind. In all of these outreaches, preparation and debriefing, conducted with the young people involved, are crucially significant in drawing out an in-depth understanding of service, solidarity, mission, community, Church and redemption. In this atmosphere, positive support should be given to those who might respond to the vocation of Priesthood or the Consecrated Life, with priests, religious, teachers, parents and peers all contributing constructively to genuine reflection over a period of time.

Young people who discover the real meaning of the Church, as life lived together with Jesus Christ in love of God and loving service of others, will carry that understanding with them into adult life. Mature faith for those people will come to mean active religious living, building up the local faith community, worshipping God, and caring for those in need. By the power of the Spirit, they will proclaim the compassion of God, known in Jesus Christ, to the world, through a life of simple witness that speaks of truth, commitment and love.

CHAPTER 6

Reaching Out in Christ's Love to All

SCRIPTURAL REFLECTION:
WE GIVE THANKS TO GOD FOR YOU ALL

We give thanks to God always for you all, constantly
mentioning you in our prayers, remembering before our God
and Father your work of faith and labour of love and
steadfastness of hope in our Lord Jesus Christ. For we know,
brethren beloved by God, that he has chosen you.

(1 Thessalonians 1:2-5a)

112. In the Gospel of St Luke, the Lord Jesus is heard to proclaim
that he has come to bring good news to the poor (Luke 4:18). It is
clear that his message is for all people, a message to share with one
another, beginning with the most disadvantaged: 'Indeed he made
himself a catechist of the Kingdom of God for all categories of
persons, great and small, rich and poor, healthy and sick, Jews and
pagans, men and women,
righteous and sinners, rulers and
subjects, individuals and groups.
He is available to all.'[1]

The perennial process of
evangelisation is a gift offered to
all people. The message of God's
love for us in Jesus Christ
reaches out, not only to all age-
groups but to all members of the
Christian community and to all
of society. The dignity of the
human person demands that
justice and solidarity be
recognised as key dimensions at
the centre of all catechetical

[1] *GDC* 163.

efforts. It is especially important that we draw into this dialogue of faith and learn from those who have sometimes been forgotten or isolated or treated as outsiders for whatever reasons. As the *Compendium of the Social Doctrine of the Church* states: 'Nothing that concerns the community of men and women – situations and problems regarding justice, freedom, development, relations between peoples, peace – is foreign to evangelisation, and evangelisation would be incomplete if it did not take into account the mutual demands continually made by the Gospel and by the concrete, personal and social life of man.'[2] The faith development processes associated with all forms of evangelisation, including initial proclamation, Christian initiation, catechesis, religious education, new evangelisation and theological reflection, should always be just and inclusive. The processes and programmes adopted to enhance lifelong learning in the Christian community should take care to welcome with Christ all those who have at times found themselves marginalised within the Church, in the parish community and in society.

INVITATION TO ACTION: OUTREACH TO ALL

There are certain special categories which deserve attention because of their intrinsic value, both from a merely human as well as an evangelical perspective. Here we have in mind those whose need for the consolation of the Christian message is all the greater because of the intensity of their isolation and suffering. These include the disabled, the elderly, the sick, and all who find themselves on the fringes of society (refugees, immigrants, nomads and prisoners). The possibility of their involvement in the Christian community is often underestimated and unappreciated. With the solicitude of Christ, catechesis will also show special concern for those in irregular situations.

ACCC 55

---

113. Some people, because of their particular situation, will require specific need-appropriate catechetical initiatives that acknowledge and support them on their faith journey: people who experience social disadvantage; people with special needs; people who are deaf; the Travelling Community; newcomers of one kind or another; and those living with illness. Responding to the particular catechetical needs of these people is the focus of this chapter.

For others, inclusion in programmes that are being provided, and the reassurance that these programmes will accommodate them reasonably, is what is essential. They do not require a catechetical methodology that is specifically designed for them, but need to

[2] CSDC 66; see also EN 29.

know that their presence is welcome in the Christian community and that they can be heard. The ongoing faith development of, for example, couples who have never married, of married couples who have separated, and of those who have divorced and remarried, but who nonetheless wish to participate in faith education and renewal, all need attention within the Christian community. The Christian family must be prepared to learn from as well as provide support for all its members.

Catechetical and other faith development programmes should be supportive of all those who wish to engage with the Church. Each individual should be ministered to, in a manner that responds to their needs. This can often seem to be a challenge. It calls for education and training on the part of those who participate in the pastoral and catechetical outreach of the Church. It requires a willingness to enter into dialogue, to be able to respect another person's position, articulate the Church's thinking, and journey together through whatever difficulties may be encountered, valuing the relationship that is built up together. Catechetical and other faith development programmes and services should never contribute to anyone feeling dismissed, patronised or marginalised further.

The Catholic Church in Ireland desires to ensure that opportunities are provided for all learners to participate fully in its education processes, regardless of need, ability or background. Difference, culture and social background are sometimes used to excuse failure to respond to the real needs of people. Alert to and encouraged by the social teaching of the Church and its development over the whole of the twentieth century, we must reach out with Jesus precisely in accordance with the specific requirements of people in their specific situations. In this way, too, the Church as a community of faith can benefit from the richness of the human condition, learning from the diversity of gifts given and callings experienced, and, in the words of Pope Paul VI, 'find again greater light, new energy and fuller joy in the fulfilment of her own mission'.[3]

[3] *ES* 18.

TRACING THE SOCIAL TEACHING OF THE CHURCH		
Leo XIII	*Rerum novarum*	1891
Pius XI	*Quadragesimo anno*	1931
John XXIII	*Mater et magistra*	1961
	Pacem in terris	1963
Vatican II	*Gaudium et spes*	1965
Paul VI	*Populorum progressio*	1967
	Octogesima adveniens	1971
John Paul II	*Laborem exercens*	1981
	Sollicitudo rei socialis	1987
	Centesimus annus	1991
Compendium of the Social Teaching of the Church		2004
Benedict XVI	*Caritas in veritate*	2009

Those Who Experience Social Disadvantage

114. Poverty is still a real issue in Ireland. There is a continuing need for awareness of those who remain disadvantaged, and for action on their behalf.[4] Literacy and numeracy difficulties among primary schoolchildren remain a matter of urgent concern. Access to primary healthcare is essential in identifying language and other developmental delays and difficulties. Education is without doubt a key element in any strategy to eliminate poverty and to address continuing dependency.

Any one of a number of personal or community issues can make it difficult to break the cycle of poverty. Lack of everyday organisational ability, inability to work, family breakdown and depression can contribute to an unstable or unsatisfying situation. Addictions, particularly addition to drugs and alcohol, continue to have a seriously detrimental effect on efforts to lift people out of poverty. They can also contribute to homelessness. The place of alcohol, 'this shadow side of our Irish heritage',[5] and its negative impact in the lives of many, needs urgent and ongoing attention in our society.[6] This reality is now further complicated by the availability of drugs and of a growing addiction to them, particularly among younger people. Interestingly, it has been pointed out that while spirituality is often a missing or underdeveloped component in treatment and rehabilitation services, people whose spirits are most traumatised by drug addiction are particularly in need of this kind of holistic support.[7]

[4] See *www.vpsj.ie; www.svp.ie; www.comhlamh.org*
[5] Irish Catholic Bishops' Conference, *The Temperate Way: Creative and Christian Responses* (Dublin: Veritas, 1999).
[6] See Irish Catholic Bishops' Conference, *Alcohol: The Challenge of Moderation*, Pastoral Letter for Temperance Sunday and Lent 2007.
[7] See E. G. Cassidy, 'A Faith Response to the Street Drug Culture: A Report from the Irish Centre for Faith and Culture', E. Walsh (ed.), *Beyond Maintenance* (Dublin: Veritas, 2000), p. 68.

It can, in fact, be very difficult to change, particularly when trying to do so on one's own. Those who have been prisoners, for instance, can find that they do not know how to move beyond their past to a new future. Education generally, as well as, specifically, pastoral and catechetical interaction, is a key need for the prison population. Many prisoners are people who missed other opportunities for education and training at a whole series of levels. They may need to be more fully resourced in order to make a personally chosen and responsible contribution to society and to the Church. If prison becomes a seedbed of recidivism, it is not serving either the individual or society.[8]

115. There are many people in Ireland today who still endure social disadvantage of one kind or another. We should find ourselves always alert to difficult and, indeed, new forms of social disadvantage and breakdown. The Church, enriched by the strong tradition of her social teaching, should see herself as a leaven in society, engaging in advocacy for those in need, pointing out the deficit that still exists between rich and poor, and contributing to governmental review, particularly regarding the need for funding of community services and the building up of strong communities as the basis of society. We should seek continuously to respond, as many have done in the Church's name in the past, to alleviate the suffering of others.[9]

> The Irish Church needs more active, articulate lay people who understand and assume their responsibilities as Christian believers in various aspects of society. Irish society and Irish democracy would benefit from a new generation of lay persons prepared and capable of informing public opinion on the contribution that can be derived from the message of Jesus to establishing values which would inspire different sectors of a pluralistic Irish political and social life.[10]

**PAUSE FOR THOUGHT:
I WAS HUNGRY, I WAS THIRSTY**

I was hungry and you gave me food, I was thirsty and you gave me drink, I was a stranger and you welcomed me, I was naked and you clothed me, I was sick and you visited me, I was in prison and you came to me.

(Matthew 25:35-36)

---

[8] See Irish Catholic Bishops' Conference, *Prosperity with a Purpose: Christian Faith and Values in a Time of Rapid Economic Growth* (Dublin: Veritas, 1999), 87-9.
[9] For a full list of Catholic organisations, societies and charities, see *Irish Catholic Directory* (Dublin: Veritas, annually).
[10] D. Martin, *Presentation of the Irish Edition of the 'Compendium of the Social Doctrine of the Church'*, St Patrick's College, Maynooth, 13 June 2005.

The Catholic Church in Ireland holds that there is a spiritual and moral aspect to overcoming poverty, disadvantage, breakdown and isolation in our community as in any community. There is a responsibility among the followers of Christ to do everything possible to overturn discriminatory practices in our community and in society. There is a duty to witness to the challenge put before us in the life of Christ. The Christian faith, based on a loving relationship with God and neighbour, has the power to transform lives and, when truly lived, to rejuvenate society:

> The Christian programme – the programme of the Good Samaritan, the programme of Jesus – is a 'heart which sees'. This heart sees where love is needed and acts accordingly.[11]

116. The invitation, therefore, should be made continuously, encouraging people, both adults and young people, to participate

in their local parish community and its faith development processes. If people have not heard the message of Jesus Christ, 'the Redeemer, the Reconciler and the Liberator',[12] or have not had sufficient religious education and catechesis to understand his significance for their lives, they will not have been given the opportunity to be transformed by Christ. An overwhelming inability to feel loved by God can block any possibility of renewal. Equally, preoccupation with material goods can stop some people from seeing their own real needs and the needs and concerns of others. Catechetical initiatives must always keep justice and generosity to the fore, seeking to overcome any sense of discrimination, prejudice or inequality. A genuine welcome that transcends any feeling of awkwardness or alienation is essential. Everyone has something to offer. Often, those who think they have least to give are, in fact, carrying with them instincts and insights that can open wide new ways of understanding and living for others. Faith should not be another of the areas in which we allow people to find themselves impoverished. Who knows when the Holy Spirit will call on any one of us to be generous to others with gifts we hardly knew were ours?

[11] DCE 31b.
[12] RP 7.

Love for others, and in the first place love for the poor, in whom the Church sees Christ himself, is made concrete in the promotion of justice. Justice will never be fully attained unless people see in the poor person, who is asking for help in order to survive, not an annoyance or a burden, but an opportunity for showing kindness and a chance for greater enrichment. Only such an awareness can give the courage needed to face the risk and the change involved in every authentic attempt to come to the aid of another...

The newness which is experienced in following Christ demands to be communicated to other people in their concrete difficulties, struggles, problems and challenges, so that these can then be illuminated and made more human in the light of faith. Faith not only helps people find solutions; it makes even situations of suffering humanly bearable, so that in these situations people will not become lost or forget their dignity and vocation.

CA 58-59.

Where people are struggling day by day to make ends meet, catechesis has sometimes been dismissed as an optional extra. This is a mistake. Faith formation can give people a sense of dignity and hope beyond their present difficulties, and present them with a whole new understanding of themselves and of life. If there is genuine conviction and outreach on the part of the local Christian community, there is every possibility that renewal within that faith community can lead to a religious awakening and a whole new way of life for those in need. The cross and resurrection of Jesus Christ gives us a new insight based on the love with which Jesus has loved us:

Social life becomes more human the more it is characterised by efforts to bring about a more mature awareness of the ideal towards which it should be oriented, which is the 'civilisation of love'.[13]

[13] *CSDC 391.*

REACHING OUT IN CHRIST'S LOVE TO ALL

People with Special Needs

117. In recent years, a great deal of reflection has led to renewed support in Irish society for those for whom special needs, physical and/or learning, are part of their personal reality. The Church, 'the place of communion and image of Trinitarian love',[14] has always endeavoured to provide for those who live with disability in one way or another. Today, we need to ask ourselves, too, what is it that these people offer the Church and society that is not only unique but also revealing of whom we all can be. Although we have become more aware of the rights of people with special needs, we have still a long way to go toward true integration.

The Church, stirred by the Spirit of Love, has much to achieve within its own local communities in this regard, as well as being an advocate in society generally. Awareness within the parish community that those living with physical and/or special learning needs often experience a sense of being excluded, and that their families and carers feel isolated and even rejected, will cause us all to plan our catechetical and other faith development initiatives, as well as our rituals and celebrations, in new ways.

Particular support needs to be provided to families of people with disability if they are to become involved in the ongoing catechesis of their children and young adults. Communication between people with particular special needs and others in the community will clarify requirements and allow appropriate adjustments to be made to the catechetical methodology being adopted. Supportive networks, and strategies such as The CEDAR Programme, developed at diocesan level, can help local parishes to be more inclusive of all.

People with special needs who live in residential settings are entitled to the best of spiritual as well as physical and emotional care and access to catechetical processes if they so wish. Diocesan faith development service-providers should give support in these areas and offer training to staff, so that they can be alert to the spiritual needs of those with whom they live and work.

People who have Physical Disabilities
118. People with special physical needs are able to participate fully with others in reflecting on their faith and its importance in their lives. They are living with the same cultural issues as their contemporaries, and require as much input as anyone else in order to be evangelised and come to know the Good News of the love of God, made available to all in Jesus Christ.

[14] *ETCS* 45.

> ### REFLECTION
>
> The beauty and wonder of God is revealed in every human person. Each person is created by God to fulfil a unique mission. His/her own special gifts are an irreplaceable part of the richness of God's image reflected in the human race… It is important that we, as a Church community, acknowledge the innate value and unique mission of all our members. The Church community is not complete without those with disabilities. We must acknowledge their vocation and the invaluable role of parents, carers and all who advocate on their behalf to live full and fulfilled lives.
>
> Irish Catholic Bishops' Conference, *Life in All Its Fullness:*
> *A Letter to Mark the European Year of People with Disabilities*
> *and the Special Olympic World Summer Games*, June 2003.

With regard to faith development strategies, then, people with physical disabilities have the same general needs as the local population. Particular attention should, however, be paid to equality of provision and to accessibility. Often, in fact, access to transport, to buildings and to an ordinary social life is still restricted for them.[15] Easy admission to religious services, to the sacraments and to faith formation programmes should be ensured. Carefully designed ramps and access to the sanctuary and to meeting rooms and toilets are essential. A convenient place to leave wheelchairs and walking aids is important for those who use such devices. For those who are visually impaired, there are now tremendous resources available through audio-technologies and computers. Larger parishes, groups of parishes, or dioceses, may be able to make appropriate services available, such as audio books, CDs, large-screen computers, scanners and equipment for reading the scanned text back to the user. Processes that seek to build up the community and invitations to serve others should all be open to those among us who are physically disabled. They, too, seek to contribute to a world where difference is accepted and valued. They have something special to offer all who are interested in developing their own personal, spiritual and moral lives. They, too, can make Christ present and available by reaching out to others.

It is important to remember that sometimes in adult life people incur physical disabilities that they have not had in their earlier years. Special care should be taken to ensure that we do not allow them, at a certain stage in life, to become isolated from their parish community. After a lifetime of participation, they should not miss out on the opportunities for growth available to others, including ongoing faith development possibilities. They have much to offer to the faith community from their life experience.

[15] See Republic of Ireland, National Disability Authority website, at *www.nda.ie*

REFLECTION: THOSE FINAL YEARS

In his final years Pope John Paul did not allow his frail physical condition to impact negatively on his public ministry... In this way his illness was a forceful and public reminder that God is appreciative of and protective of every single human life... In the final months of his life John Paul II bore eloquent witness to the central Christian truth that old life, injured life, disabled life – every life – is God's own life, God's own special gift and task.

J. Scally, 'John Paul II: A Champion of the Disabled', *Doctrine and Life* 55(2005)5, p. 20.

PARISH PASTORAL COUNCIL: SEEKING INCLUSION

- Is our Parish Pastoral Council representative of all?
- Is the access and welcome to our church and parish centre inclusive of all?
- Are children and young people with disabilities welcomed and encouraged to participate in parish groups and events?
- Is it possible for us to broadcast our parish celebrations on Parish Radio?
- Could we make our parish information available in a variety of formats (Braille, written formats, audio tapes)?

Adapted from Irish Catholic Bishops' Conference, *Life in All Its Fullness*.

People with Special Learning Needs

119. The term 'intellectual disability' encompasses a great variety of personal realities. These include experiences from academic learning disabilities (such as reading, maths, writing and spelling) through developmental learning difficulties (attention, memory, perception, thinking and oral language skills) to profound and multiple learning difficulties, as well as those on the autistic spectrum and also the emotionally disturbed.

For the Christian, everyone is a gift and everyone has gifts to share. Through the Incarnation, Jesus, the Son of God, has united himself with every individual in the human family. Christians are consciously aware of the need to reach out and embrace all members of our communities. At the time of the Special Olympics World Summer Games in Ireland in 2003, the Irish Catholic Bishops' Conference observed: 'The games are a magnificent symbol of what may be achieved when we focus on the abilities and skills of people rather than on their disabilities.'[16] Indeed, those days had a profound effect on the hearts and on the thinking of the

[16] Irish Catholic Bishops' Conference, *Life in All Its Fullness*.

whole nation. They are days we should never forget. The Christian community is faithful to the love of God when it comes to understand that everyone is indispensable to God, and thus should be indispensable to us. We must be present to each other just as God is present to all.[17]

Intellectual disabilities manifest themselves in a variety of ways: disorders of attention; poor motor abilities; perceptual and information-processing difficulties; language difficulties; and difficult social behaviour. They require different responses and a differentiated approach to learning which treats pupils as individuals. This applies as much in catechesis and religious education as in other forms of education. The lack of adequate resources in this area, as well as the need to suggest ways of adapting material that is available, is a significant problem that requires immediate attention.[18] The presence of people with special learning needs brings the requirement for individual attention to the fore. Their teachers need to be supported and trained in the development and provision of personalised programmes of catechesis where necessary, and helped to explore a variety of approaches to faith development. Even people with profound and multiple learning difficulties can be encouraged to recognise emotional and spiritual needs within their social circumstances. Their own life experiences, as with all people, provide an essential framework for participating in religious ritual, prayer and worship, and for understanding religion.[19]

Growth in our understanding of special learning needs, and progress in specialised teaching and learning methodologies, as well as the advent of the Special Needs Assistant in schools, makes it desirable and possible for all to have religious education and catechesis adequate to their requirements.

[17] See P. J. Wadell, 'Pondering the Anomaly of God's Love: Ethical Reflections on Access to the Sacraments', E. Foley (ed.), *Developmental Disabilities and Sacramental Access: New Paradigms for Sacramental Encounters* (Collegeville, MN: The Liturgical Press, 1994), p. 70.

[18] See M. Ní Ceallaigh, 'Towards Inclusivity in Religious Education', R. Topley and G. Byrne (eds), *Nurturing Children's Religious Imagination: The Challenge of Primary Religious Education Today* (Dublin: Veritas, 2004), pp. 66-76.

[19] See B. Carpenter, R. Ashdown and K. Bovair, *Enabling Access: Effective Teaching and Learning for People with Learning Difficulties* (London: David Fulton, 1997), p. 149.

SPECIALISED PEDAGOGY

A growth in social and ecclesial consciousness, together with undeniable progress in specialised pedagogy, makes it possible for the family and other formative centres to provide adequate catechesis for these people, who, as baptised, have this right and, if non-baptised, because they are called to salvation.

GDC 189.

Catechetical and religious education programmes for those with special learning needs should use every available form of modern pedagogical methodology, and should, as far as possible, be in the mainstream of parish and school life. Teachers fulfilling the role of catechist in special education settings should be recognised by the Church and receive ongoing training and pastoral support. Equally, clergy and other parish personnel who support catechetical endeavours for people with special learning needs, whether their involvement is in special or mainstream schooling, should receive appropriate training. They should seek to encourage people with special learning needs to learn through their senses[20] and share experiences of becoming aware that people, objects, symbols, places, food and occasions have special importance. People with special learning needs should be facilitated in celebrating their achievements and joining enthusiastically in a variety of occasions when people meet for worship and celebration. It is significant for people with learning difficulties to realise that they belong to a community.[21] It is important, too, for the community to realise that those with intellectual disabilities are equal members of the community and have much to offer.

[20] See F. Longhorn, *Religious Education for Special Children* (Wooton Catalyst Education Resources, 1993).

[21] See S. Treanor, 'Special Needs and the Faith Community', T. Hanna (ed.), *Strategies for Building Faith Communities in Schools* (Dublin: Marino Institute of Education, 2005), p. 164. See also *Special Religious Education* (SPRED) programme operating in parishes throughout Ireland.

The Deaf Community

120. People who are deaf form a particular cultural, linguistic minority within society and within the Christian community. As such, they deserve to have their language and culture respected and valued in all aspects of life, including their faith life. They often experience the environment in which they live and work and worship as disabling. In their interaction with hearing people, deaf people have much to give as well as much to receive. All of us are invited to accept and recognise God alive within the other. God is available to us through that person as they are. There is a world of spiritual life, reflection, celebration and challenge that is available to each of us, by the grace of the Holy Spirit, in and through every member of the Christian family, including deaf people in our community.

Generally, any form of catechesis, or more broadly of faith development, involving deaf people, must be visual. Art, mime, dance and banners, for instance, should be used whenever possible. Written presentations can also be very useful, but it should be remembered that sign language is the primary language of the Deaf Community. English is a secondary language not easily understood by all deaf people. Deaf people, and their knowledge of a variety of ways of communicating, can help enhance and enrich how the liturgy is celebrated, how teaching and learning takes place, and how meetings and events are organised in the Church.

The Deaf Community continuously provides opportunities for others to communicate and build up relationships with its members:

● Deaf adults within a parish community should be consulted and asked to articulate their needs in relation to faith development and participation in parish life.

● Parish Pastoral Councils can contact the National Chaplaincy for Deaf People, who can put them in touch with deaf adults who have studied and trained and have the experience to advise parishes. They may also be able to provide people who can interpret, in a volunteer capacity, for parish meetings, liturgy, events and courses.[22]

● Catholic schools for deaf children have enormous experience and expertise, which could be used to inform parish communities about the catechesis of deaf children and youth.

[22] See *www.ncdp.ie*

- Each diocese should have someone experienced (preferably with sign language) to act as adviser to parishes, and to act as a contact with the National Chaplaincy for Deaf People.

If language questions are not addressed, deaf people have no access. Their experience is that they have often been excluded from their local worshipping communities, neglected in their faith development and, some would say, starved of spiritual nourishment. The Church at diocesan and parish level must deal with these needs, if it is to live up to its duty and responsibility of bringing all people to God in Jesus Christ. It must seek to create open interaction between deaf and hearing people. This is a good time for all members of the Church, encouraged by the Spirit, to become involved in the real and sometimes challenging story of human living, in all its richness and diversity. Deaf people are a vital part of Church. The whole Christian community should be stirred to consider their practical needs and to respond to them appropriately and actively in love.

The Travelling Community

121. When members of the Travelling Community engage in catechetical and ongoing faith development activities, their cultural heritage, their values, language, customs, family life, shared history and traditions should be acknowledged and valued. Family, both immediate and extended, is at the heart of the Travelling Community.[23] Nomadism, that is, being able to pick up and move whenever it is necessary, useful or desirable, is a defining characteristic of Traveller life, even when living in houses. Greater awareness among the settled community of what is important within the Traveller way of life is essential. Traveller craft and work patterns, Traveller language and culture, ought to be recognised and encouraged. They are an ethnic minority that has been part of Irish society for centuries. Their experience, however, is often one of rejection, discrimination and exclusion.[24] Certainly, the Travelling People, whether wealthy or poor, have continued to find themselves marginalised in Irish society in relation to education, accommodation and health.

Travellers should have access to all forms of education and to education in faith. There is a new appreciation for education, generally, within Traveller families, with 90 per cent of Traveller parents aspiring to greater participation by their children in second-level schooling.[25] This can be difficult when their lifestyle and values are not celebrated in the Curriculum. Many schools, have, however, with Government funding, worked hard at finding an approach that allows Traveller children to feel at ease in school and be supported as necessary. In general, the richness of

[23] See E. Gormally, *Whiddin to the Guaras, Talking to Our Own: Traveller Researchers Talk to Limerick Traveller Children* (Dublin: Veritas, 2005).
[24] See 'Pavee Point Factsheets – Culture and Heritage'. Available at *www.paveepoint.ie*
[25] See Citizen Traveller Campaign 2000.

cultural diversity should be made known in the visuals, examples and information offered to all pupils. An intercultural curriculum, focusing not just on 'exotic' customs of Travellers and other minority groups, but also examining majority ethnic and cultural understandings and traditions, should be the norm.[26]

Resources and materials with an intercultural basis need to be developed and made available for all age-groups. When it comes to religious education, Traveller children may well have a stronger basic religious belief than some of the other children in their class, and provide a positive counter-cultural witness for their peers.

WORKING WITH THE TRAVELLING COMMUNITY

- Be sensitive to Traveller culture, customs and values.
- Be aware that family is at the heart of Traveller life.
- Be open to learn from the Travelling person.
- Be prepared to challenge your own prejudices.
- Be willing to help Travellers challenge their prejudices.

---

122. For most Travelling People, the Catholic faith is part of their way of life. God is experienced as close by, within everyday things and events. Travellers call on God, believing He hears their prayers and will respond. God is to be found in blessings, which are understood as the hand of God at work in a Traveller's life.[27] They have a particular respect for 'holy people', pilgrimages and pledges. Catechetical moments focused on significant times of the year, such as Lenten programmes and remembering the dead in November, often create a positive response. The sacraments, Baptism, Confirmation, First Communion and Matrimony, are celebrated enthusiastically. In Dublin, the Parish of the Travelling People provides catechists to support sacramental preparation. These catechists offer very important out-of-school preparation for Holy Communion, Reconciliation and Confirmation. For the more nomadic families who may have missed out on sacramental

[26] See *Report of the Task Force on the Travelling Community* (Dublin: The Stationery Office, 1995), pp. 154-63.
[27] See F. Murphy, C. McDonagh and E. Sheehan, *Travellers: Citizens of Ireland* (The Parish of the Travelling People, Dublin, 2000), p. 198; see also The Parish of the Travelling People, *The Light Within: The Faith of the Traveller Community* (Dublin, 2000), brochure and video.

preparation, this is essential.[28] When the time comes, being married 'in the eyes of God', that is, in Church, is the only form of marriage accepted generally in the Travelling community.[29]

Travellers often find that they do not have easy access to local parishes, experiencing instead a sense of isolation or rejection. The Faith Development Services of a diocese need to work out an approach that is supportive and helpful in bringing Travellers and the settled community into closer co-operation. Often, it has been a parish Sister who helped create the necessary openness and accessibility. The Parish of the Travelling People highlights the need for ongoing work in this regard, seeking to encourage and resource Church leaders and local parish teams to actively include Travellers in the lives of their local parishes as equal and full members of their local church.[30]

31

Faith Development Coordinators should, in the future, pay particular attention to the catechetical needs of Travellers living or passing through their parish or parishes, building bridges between them and the local community. All those who seek to work with Travellers must become immersed themselves in the reality of Traveller understandings, needs and hopes. They will require cultural awareness training, to challenge their own prejudices and open them to the richness of Traveller life. They may also be able to learn appropriate ways of helping Travelling People consider their prejudices and together move forward to a new vision of the life to which Jesus is calling us all. They will need to work closely with those providing leadership within the Travelling Community, and enable Travellers who are interested to be educated and trained as catechetical leaders within their own communities. The ongoing education in faith of Travellers needs not only to be accessible but also to be informed and led by trained Travellers. Where and how to instigate adult catechesis requires thought, prayer and consultation. Particular attention should be paid to those families who find themselves on the edge of their own community and outside any formal inter-family

[28] See *The Parish of the Travelling People* (Dublin), p. 2.
[29] See T. Barry, Masters Thesis in Pastoral Care and School Chaplaincy, Mater Dei Institute of Education, 2004, pp. 29-35.
[30] See Parish of the Travelling People, *Mission Statement*.
[31] Details of mural created for St Joseph's Training Centre, Ennis, County Clare.

structures. Adult faith development is as much an issue for Travellers as it is for the population, generally, within the Catholic Church in Ireland.

Migrant Workers and Other Newcomers

123. Our world, as observed in Chapter 1, has become an increasingly interdependent and globalised one. Migration from one country to another in search of an improved way of life, has always been an issue, as we in Ireland know from experience. Indeed, we should never lose sight of those who have left Ireland in search of better times. Among the Irish Diaspora, there remain some who are down and out and have never been able to live up to the dreams they had for themselves. Their pastoral care is still as much a concern to the Irish Church as it was in the past. Today, international migration on unprecedented scales, the greatest movement of persons, if not of peoples, of all time, contributes to a new diversity among the populations of more and more countries. 'International migration must therefore be considered an important structural component of the social, economic and political reality of the world today'.[32] In 1996, the Republic of Ireland became one of the last of the then EU countries to reach its migration turning point, moving from being a country of emigration to becoming a country of immigration. Over the past decade, as one of the dividends of the Peace Process, large numbers of migrant workers have also begun to arrive in Northern Ireland.

Migrant workers have come to Ireland for economic reasons, often to break out of extreme poverty and improve their chances in life. Some newcomers have also left their countries for political reasons, escaping persecution and oppression. Economic, political and personal motivation, in fact, frequently overlap. Because immigration has been largely market-driven, we in Ireland have placed little emphasis on long-term integration. It is becoming clear, however, that this is not a small-scale or short-term situation. While some of those who came to Ireland have returned home after a period, many are here to stay, and they will, indeed, contribute to the building up of local communities and of society generally. We have rapidly become and will continue to develop as an inter-cultural society. A new situation is

[32] EMCC 8.

at hand, 'creating fresh opportunities for contacts and cultural exchanges, and calling the Church to hospitality, dialogue, assistance and, in a word, fraternity'.[33] In fact, it is useful to distinguish, here, between *assistance*, a concerned first short-term welcome, and *integration*, a welcome pursued constantly over a long period and in the true sense of the word.[34] The Church, 'the community of those who have been brought together by the Risen Christ',[35] with all its experience of the richness of society and culture around the world, is well placed to make a positive contribution to integration and to the public debate on the changing nature of Irish society. 'Welcoming the stranger, a characteristic of the early Church, thus remains a permanent feature of the Church of God.'[36] Migrants continually thirst for some gesture that will make them feel at ease, recognised and

acknowledged in their new home. We should all encourage our local faith communities to open their doors to these newcomers, to grow in knowledge and experience, to overcome any inclination toward racism, and to educate themselves to embrace, wholeheartedly, true hospitality. Together, in response to Christ's call to sow the seeds of faith and love among all the nations of the earth, we can build a renewed vision of what it means for the Church to be missionary: 'Being *missionary*, the Church's ministry is *outward* looking, passing on its own treasures to others and being enriched with new gifts and talents.'[37] This interaction is no longer determined by geographic distance. Differences of culture and religion are experienced in our home towns and villages. Together we can grow in holiness as well as in wholeness, discovering new riches, new ways of worshipping God, new ways of understanding the Gospel message for our time.

124. The Catholic Church seeks to contribute to a strategic, long-term approach to inclusion and integration. We seek to celebrate the richness and variety of the religious and ethnic customs that we are becoming more aware of in our newly revitalised society. We hope to become alert to important and fascinating new issues in faith formation, arising from the diversity of people who live in our society. God has created us in all our variation, and gifted us

[33] *RM* 37.
[34] See *EMCC* 42.
[35] *CSDC* 49.
[36] *EMCC* 22.
[37] *EMCC* 37b.

with the possibility of creating new forms of dialogue. The pedagogy of God is ever new, helping each generation to learn in new ways to know God better and understand more clearly what it really means to love one another:

> The passage from monocultural to multicultural societies can be a sign of the living presence of God in history and in the community of mankind, for it offers a providential opportunity for the fulfilment of God's plan for a universal communion.[38]

Some newcomers have come to Ireland as practising Catholics or members of other Christian traditions, including the Orthodox Church. They carry with them much that can be inspirational for Irish Catholics. New forms of inter-Christian dialogue are welcome. Such dialogue has the potential to help us to grow in our understanding of Christ's message. It is essential that churches of departure and arrival establish an intense collaboration with one another.[39] In particular, good relations should be built up with those Catholic dioceses from which many people have come to live and work with us. Chaplains from their home country can make a significant contribution to the pastoral care of such migrants, seeking always to encourage them to participate fully in the life of the diocese to which they now belong. The Church in Ireland, listening to the Spirit, must become a sign of a new kind of unity, embracing the prospect of a renewed humanity.

Among those who have come to live in Ireland, there are also many who belong to religious traditions other than Christianity. In our society today, as well as our brothers and sisters in the Jewish community, who have long been a blessing to us all, we now have many Muslims, Hindus, Buddhists and members of other religions. There are also, among our newcomers, some who have been brought up without any religious tradition. The Catholic Church reaches out to welcome them all, seeking to offer them an experience of the love of Christ, who spent his public life on the move, going through towns and villages (Luke 13:22; Matthew 9:35), with nowhere to lay his head (Matthew 8:20; Luke 9:58). Local parish communities should make it their business to be gracious and generous to newcomers, and, at an appropriate moment, invite them to become aware of the spiritual traditions of the parish community and of the Church.

125. Some of those who have come to Ireland may wish, in the future, as is already happening, to take instruction in the Catholic

[38] *EMCC* 9.
[39] See *EMCC* 70.

faith and come to belong to their local worshipping community. Parishes, indeed, or groups of parishes, should be fully prepared to introduce the RCIA whenever required, and be ready to initiate adults and children of catechetical age into the Christian faith. Priests, Faith Development Coordinators, volunteer catechists and others who make themselves available for this work, will themselves benefit greatly from the cultural diversity and rich traditions with which they will, as a result, become familiar. In such a way, the gifts brought to us by newcomers can be absorbed and become a source of renewed faith within the Christian community.

The Catholic Church offers newcomers open access to its education endeavours. All are welcome to partake as appropriate in the education in faith programmes offered locally by the Church in parishes, schools and education centres. Faith development processes of one kind or another will seek to inform and support individuals and the community in reaching out to newcomers in their needs. They will also invite those who are new to participate and belong, coming to experience Christ in their Christian neighbour:

> In migration faith discovers once more the universal message of the prophets, who denounce discrimination, oppression, deportation, dispersion, and persecution as contrary to God's plan. At the same time they proclaim salvation for all, witnessing even in the chaotic events and contradictions of human history, that God continues to work out his plan of salvation until all things are brought together in Christ (see Eph 1:10).[40]

It is very important that all those who offer faith development initiatives at whatever level in the Church, use material reflecting the lifestyles and cultural background of a wide variety of people, and are aware of the rich cultural heritage, histories and civilisations of the people with whom they are engaging. It will always be important for teachers and catechists to be aware of their responsibility to adapt textbooks and resources to the particular needs and various cultural backgrounds of the students in their care. When we educate ourselves to welcome, to solidarity and openness toward foreigners, we may discover the seeds of the Word of God in different cultures. At the same time, we will always be proud to show others an insight into the great Irish Christian tradition and the gift it has continually made available around the world. In the context of growing religious pluralism, we must be able to give reasons for our faith and the hope that is within us.[41] In this way, we may expect to strengthen our own faith by involving ourselves in educated dialogue with others.

[40] EMCC 13.
[41] See 1 Pet 3:15.

People Living with Illness

126. Illness changes a person's life. In sickness, we experience powerlessness and limitation. Apart from the debilitating nature of illness, people also often find changes in their lifestyle difficult. Sickness sometimes leads to anxiety and despair. It can also affect us, at the same time, in more positive ways, bringing us to new maturity, helping us to discern what is not essential, and encouraging us to turn toward that which is. Very often, illness provokes a search for God and a return to God's embrace.[42] The celebration in February each year of World Day of the Sick, close to the feast of Our Lady of Lourdes, is a moment for timely catechesis on illness and suffering. It has drawn particular attention to the needs of those who are ill, and to the gifts they present to the Church and to the world. A variety of creative initiatives, such as gatherings organised by hospital chaplains at this time and celebrations of the Sacrament of the Sick at parish liturgies, have strengthened awareness of mutual support and concern. The mystery of Jesus Christ, crucified and risen, in the life of the Christian, is heightened when one is confronted with illness or finds oneself close to death. Suffering linked with the suffering of Jesus Christ, the Son of God and Son of Mary, becomes something

new. His self-sacrifice is an invitation to make of our suffering and of our whole lives a sacrifice with him for the salvation of the world: 'The lives of the faithful, their praise, sufferings, prayer and work, are united with Christ and with his total offering, and so acquire a new value.'[43]

Those who have become ill will vary greatly in their understanding and experience of lived Christian faith. For some, because of their closeness to the sacraments, there will be little need for explanation of the healing ministry offered by Christ in his Church through the sacrament of Anointing of the Sick, the sacrament of Penance and Reconciliation, and in the Eucharist. Some, although connected with parish, will have little knowledge of the ministry that can be given them. Others who may be unfamiliar with the faith can, in this moment, find themselves enquiring about Christian belief. In different ways, illness can be a moment when a special kind of

[42] See CCC 1500-1501.
[43] CCC 1386.

catechesis, based as always on a tender compassion for the other, is appropriate. Such support seeks to be wise, discreet and patient. Speaking of Jesus' healing ministry as a sign that 'God has visited his people' (Luke 7:16), and that the Kingdom of God is close at hand, the *Catechism of the Catholic Church* observes:

> His compassion toward all who suffer goes so far that he identifies himself with them: 'I was sick and you visited me' (Matthew 25:36). His preferential love for the sick has not ceased through the centuries to draw the very special attention of Christians toward all those who suffer in body and soul. It is the source of tireless efforts to comfort them.[44]

127. While physical illness is generally acknowledged for what it is, many people find mental health issues difficult to accept and come to terms with. Priests, religious, pastoral workers and parish leaders have a supportive role to play in promoting good mental health in the community, and in assisting those who have difficulties of this kind. They can also help to promote acceptance of people who experience mental anguish and require care and assistance, encouraging family and others in the faith community to continue caring for them in an appropriate way. Loving pastoral care is significant in itself, but counselling skills and an understanding of emotional interaction are at times very important. Education in understanding how groups work and how individuals seek to satisfy their own needs within groups, can also be particularly useful to those working in ministry. In order to facilitate good relations in any setting and, in particular, to be able to offer sound pastoral support to those suffering mental distress, education in human relations, family dynamics and community development can be of great benefit. Catechetical input can lift the discussion further by offering an experience of love and hope in Jesus Christ. Those involved in pastoral outreach to others need always to be alert that they, too, are taking good care of their own mental health and have not become isolated. The care we are willing to pay to our own faith development is a significant indicator of how we are in our own lives.

[44] CCC 1503.

128. Education in providing a good listening ear is essential when working with people who are ill. Those providing hospital chaplaincy services and others who work pastorally with people who have serious illness should be professionally trained. Prayer, reflection and ongoing conversation with the sick have no preconceived pattern. Spiritual direction, that is, intimate spiritual conversation, can come about in response to any of a number of starting points. Everything will depend on the needs of individual patients. While praying for the sick is of itself a very practical and significant support, praying with the sick is more personal and penetrating. It should be positive and persistent, but will also include periods of quiet and stillness. The purpose is to instil faith and expectancy without raising false hopes. Education in how to pray is something we are always in need of. It is something we learn from one another, under the careful direction of the Holy Spirit, our ultimate spiritual director. Illness, then, can provide extraordinary opportunities for learning about life and growing in love, not only for the person visited by sickness but also for their family, friends and others with whom they come in contact.

There will come a time, too, to help the person prepare for a dignified and Christian death. The person who is dying is supported by the prayers and faith of others in their family, in the hospital and in parish. They are helped to know that they are being embraced within the wider healing ministry of the whole Church. 'People who are dying want to know that, even though there is no prospect of recovery, they will not be abandoned. It is important that the kind of care a sick person receives is not dictated by the fears and conveniences of others.'[45] All of us have to recognise our own need for education in faith around death, so that we can offer our very best to those who will appreciate our presence in their last days and moments.

[45] Irish Catholic Bishops' Conference, *Cherishing the Evening of Life*, Day for Life, 2 October 2005.

REFLECTION

A person who is dying is more than a sick body. Every person is created for relationship with God. The last days and weeks of life are the closing stages in a lifelong journey. We Christians, in common with many others, believe that this journey finds its fulfilment in eternal happiness with God. Once the initial shock of life-threatening illness has been dealt with, people who are sick can often be drawn to reflect on the meaning of their lives and on their relationship with God. This is often a time for giving thanks, and for reconciliation. Good palliative care, because it frees the sick person from excessive anxiety and pain, facilitates good pastoral and sacramental care.

Irish Catholic Bishops' Conference, *Living with Dying: A Letter from the Irish Bishops to Mark the Day for Life* (Dublin: Veritas, October 2002).

Funeral time, too, offers a moment of significant catechetical possibility, formally and informally, as family, friends and parish gather to honour the dead and reflect on life, death and life everlasting in the loving embrace of Jesus Christ.

May he support us all the day long,
till the shades lengthen and the evening comes,
and the busy world is hushed,
and the fever of life is over and our work is done!
Then in His Mercy may He give us a safe lodging
and a holy rest
and peace at the last.
Blessed John Henry Newman.

SECTION D
SUPPORTING THE GOOD NEWS

CHAPTER 7

Resources and Implementation

129. Looking back on the great Jubilee Year 2000 and all the events that marked its celebration, Pope John Paul II spoke about how 'the experiences we have had should inspire in us new energy, and impel us to invest in concrete initiatives the enthusiasm which we have felt'.[1] At the beginning of the Third Millennium, living a particular moment in the life of the Church in Ireland, shaped by our past and looking forward full of hope, we are reminded that it is Jesus Christ upon whom we depend. It is he 'who is to be known, loved and imitated'.[2] With the love of Christ as our inspiration, new energy and enthusiasm can be found for a catechetical renewal in Ireland, requiring that practical initiatives be taken, adapted to the circumstances of the local Christian community. Dependence on human effort alone is to be avoided, for the Spirit is always capable of new surprises. At the same time, an enthusiastic programme of rejuvenation, supporting in a strategic way that which is already in place, is very much to be welcomed:

> It is in the local churches that the specific features of a detailed pastoral plan can be identified – goals and methods, formation and enrichment of the people involved, the search for the necessary resources – which will enable the proclamation of Christ to reach people, mould communities, and have a deep and incisive influence in bringing Gospel values to bear in society and culture.[3]

In this final chapter, objectives are presented at a variety of levels, suggested by what has gone before. These objectives set out the policy to be pursued within each area of responsibility. Alongside each objective, some indicators of achievement are provided, suggesting steps to be realised along the way in addressing the particular objective. A graduated approach, building practically on what has already been achieved locally, and targeting the particular needs of the faith community, is what is envisaged. Practical measures are helpful in giving people a sense of the parameters within which, inspired by the Spirit of Life, they relate and build

[1] NMI 15.
[2] NMI 29.
[3] NMI 29.

one another up. There can be a sense of ease when responsibility is clearly established and shared. Many of the needs recognised here will be responded to at a volunteer level. With the declining number of priests and religious, however, it is clear that some of the lay faithful will have to be further educated, trained and paid at appropriate levels if we wish to offer coming generations the Good News we have been given. The influence today of other, often conflicting worldviews, makes it imperative that the healing and the challenge presented to us by Jesus Christ are made known in our world by the People of God. We are invited to support, financially as well as in other ways, especially by our prayers, the Spirit's ongoing evangelisation of the Church and of society. Each Catholic community of faith is asked, therefore, to set out short-, medium- and long-term catechetical goals within its own given situation, in order to achieve what is possible in an appropriate timescale. It is envisaged that this *National Directory for Catechesis in Ireland* will have a ten-year life-span. It is recommended that the objectives highlighted here be agreed locally with relevant modifications and put in place within five years of publication. The second five-year period should be used to review structures and strategies that have been established, consolidate what has been positively achieved, and carry out, according to local need, that which has remained incomplete. Individual Catholics are urged to take responsibility for their personal faith education, both for their own good and for that of their community. A fully formed and empowered Church community, guided by the Holy Spirit, will have so much to say, in union with Jesus Christ, for our world today.

The Parish Community as Agent of Faith Development

130. The parish community is the focal point of faith development in all its forms. Initial proclamation, Christian initiation, catechesis, religious education, new evangelisation and theological

reflection all find a home within the parish community. The task of catechesis and faith development generally underpins the other principal tasks of the parish. In parish, the adult members of the local faith community, together with their children and young people, seek to support one another in faith and to grow continually in understanding, sharing and living that faith.

STARTING POINT:
THE PARISH AT THE CENTRE OF EVANGELISATION

The parish is, without doubt, the most important *locus* in which the Christian community is formed. This community is called to be a fraternal and welcoming family, where Christians become aware of being the people of God. In the parish, all human differences melt away and are absorbed into the universality of the Church. The parish is also the usual place in which the faith is born and in which it grows. It constitutes, therefore, a very adequate community space for the realisation of the ministry of the Word at once as teaching, education and life experience.

Today, the parish is undergoing profound transformation in many countries. Social changes are having repercussions on the parish, especially in big cities 'shaken by the phenomenon of urbanisation'. Despite this, 'the parish is still a major point of reference for the Christian people, even for the non-practising'. It must continue 'to be the prime mover and pre-eminent place for catechesis', while recognising that in certain occasions it cannot be the centre of gravity for all of the ecclesial functions of catechesis and must integrate itself into other institutions (cf *CT* 67 b).

GDC 257.

PARISH FAITH DEVELOPMENT OBJECTIVES

131. *Parish Objective 1:* Each parish will place the faith development of all its members at the centre of its stated mission and goals, promoting the parish's Faith Development Plan at every opportunity.

Some Indicators of Achievement

- The parish will have a graduated Faith Development Plan to be realised step by step over a set period of time. The Parish Priest will ensure that personal and community catechesis is kept to the fore in the parish and in the minds of parishioners.

- Prayerful reflection on the Gospel will form the basis upon which the parish engages in catechetical and other forms of faith development planning.
- The Parish Priest will see that a professionally qualified and experienced person is appointed as Faith Development Coordinator for the parish, possibly in conjunction with neighbouring parishes.
- Suitably trained volunteer parishioners, working as part of various parish teams, chosen according to the particular needs of the parish, will fulfil, as catechists, a mentoring role with adults and young parishioners who are growing in their faith.
- The Parish Priest will identify faith development goals specific to the particular requirements and resources of parish members.
- The parish will collaborate with other parishes, the deanery and diocese in initiating and overseeing local catechetical and other faith development projects.
- The parish will strive to meet the faith development needs of everybody within its remit, particularly those who might not have a strong voice.

132. *Parish Objective 2:* **The priest in the parish will demonstrate a clear commitment to the evangelising and catechetical nature of his ministry, and strive, with the support of parishioners, to give the various levels of faith development due priority.**

Some Indicators of Achievement

- The Parish Priest and those who collaborate with him will demonstrate a commitment to support and encourage one another and those volunteers who have been given particular faith development roles in the parish.
- The parish will encourage the priest in the particular role he plays in its evangelisation. It will provide practical support, especially in his celebration of the sacraments, his delivery of homilies and his other catechetical inputs in the parish.
- The priest as presider at the celebration of the liturgy will ensure that catechetical opportunities intrinsic to the liturgy are used appropriately.
- The parish as a community will seek to nourish and support the priest, personally and spiritually, helping him to grow with them in faith.

SMALL GROUP DISCUSSION:
THE PRIEST AS EVANGELISER

As pastors we have been chosen by the mercy of the Supreme Pastor, in spite of our inadequacy, to proclaim with authority the Word of God, to assemble the scattered People of God, to feed this People with the signs and actions of Christ which are the Sacraments, to set this People on the road to salvation, to maintain it in that unity of which we are, at different levels, active and living instruments, and unceasingly to keep this community gathered around Christ faithful to its deepest vocation. And when we do all these things, within our human limits and by the grace of God, it is a work of evangelisation that we are carrying out.

EN 68.

---

133. *Parish Objective 3:* Adult faith development will be at the centre of parish life, helping the community to grow vigorous in its conversion to Jesus Christ.

Some Indicators of Achievement

- The Parish Priest and those who assist him will demonstrate a clear commitment to lifelong education in Christian faith, highlighting continuing adult education in the parish's Faith Development Plan and in their day-to-day work.
- Where there are adults preparing for initiation into the family of the Church, priority will be given in the parish to the RCIA process. All those who minister in the parish will be educated in the principles underlying, and implications of, the RCIA.

- The Faith Development Coordinator, involved personally in ongoing faith education, will assume responsibility for overseeing a ministry of adult faith development in the parish.
- Opportunities for members of the parish to participate in theological reflection will be encouraged. Ongoing conversation will be entered into with local third-level colleges offering theology, philosophy and pastoral ministry modules, with a view to encouraging participation by interested adults from the parish.
- The parish will strive to proclaim the Gospel to adults who are alienated or who have drifted into religious indifference.

- At regular intervals, the parish will initiate adult programmes to accommodate specific groups, such as young adults, parents/guardians, those who are single, the elderly and people on the margins of the community, inviting them to partake in an adult conversation about faith in their lives.
- Marriage education, including preparation for marriage and ongoing marriage enrichment, will be given particular support by the parish community.
- Regular in-service will be provided for priests, deacons, religious and those who collaborate with the Parish Priest, seeking to support them spiritually, affectively and intellectually in their own faith commitment, and encourage them to develop further their pastoral skills.

ADULT FAITH DISCUSSION:
BECOMING THE CHRISTIAN WE SAY WE ARE

All through our lives, we must all be working at becoming the Christian we say we are… In a world which is more and more sophisticated, adults cannot be content with primary school religious knowledge. Doubts and difficulties about faith nearly always come from misunderstanding or lack of adult knowledge about our religion. Adult education in religion is one of the urgent religious needs in Ireland in our time. An educated world needs an educated faith.

HFH, p. 37

134. *Parish Objective 4:* **The catechetical and religious education needs of young people will be given high priority in the life of the parish.**

Some Indicators of Achievement
- The parish will have an established support system for family catechesis, helping parents/guardians, grandparents and young people to speak and pray together in the light of their everyday experience.
- A Family Mass ministry in the parish will encourage families to participate in parish liturgy and community-building, as well as in reaching out to those in need.
- The parish, facilitated by the Faith Development Coordinator, will provide parish preparation for the sacraments of initiation, in conjunction with parents and with the local schools. Parish volunteers will receive training to become members of parish Baptismal, Confirmation and First Communion Teams.

- A designated priest of the parish and the Faith Development Coordinator will visit the parish primary schools, working in co-operation with the school Principal, Religious Education Co-ordinator, and teachers of students preparing for the sacraments.
- The parish will develop a youth initiative to support, in a variety of ways, the faith development needs of adolescents. Priests and Faith Development Coordinators will be in touch with local post-primary schools. The parish will facilitate the commitment to service in Church award scheme for the senior cycle age-group, mentioned in Chapter 5 above.

PARISH PASTORAL COUNCIL: MINISTRY TO YOUNG PEOPLE

An explicit ministry to young people is essential, not an optional extra. That ministry cannot be uniform. People have different needs and we must reach out by providing a full 'cycle of care'. Some hunger for spiritual support. Others have little experience of spiritual nourishment. Others are disinterested or burdened by pain and guilt – for many have grown up with suffering or abuse. The experience of being bullied is widespread. This can happen on the basis of race, disability, gender, sexual orientation or social class.

Any such victimisation of individuals or groups is unacceptable and to be condemned. These all make it difficult for people to believe in a God who believes in them. Everyone has the right to hear the Good News wherever they are on life's journey.

Irish Catholic Bishops' Conference, *Building Faith in Young People* (Dublin: Veritas, 2005), p. 9.

---

135. *Parish Objective 5:* The parish Faith Development Plan will be inclusive, giving significant attention to those who have specific needs in relation to faith development.

Some Indicators of Achievement
- Those who are experiencing family, financial or other difficulties will find support in their faith community.
- There will be easy access to the parish church, parish centre and school buildings, such that those with special physical needs feel welcome.
- Those with special learning needs will be integrated into the parish, including its liturgical rituals and community events.
- The linguistic concerns of the Deaf Community will be attended to in the parish.

- Migrants and other newcomers, as well as Travellers, when present as part of the local worshipping community, will experience the hospitality of the faith community, and contribute to its growth.
- Ecumenical, intercultural and inter-religious outreach will be considered an essential part of parish life.
- Those who are living with illness will receive special attention from the parish. Their contribution to the parish's sense of care, community and prayer life will be cherished.

**PAUSE FOR THOUGHT:
INCLUSION AND ACCOMPANIMENT**

Inclusion begins in our hearts. It begins with a decision to love. We can open our hearts to one another and recognise the strengths of every person. When each person is allowed to share their gifts, our community is strengthened.

We experience accompaniment in all sorts of ways. Accompanying a person to attend an event or function is often a wonderful expression of inclusion.

Dublin Jubilee – AD 2000 Office, *It's My Church Too! The Inclusion of People with a Disability in the Life of the Church* (Dublin: 2000), p. 14.

Diocesan Faith Development Services

136. The Catholic Church in Ireland, as elsewhere throughout the world, is a communion of Particular Churches or Dioceses, each led by a Bishop. Under his care and encouragement, members of the Catholic community, lay people, religious, priests and deacons strive to live a Christian life within the particular socio-cultural context they experience where they live. Parishes, schools, religious communities and ecclesial movements draw sustenance from the diocese and are supported by structures and resources put in place by the diocese. Every diocese is the realisation of the universal Church in a particular place, and every parish is an integral part of the diocese, contributing to the diocese's faith development and missionary outreach. All the constituent parts of a diocese contribute to the development of its particular characteristic spirit, and work to ensure its continued growth and well-being.

DIOCESAN FAITH DEVELOPMENT OBJECTIVES
137. *Diocesan Objective 1:* **The diocese will have a clearly defined vision of evangelisation at the heart of its Diocesan Faith Development Plan.**

Some Indicators of Achievement

- The bishop will have an identifiable central role as the chief catechist of the diocese. He will provide for initial proclamation, ongoing catechesis and lifelong faith enrichment processes in the diocese.
- Significant financial resources will be sought and put in place to facilitate an effective and unified support system for faith development within the diocese.
- The bishop will put in place a coordinated team of faith development personnel, working in co-operation and together designated as the **Diocesan Faith Development Services**. This may be achieved by a number of smaller dioceses establishing such services together.
- This revitalised and flexible manifestation of the diocesan catechetical office[4] will seek to encompass and coordinate the diocese's interest in faith education at all levels, in homes, parishes and schools, for adults, young people and children.
- The team cooperating as Diocesan Faith Development Services will keep an eye to particular areas of concern, such as Catholic schools, special needs, family ministry and youth ministry, justice and social solidarity, liturgical catechesis and, above all, structures to support home, parish and school working in partnership.
- The Faith Development Services team, in collaboration with the bishop and other diocesan officials, will set out and seek to implement a Diocesan Faith Development Plan. Such an initiative will be part of the general Diocesan Plan.
- Support for the ongoing formation and training needs of priests, deacons, Parish Pastoral Councils, Faith Development Coordinators and other pastoral workers, volunteer catechists, members of parish teams and religious educators will be provided.

[4] See *GDC* 126.

INTER-DIOCESAN ACTION:
COMBINING RESOURCES FOR COMMON BENEFIT

It is useful for a number of Dioceses to combine their actions, bringing together for common benefit their experiences and undertakings, their offices and equipment; for the Dioceses that are better provided to give help to the others; and for a common action programme to be prepared for the region as a whole.

GCD, 127.

138. *Diocesan Objective 2:* **The diocese will promote a faith development strategy that embraces faith development as lifelong learning.**

Some Indicators of Achievement

● The Diocesan Faith Development Services team will be led by an appropriately qualified, experienced and skilled **Diocesan Director of Faith Development.**[5] The Director will oversee reflection on present needs and provision, as well as identifying and putting in place strategies to provide for future evangelisation, catechetical and religious education challenges facing the diocese, its people, its parishes and its schools.

● The Diocesan Faith Development Services, under the leadership of the Director of Faith Development, will be composed of a number of **Diocesan Advisers,** depending on the size of the diocese and sometimes in collaboration with other local dioceses, each with their own area of responsibility, such as, for instance: Adult Diocesan Adviser; Primary Diocesan Adviser; Post-Primary Diocesan Adviser.

● This Team will be structured in such a way to provide an Education Office supporting the management of Catholic schools. It will also incorporate Family Ministry, Youth Ministry and Special Needs Faith Support. A unified approach, which prioritises partnership between home, parish and school in the faith development of adults and children, will be sought.

[5] Adapted from the GDC 265-268.

- The Liturgy and Music Office, Pastoral Development Office, Justice and Social Affairs Office and those with responsibility for ecumenical and inter-faith dialogues, will also be significant contributors to the Diocesan Faith Development Services.
- Those appointed to the position of Diocesan Adviser will have previous catechetical and religious education experience in parishes or schools, with adults or with young people, as well as professional qualifications and practical training.

139. *Diocesan Objective 3:* **Adult faith development will be clearly visible as the chief form of faith development in the diocese.**

Some Indicators of Achievement

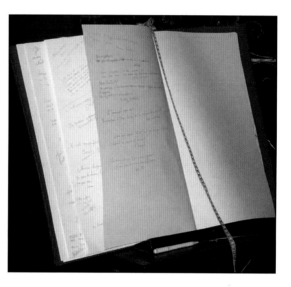

- The diocese will have a clearly stated vision of lifelong learning in parishes and deaneries, which promotes adult faith development as the chief form of faith development.
- The diocese will engage in financial planning to secure sufficient resources to provide for adult faith development in the diocese.
- The diocese will have a clearly defined strategy for developing parish adult faith development leaders and teams, including appropriate education and training.
- There will be a particular policy, at diocesan level, for outreach to young adults, parents/guardians and the elderly, among other groups.
- National programmes focused on adult needs, such as marriage education, will be encouraged at local diocesan level.
- The diocese will ensure that each parish has access to trained Faith Development Coordinators.
- The diocese will support third-level evangelisation and catechetical programmes of various kinds and IT initiatives in the whole area of faith development. A diocesan website will have been developed, with priority given to faith development initiatives.

STARTING POINT: YOUNG ADULTS ARE OUR PEOPLE

Young adults are not an indifferent, consumer-driven, narcissistic group who care little for what the church is or does. They are our people. They keep telling us so. They are God's people. They are not the future of the church. They are the present church waiting to be welcomed. We have much to offer; they have much to learn. They have much to give; we have much to receive.

J. C. Cusick and K. DeVries,
The Basic Guide to Young Adult Ministry
(New York: Orbis, 2001), p. 8.

140. *Diocesan Objective 4:* **The catechesis and religious education of the young will be given priority in the diocese.**

Some Indicators of Achievement
- A strategy for supporting Family Ministry will be in place in the diocese.
- The diocese will have a coordinated approach to Youth Ministry, supporting a variety of faith development initiatives for young people.
- The diocese will support a programme organised at parish level to enable parents/guardians to participate fully in the sacramental initiation of their children. This programme will involve a partnership between home, parish and primary school.
- The diocese will promote opportunities for parents/guardians to support them and help them reflect on the ongoing catechesis and religious education of their children beyond sacramental initiation.
- The diocese will have in place an Award Scheme to encourage young people at senior cycle level to become involved in activities associated with faith development and commitment to service in the Church.

141. *Diocesan Objective 5:* **There will be strong diocesan-wide collaboration with religious congregations in providing for faith development initiatives at a variety of levels.**

Some Indicators of Achievement
- Close attention will be paid at diocesan level to faith development partnerships with local religious congregations.
- The diocese will be in discussion with religious congregations and their Trustee bodies in developing new models of Catholic second-level schooling in the diocese and in establishing appropriate networks and strategies for the up-skilling of school management and staff.

- Religious who have worked in other parts of the world and have come home to live in Ireland will be acknowledged as a particularly rich resource in the diocese.

National Co-operation

142. The Irish Catholic Bishops' Conference gladly supports all faith development initiatives in the Catholic Church in Ireland. It seeks to ensure that professional standards are maintained in all the works of evangelisation, catechesis and religious education undertaken within the community of the Church, whether nationally, at a diocesan level or in parish, school and home. It persists in requiring strong preparation and ongoing in-service of priests and religious in this vital area of their ministry. It encourages new evangelisation projects and theological reflection among adult Christians. It seeks to be certain that the highest standards are upheld in the formation of Faith Development Coordinators and teams of volunteers, to work in parishes and connect with schools. It highlights the significance of respectful ecumenical, inter-cultural and inter-religious dialogues at the heart of the Christian life. It supports a professional approach to the running of Catholic schools and to the training and in-service appropriate for Catholic-school boards of management, principals and teachers. It encourages lay people to deepen their own faith, and supports parents and guardians in taking up their responsibilities and rights in relation to sharing their faith with the young.

NATIONAL FAITH DEVELOPMENT OBJECTIVES
143. *National Objective 1:* **The Irish Catholic Bishops' Conference will give priority to the faith development of both adults and young people.**

Some Indicators of Achievement
- Catechesis and other forms of faith development will, with the publication of this *Directory*, have been defined by the Irish Catholic Bishops' Conference as an area for priority attention over the coming ten years.

- The Bishops' Conference will attach primary importance to developing personnel and financial resources for catechetical and other faith development initiatives at national, diocesan and local levels.
- The position and mission of the Catholic Church in education in Ireland will be confirmed and developed.
- A review will establish the most appropriate way of dividing responsibilities among various Episcopal Commissions/ Councils concerned with faith development, including initiation and catechesis, Catholic education and missionary evangelisation, always acknowledging also those with special needs.
- The Catholic Bishops will have a policy outlining support for ongoing research initiatives to ascertain and review priorities in catechesis and in all the areas of faith development.

144. *National Objective 2:* The Bishops' Conference will have a National Faith Development Team which will have responsibility for supporting national co-operation across the various types of faith development for all ages and needs.

Some Indicators of Achievement
- The executive secretaries to the relevant Episcopal Commissions/Councils together will be established as the **National Faith Development Team.** One of their number will oversee the Team.
- The National Faith Development Team, supporting the National Catechetical Office, will encourage a nationally agreed approach to initial proclamation, Christian initiation, catechesis, religious education, new evangelisation and theological reflection in dioceses throughout Ireland, listening, supporting and encouraging all those who collaborate in these forms of ministry. The focus of the Team will be communication, facilitation and resourcing. This will be achieved under a number of headings:
  - Overseeing evangelisation needs nationally across dioceses.
  - Coordinating a sustained dialogue nationwide between faith and culture, providing for a continuing socio-cultural analysis, and encouraging an ongoing evangelisation of culture.
  - Facilitating familiarity with the needs and requirements set out in this *National Directory for Catechesis in Ireland.*
  - Initiating and supporting a research strategy to identify national and local faith development needs and suggest appropriate interventions.

- ◆ Supporting dioceses in the formulation of faith development elements of their Diocesan Plan.
- ◆ Helping dioceses establish good practice within their Faith Development Services.
- ◆ Supporting dioceses in the management of their schools through the resourcing of their Education Office.
- ◆ Drawing attention to local adult faith development needs and supporting dioceses in providing for those needs nationwide.
- ◆ Briefing the various national associations of Diocesan Advisers for Religious Education.

- ◆ Maintaining a centre for information on all faith development matters.
- ◆ Initiating new projects nationwide and expanding existing ventures in the various areas of faith development.
- ◆ Providing ongoing access to initiatives and resources through its website.
- ◆ Advising writers working on catechetical and religious education syllabuses and programmes.
- ◆ Producing an annual report, detailing national faith development initiatives.
- ◆ Reviewing the national policy for faith development at regular intervals.
- ● The National Faith Development Team will work closely with the Catholic Communications Office and other national offices of the Catholic Church to ensure a common understanding and continuity of approach to faith development throughout the Catholic Church in Ireland.

Faith Development in Catholic Schools

145. An open and respectful approach to religion and its contribution in shaping our daily lives is a necessary component

of every school community. Good religious education, strong pastoral care and effective chaplaincy support are essential for the holistic development of the young. The Board of Management of the Catholic school is responsible for the development of the school on behalf of the Patron/ Trustees, with the support of management bodies such as the Catholic Primary School Managers Association and the Association of Management of Catholic Secondary Schools. It appoints teachers and principals to the school, sets priorities and ensures the resourcing of its approved projects. School mission statements and policies, approved by the Board of Management, should reflect a transparently open approach to the established ethos of the school, to its young people themselves and to their religious tradition, experience and beliefs. The Principal and Deputy Principal, the Head of the Religious Education Department (Post-Primary), the Coordinator of Religious Education (Primary), and where possible the Coordinator of Chaplaincy Services and the Coordinator of Pastoral Care in a school, as well as others in leadership roles, should be carefully considered positions, supported, as a priority, by ongoing education and training.

FAITH DEVELOPMENT OBJECTIVES IN RELATION TO SCHOOLING
146. *Schools Objective 1:* **The members of the Catholic Church in Ireland will contribute energetically to developing a holistic understanding of education in school.**

Some Indicators of Achievement
- Catholic parents/guardians will be encouraged in their role as the first educators of their children in their religious growth and development.
- Parents who choose to send their children to a Catholic primary or post-primary school will be aware of, understand and support the school's Catholic ethos.

- Catholic leadership at all levels, local, diocesan and national, with the support of the faithful, will give high priority to maintaining and developing Catholic schooling, ensuring that the specific responsibilities of the Catholic Church as Patron of schools, in partnership with the State as the main provider of education, are honoured.
- The national Catholic Education Service for the whole of Ireland, instigated by the Irish Catholic Bishops' Conference and the Conference of Religious in Ireland in 2008, will oversee partnership within the Catholic schools sector.

147. *Schools Objective 2:* The Catholic school will operate according to a Mission Statement and Ethos Policy that openly reflects its Catholic spirit.

Some Indicators of Achievement
- The mission and objectives of each Catholic school will be developed, in conformity with its traditions, through partnership between the Patrons/Trustee bodies, Board of Management, principal, teachers and parents/guardians.
- The mission and objectives of the Catholic school will be based on Gospel values, respect for each individual and for the common good, and a commitment to the search for truth and the development of the whole person.
- There will be an awareness on the part of all involved in a Catholic school that they are contributing to the promotion of a particular educational experience, founded upon a Catholic anthropology of the person, vision of society, understanding of teaching and learning and of knowledge itself.
- The Catholic primary school, as an outreach of the local parish, will seek to nourish the faith of its Catholic students and assist in their Christian initiation. It will respect the religious tradition of other students and facilitate them in every way.
- In a Catholic post-primary school, the educational needs, including religious education needs, of all will be given priority. The faith of Catholic students will be informed and supported.
- School policies will reflect the openly Catholic atmosphere of the school.
- Alternative models for Catholic schools, which seek to meet the needs of a wide diversity of pupils, will be encouraged. Where there are special benefits to a local community, an interdenominational school may be sponsored in conjunction with other Christian denominations.

RENEWED VISION:
RE-EXAMINING THE CATHOLIC SCHOOL

Our Catholic schools have been the result of huge generosity and commitment on the part of thousands of people over generations. Education was provided for millions when the State could not or would not provide it. We owe a huge dept of gratitude to these people – lay, religious and clergy. But we have to re-examine what role our schools can play in an increasingly pluralist society. When we see how much faith-based schools are in demand in most other countries, we must ensure that we are offering a Catholic education to all and not just a good secular education for ethnic Catholics. And we are committed to resisting the pressures that would seek to replace education of the whole person with little more than job training.

Irish Catholic Bishops' Conference, *Building Faith in Young People*, p. 10.

148. *Schools Objective 3:* The Catholic school, primary or post-primary, will be characterised by respect, generosity, justice, hospitality and critical reflection.

Some Indicators of Achievement

● Catholic schools will be known to be open to pupils from all cultural and religious backgrounds.

● The Catholic school, utterly respectful of everyone's belief system, will invite all those who participate in its education system (teachers and parents/guardians as well as students) to know, understand and honour the characteristic spirit within which it builds its education community.

● Recognising and responding to the educational needs of all children, the Catholic school will exercise an option for justice, especially for the poor and disadvantaged.

● The Catholic school will contribute to the future of the Church and of society by developing an informed, critically reflective pupil and teacher body.

PAUSE FOR REFLECTION:
THE CATHOLIC SCHOOL, OPEN TO ALL

The Catholic school's public role is very clearly perceived. It has not come into being as a private initiative, but as an expression of the reality of the Church, having by its very nature a public character. It fulfils a public usefulness and, although clearly and decidedly configured in the perspective of the Catholic faith, is not reserved to Catholics only, but is open to all those who appreciate and share its qualified educational project.

CSTTM 16.

149. *Schools Objective 4:* The Board of Management in a Catholic school will take responsibility, on behalf of the Patron/Trustees, for developing the school, overseeing its Catholic ethos, and supporting the Principal in the daily management of the school, according to that ethos.

Some Indicators of Achievement
- The Board of Management of a Catholic school will take on the role of overseeing the provision of a clearly defined mission statement, codes and policies reflecting the Catholic ethos and characteristic spirit of the school.
- The Principal and staff of the school will be actively supported by the Board of Management in providing an atmosphere in the school commensurate with its open and respectful Catholic ethos.
- Initial training courses for boards of management will include a specific section on understanding Catholic ethos and its implications for decision-making.
- Board of Management members will have an opportunity, at least once a year, to review issues related to the Catholic ethos in the school and to report on this to the Patron.

150. *Schools Objective 5:* The Principal will ensure that the decisions of the Board of Management, and particularly the ethos statement set out by the Board, are lived out in the day-to-day running of the school.

Some Indicators of Achievement
- The Principal of a Catholic school will be employed on the understanding that he or she is delegated by the Board of Management and has responsibility to encourage, develop and promote the ethos associated with that particular Catholic school.
- Arrangements will be made for the provision of courses/modules in the management of Catholic schools. In-career support for those who are already in position will also be provided.

- The school Principal in a Catholic school, at the behest of the Board of Management, will take responsibility for providing suitable occasions for reflection on the spiritual and religious well-being of the school community. Retreat days for students, with appropriately trained retreat teams, will take place at frequent intervals.

151. *Schools Objective 6:* Staff in a Catholic school will know, understand and sustain the Catholic ethos within which they are employed.

Some Indicators of Achievement
- The teaching staff of a Catholic School will be actively involved in promoting the Mission Statement and policies approved by the Board of Management.
- Teachers will be employed on the understanding that they will commit themselves actively to supporting the ethos of the school. At the same time, the school will respect the freedom of conscience of teachers in matters of personal religious belief and practice.
- New teachers, as part of their induction to the school, will have an opportunity to focus on the Catholic character of the school.
- School staff will take the opportunity to review some aspects of the Catholic ethos of the school at least once a year.

FOCUS GROUP: THE CATHOLIC SCHOOL PRINCIPAL AS SPIRITUAL LEADER

The next generation of principals will need to generate new expressions that inspire, teach, captivate and support the faith in schools. This will require new skills at an intellectual and a human level. Principals will need a more explicit understanding of the philosophical, theological and spiritual underpinnings of Catholic education, and also to develop skills that help teachers, parents and students grasp the importance and challenge of the Christian message in a way that is appropriate to their development.

D. Tuohy, M. Maume and R. Maxwell, *Beyond Nostalgia: Issues In Trusteeship with Regard to The Catholic Ethos of Post-Primary Schools* (Portlaoise: Presentation Ministries Office, 2000), p. 66.

---

152. *Schools Objective 7:* Religious education and faith formation will be evident strengths in the schooling provided by a Catholic school.

Some Indicators of Achievement

- Religious Education will be one of the crucial elements supporting the characteristic spirit of a Catholic school. Trained Diocesan Advisers for Religious Education will support the Principal and those teaching Religious Education, encouraging and resourcing the school in supporting and informing the faith of Catholic students.

- The Catholic school will establish and maintain strong contact with local Catholic parishes. A nominated member of the school staff will coordinate school input into celebrations of sacramental initiation in the local parish.

- The Catholic primary school, as part of the parish community and with that community, will assist parents/guardians in providing sacramental initiation support for children. School and parish programmes will be coordinated, with the help of parents/guardians, in such a way that home, parish and school develop and maintain close co-operation in the preparation of children for sacramental initiation.

- Teachers of Religious Education in post-primary schools will be fully trained specialist teachers. Religious educators working in a Catholic second-level school, as well as having responsibility for the religious education of all students, will be acknowledged as having a faith formation responsibility to their Catholic students.

- The Bishops' Guidelines for Junior Cycle (1999) and Senior Cycle Religious Education (2006) will be adopted, and a Religious Education Policy will be put in place as recommended in the Bishops' document on such policies (2003).
- Religious Education as a subject will be embraced with Catholic students from a Catholic perspective, and discussed with other students from their perspective. An approach that only speaks of the phenomenon of religion, rather than the students' experience of faith, will be considered insufficient in a Catholic school.

STARTING POINT: BALANCING FAITH
DEVELOPMENT NEEDS IN CATHOLIC SCHOOLS

The challenge of the future will clearly lie in defining the place of faith development in the schools, balancing the needs of pre-evangelisation, evangelisation and faith support for the school community, and linking the school with the faith life of the Church.

Beyond Nostalgia, pp. 64-5.

Ecclesial Movements, Groups and Organisations

153. Often in the Church, particular groups and organisations have gathered for support, prayer, celebration and service. In Ireland, the St Vincent de Paul Society, the Legion of Mary and the Pioneer Total Abstinence Association are traditional examples of enthusiastic, courageous and faith-filled commitment. More recently, prayer groups, parish folk groups and a variety of charitable organisations have provided a home for the spiritual and missionary energies of lay people.

Small Christian Communities have now been established in some parishes, helping members of the parish to discover their full Christian calling in the company of a group of parish members who support one another in faith. Praying with Scripture, community building, and service within and beyond the parish, along with active participation in liturgical celebrations, are the centre and source of renewal for such smaller gatherings within parish.

A further development has been the arrival in Ireland of ecclesial movements in the Church, which have much to offer adults, and young adults in particular. These communities seek a particular type of commitment, celebrating within a specific charism the importance of religious faith in life. They are often very close-knit communities, celebrating the Eucharist together and introducing the lay person to a life of service rooted in the faith of the Church. When this way of life helps them to build up the local parish faith community and to grow in communion with other ecclesial groups and organisations and with the bishops, it is a further blessing for the Church.[6]

[6] *EE 29.*

FAITH DEVELOPMENT OBJECTIVES FOR CHURCH ORGANISATIONS, SMALL CHRISTIAN COMMUNITIES AND ECCLESIAL MOVEMENTS

154. *Communities Objective 1:* Church organisations, Small Christian Communities and ecclesial movements will embrace their role in evangelisation and in building up the Church in Ireland, supporting the catechetical life of the parish and diocese, seeking to put their particular mission at the service of people, the Church community and society.

Some Indicators of Achievement
● Church organisations and groups will establish faith development, either directly or indirectly, as a key element of their mission.
● Small Christian Communities, who are involved in ongoing personal and community catechesis, will see this as central to their existence, and put themselves at the service of faith development in the parish.
● Ecclesial movements will have a formulated plan for faith development among all their members. Members will have good relations with their local parish, supporting its education in faith programmes and its life and growth generally.
● Lay people involved in all such movements, groups and organisations, will be present at and participate in parochial, diocesan and national initiatives, particularly those involving evangelising outreach of one kind or another.

> ### REFLECTION:
> ### OUR COMMON CHRISTIAN SPIRITUALITY
>
> Education in the spirituality proper to a particular movement or association enriches the Church and is a natural continuation of the basic formation received by all Christians. Firstly, it is necessary to educate in what is common to all the members of the Church, before educating in what is particular and diverse.
>
> *GDC 262(a)*

Education and Training for Faith Development

155. An area of particular concern for the Catholic Church in Ireland is the expectation that those who are invited to act as Faith Development Coordinators, catechists and religious educators within the Catholic community, have an opportunity in their training to grow in knowledge and understanding of their Catholic faith, to nourish their faith and to experience its fullest meaning in their lives. Highly motivated young adults, desiring to be educated and trained as teachers and for collaborative ministry, should find themselves fully supported by the Catholic community. The *Catechism of the Catholic Church*, the *General Directory for Catechesis* and this *National Directory for Catechesis in Ireland* should form the basis upon which members of the Catholic Church in Ireland are informed about and interact with Jesus Christ, whom they seek to know deeply in their hearts. It is in knowing him as he truly is that we can share his message lovingly with one another.

FAITH DEVELOPMENT FORMATION OBJECTIVES

156. *Formation Objective 1:* A system and programmes will be in place within the Catholic Church, in association with other providers, for the education and training of experienced lay persons, enabling them to become available to their parish and diocese to help others to grow deeply into their Christian faith.

Some Indicators of Achievement

- A process of education and training for Parish Pastoral Workers, and specifically for Faith Development Coordinators, will be developed and supported, such that in time professionally qualified lay people with considerable experience are available throughout the country.
- In addition to initial qualification, ongoing training and supervision will be available in order to heighten their collaborative skills and to maintain registration in the role of Faith Development Coordinator.
- Seminarians will be formed in catechetical outreach and instruction and be familiar with the nature of the lay apostolate and the right ordering of the collaboration of the non-ordained faithful in the ministry of priests.[7]
- In-service will be provided at regular intervals for priests, deacons and religious working in parishes, with a view to supporting them in developing suitable collaborative strategies.
- Volunteers will be trained at diocesan and regional levels to work within their parish as members of the Parish Pastoral Council, and within initiatives deemed appropriate to the particular parish, such as Baptism Teams, Liturgy and Music Teams, Family Mass Teams, Justice Groups, Bereavement Teams, etc., helping others to engage with and grow in their faith.

[7] See Congregation for the Clergy, *The Priest, Pastor and Leader of the Parish Community*, 4 August 2002; also *Ecclesia de Mysterio*, along with other documents of that and other Roman Dicasteries.

- Trained volunteer catechists will be visible within their local parish.
- Distance Learning programmes will become available within the Irish context, enabling parish volunteers, for example, to engage with their own faith development needs.

157. *Formation Objective 2:* All those teaching in schools will be fully informed about the life and teaching of the Catholic Church, so that they can initiate genuine dialogue between their pupils and the Catholic community to which many of the students belong.

Some Indicators of Achievement
- Teachers, in their training, will gain familiarity with the religious traditions of young people in Ireland and their families, and demonstrate true knowledge of the Catholic faith and other religions.
- School students of all faith traditions and none will be encouraged to display an informed understanding of membership of the Catholic Church, its teachings and tradition.
- Catholic students in schools other than Catholic schools will be educated in a manner that is appropriate to their religious faith. Their parents or guardians will ensure that catechesis and preparation for sacramental initiation continues at home and in parish.

158. *Formation Objective 3:* Education and Training in Religious Education, Catholic Teaching and Christian Initiation, will be considered an essential element in the qualification of all teachers who wish to teach in Catholic primary schools.

Some Indicators of Achievement
- Colleges of Education that prepare teachers who may wish to work in Catholic primary schools, will ensure that they have access to the fullest possible training as religious educators.
- Evidence of training in Religious Education, Catholic Teaching and Christian Initiation will be required by a Catholic primary school employing new teachers.
- In Colleges of Education with a Catholic ethos, resources will be set aside for chaplaincy services. A programme of personal faith development will be available, suitable for encouraging young adults of varying commitment to connect more fully with their Catholic faith tradition.

159. *Formation Objective 4:* Religious educators working in post-primary Catholic schools will be professionally trained as subject-specific teachers whose background in theology, as well as religious education methodology, prepares them to contribute in a focused way to the religious education and ongoing faith development of young people.

Some Indicators of Achievement

- The religious educator in a post-primary Catholic school will be a subject-specific teacher who has completed undergraduate studies in theology, has fulfilled the requirements for the teaching of religious education laid down by the relevant authorities, and is willing to support the characteristic spirit of the school.
- The religious educator in Catholic second-level schools, even when taking Religious Education classes for State certification, will engage with the material in a manner that contributes to the spiritual and moral development of the students.
- Religious educators in a post-primary Catholic school will contribute in many ways to the school's ethos, mission and policies. They will do this as part of the whole-school team, not on their own.
- The religious educator will be open to the variety of faith questions that emerge in his or her own life as well as that of their students, participating regularly in renewal activities such as spiritual direction and retreat time, as well as in peer-support and supervision.

160. *Formation Objective 5:* Those who provide chaplaincy services in post-primary schools will be experienced people who have completed post-graduate studies relevant to school chaplaincy.

Some Indicators of Achievement

- Where possible in post-primary schools, qualified personnel will provide chaplaincy support for Catholic and other students and for staff.
- Those who provide chaplaincy services will have training in practical liturgy, pastoral care, personal counselling and bereavement counselling, as well as theology.
- Those providing chaplaincy in schools will engage in supervision and ongoing spiritual direction.

161. *Formation Objective 6:* All Catholic Colleges of Education, Theological Faculties and Pastoral Institutes will provide their students with relevant opportunities for formation as well as study.

Some Indicators of Achievement

- This *National Directory for Catechesis in Ireland*, the *General Directory for Catechesis* and the *Catechism of the Catholic Church*, will be key focuses in the teaching, learning and research activities of third-level courses at these colleges.
- Planning and resources to support the ongoing provision of Theology at third level will be given priority by the Irish Catholic Bishops' Conference in conjunction with religious congregations and the University Colleges.
- Optional modules, which provide opportunities for students to grapple with their own faith and acquire support mechanisms for growth in faith, will be offered.
- Chaplaincy support services will be available to third-level students in a way that encourages the ongoing catechesis of all participants, including those providing the service.

Provision of Materials for Faith Development Activities

162. As well as the personnel and financial resources that are necessary for a renewal in catechesis and in faith development at all levels, investment in the provision of material resources is crucial. A tremendous contribution can be made with the production of good programmes, textbooks and other resources for all age-groups and need-groups. Books for adults dealing with catechetical and theological concepts in an accessible manner are essential. Posters, videos, CDs, DVDs, drama- and action-based resources, as well as imaginative materials that allow artistic expression through music, liturgy and painting, for instance, are all helpful for teachers, priests, deacons, Faith Development Coordinators, catechists, parents/guardians and others building a learning relationship with adults and young people. A variety of faith-filled computer software and websites can create new interactive ways of coming into contact with religious questions. Healthy informed discussion in the press and on radio and television, as well as the use of other forms of mass communication, can raise public awareness of the role, meaning and value of religion in people's lives.

OBJECTIVES CONCERNING MATERIALS FOR FAITH DEVELOPMENT

163. *Resources Objective 1:* Adult resources for faith development, employing adult learning processes, will be made available at a variety of levels.

Some Indicators of Achievement

- A wide variety of reading material for adults, opening up their faith experience and introducing them to Catholic spirituality, scriptural meditation, the teaching of the Church, ecclesiology and so on, will be made available to encourage adults to delve deeper into their faith.
- The *Compendium of the Catechism of the Catholic Church* will be available and a local catechism for adults will be developed.
- A variety of appropriate theological and catechetical material will be suggested for libraries across the country.

164. *Resources Objective 2:* A renewed syllabus/curriculum and programme, suitable for religious education and formation in Catholic primary schools, will be developed, responding to the realities of today's cultural and religious context in the light of the teaching of the Church, indicated in the *Catechism of the Catholic Church*.

Some Indicators of Achievement

- A renewed syllabus/ curriculum for religious education and formation in Catholic primary schools will be developed, based on the principle of connecting home, parish and school in the formation of Catholic pupils.
- The syllabus/curriculum will uphold a direct connection with parents and parish in the preparation of Catholic pupils for sacramental initiation.
- The syllabus/curriculum will acknowledge the variety of pupils in a Catholic school and recognise the religious duties and responsibilities of their parents.
- This syllabus/curriculum will take account of the breadth of special education and inclusion needs.

- With such a syllabus in place, a new programme will be developed in Catholic primary schools, using the best methodology available, and appropriate for the particular age-group and stage of faith of the children involved.

165. *Resources Objective 3:* Faith development resources for use in the family will be given new priority within the Catholic community.

Some Indicators of Achievement
- Family prayer and ritual will be promoted within Catholic homes as a normal part of family life.
- Materials to help parents/guardians and members of the parish in preparing children to receive the sacraments will be readily available.
- Resources to help young adults to reflect as they make important life choices, prepare for marriage and anticipate parenthood, or consider a vocation to priesthood or religious life, will be developed.
- Accessible reading and audio-visual material will be provided for adults seeking to build up their family life in a Christian context.

166. *Resources Objective 4:* Post-primary religious education programmes, responding to the various syllabuses and frameworks for second-level Religious Education, and appropriate for use in Catholic schools, will be made available.

Some Indicators of Achievement
- At post-primary level, the Irish Catholic Bishops' Conference will provide suitable programmes for the religious education of Catholic students.
- These programmes will be renewed regularly, and the syllabuses underlying their production responded to creatively from a Catholic perspective.
- The Bishops' guidelines and policy documents for the faith development of Catholic students, together with this Directory, will be the basis upon which Religious Education is being taught in Catholic schools.
- The syllabuses themselves will be given ongoing attention.

167. *Resources Objective 5:* Catechetical programmes designed specifically for use within the parish community will also be provided.

Some Indicators of Achievement

● Support material for good liturgical celebration will be available and reasonably priced.

● Resources for homilies will be widely available, helping the priest identify themes from the three-year lectionary cycle.

● Music will be recognised as a deep source of spirituality. An agreed hymnal, the material chosen with an eye to its catechetical value, will be made available as the basis of parish celebrations.

168. *Resources Objective 6:* Human dignity, justice, social solidarity and inclusivity will be characteristic elements of all Catholic programmes, resources and materials produced at all levels for adults, adolescents and children.

Some Indicators of Achievement

● All possible efforts will be made so that those who have been disadvantaged in any way are not marginalised further within faith development programming.

● Materials will be produced that will enable the social teaching of the Church to be made accessible to a wide variety of people and groups.

● The perspective of people with physical disabilities will be acknowledged and valued in faith development processes and programmes.

● People with special learning needs will be addressed, with specific programmes adapted to their requirements.

● The linguistic concerns of the Deaf Community will be embraced in resources for schools and parishes.

● Through parish catechesis and school religious education and formation programmes, dialogue between Travellers and the settled community will be supported.

● Textbooks and resources will encourage migrants and other newcomers to share their gifts within the Christian community. Respect for difference will be celebrated.

● Ecumenical and inter-religious dialogues will be attended to respectfully in catechetical and other faith development materials.

● Those living with illness will be provided with specialised catechetical material and treated thoughtfully in resources available at all levels.

169. *Resources Objective 7:* The Catholic Press and other forms of Catholic media will support efforts within the Catholic Church to renew its approach to faith development today.

Some Indicators of Achievement

● Catholic newspapers, newsletters and pamphlets will contribute to raising public awareness of the evangelising mission of the Church.

● Radio stations will be supported locally in giving time to in-depth spiritual and religious matters.

● Catholic websites, noticeboards and chat rooms will have come on line. Distance Learning modules will be provided within the Irish context.

● Diocesan and parish websites will be available and used to good catechetical effect.

'Man's real, true hope which holds firm in spite of all disappointments can only be God – God who has loved us and continues to love us "to the end" until all "is accomplished" (cf. John 13:1 and 19:30). Whoever is moved by love begins to perceive what "life" really is.'

Benedict XVI, *SS* 27.

Conclusion

170. If we have heard the Good News of God's love for us in Jesus Christ, we too can be good news for one another and for the world. 'The vocation to love ... makes the human person an authentic image of God: man and woman come to resemble God to the extent that they become loving people.'[1] As members of the Catholic Church in Ireland, we hope to support one another in love and to encourage one another to speak openly about what our deep-down faith in Jesus Christ means for us. Together we seek a fuller knowledge of the Son of God in his words and deeds. We can open our hearts to the challenge and to the peace that Christ our Teacher offers us in our daily lives. Led by his Spirit, we journey toward the fullness and completion of the Kingdom of God, the Kingdom already set in motion by Christ's presence among us. His call finds a home with us and resounds in us to the ends of the earth: Live the good news! Share the good news! Be good news!

OUR FERVENT HOPE:
LIFE LIVED IN THE JOY OF CHRIST

May the world of our time, which is searching, sometimes with anguish, sometimes with hope, be enabled to receive the Good News not from evangelisers who are dejected, discouraged, impatient or anxious, but from ministers of the Gospel whose lives glow with fervour, who have first received the joy of Christ, and who are willing to risk their lives so that the Kingdom may be proclaimed and the Church established in the midst of the world.

EN 80

Now is the time to rediscover our mission, to clarify our objectives and to set ourselves appropriate goals. In order to be an evangelising and catechising Church, we commit ourselves fully to the vision laid out in this Directory, as an expression of who we

[1] Benedict XVI, Address to the Participants in the Ecclesial Diocesan Convention of Rome, 6 June 2005.

are. It is an ambitious project. The objectives put before us in the final chapter set us on a journey together. The challenge now is to revitalise our Christian lives and find the new direction that our times and circumstances require. In all the different situations considered in this reflection, whether at home, in parish, in school, at diocesan, regional or national level, our purpose is the same: to reach out and together touch and feel and bring alive the coming Reign of God.

171. In-depth reflection can bring meaning, certainly, to individual lives. Unless, however, we are willing to act as one, we will not know the full power that the Christian community has to transform our lives and the lives of others in God's love. Home, parish and school are not only important for one another, they form a partnership that is dependent on one another. The Church at parish level, and also at diocesan and national level, draws energy and strength from all those who play their part. The greatest resource of the family of the Church, along with Christ and the Spirit he has sent us, is its people.

As members of Christ's Church, we try to live life to the best of our ability, by reaching out to others in Christian love. However, as we journey with Jesus Christ toward the fulfilment which he promises can be ours, we are often unaware of the efforts being made to live the Gospel, quietly, unobtrusively, but with determination, by others. It is good from time to time to highlight the variety and depth of the work that the Christian community and its individual members involve themselves in. The never-ending prayer of monastic and contemplative communities is a gift, too, that should be recognised and cherished as an active contribution at the heart of the Christian community's ministry of love.

172. We wish to acknowledge all the efforts that will certainly be made as a result of the publication of this *National Directory for Catechesis in Ireland*. By seeking to implement a renewed vision, with new planning and procedures in place, we are stating once more our belief that the Church does indeed exist in order to evangelise and catechise, bringing the light of Christ to bear on the world and its peoples. We seek to begin again to convert our hearts, to ask one another for forgiveness and reconciliation, and to renew our trust in God's continuing revelation of what we can be and do together.

Renewal takes place from both the bottom up and the top down. A personal decision by all of us who have read and reflected on this Directory to involve ourselves in ways appropriate to our own situation and talents, and to be open to working with others for renewal at all levels of faith development, will have an enormous effect on what can and will be achieved.

173. All of this, we recognise, depends on God's Spirit and on Christ Jesus our Saviour, whom we seek to know, follow and serve with commitment, energy and imagination. We ask Mary, his mother and our mother, the mother of Salvation and the mother of the Church, the first evangeliser, to draw us ever closer to her Son and to remind him constantly of our need:

Mary, mother of Christ,
pray for us.
Mary, mother of God,
pray for us.
Mary, mother of the Church,
pray for us.
Mary, our mother,
pray for us.
Mary, Queen of Ireland,
pray for us.
Mary, Queen of Peace,
pray for us.

SCRIPTURAL REFLECTION:
'DO WHATEVER HE TELLS YOU.'

The greatest temptation of the Church is to put other things, other people, at the centre and inevitably things fall apart... The greatest task of the Church in every generation is to keep restoring Christ to the centre and by listening, to his word with open lives, attend to the world we live in. This is the only way to be the Church today in every generation.

Our Catholic tradition strongly reflects the second important element of the Church that is found at Cana, namely that Mary is very close to the centre. It is through her dialogue with her Son and with the people around them that the miracle of transformation is set up. She speaks the needs of the people to Jesus – 'they have no wine' – and she gives her one and only command to the servants – 'do whatever he tells you'. This ongoing interaction is a very important part of our understanding of our spirituality... 'Do whatever he tells you.' That is still Mary's only command to the Church.
Think Big, Act Small: Working at Collaborative Ministry Through Parish Pastoral Councils (Dublin: Veritas, 2005), pp. 129-30.

CONCLUDING MEDITATION:
LOOKING FORWARD TO NEW BEGINNINGS

Pray with the Lord, using the Scripture provided here, or other favourite pieces, renewing your commitment to go out into the whole world, to be good news, sharing with all-comers the good news of Jesus Christ, that we are loved by God for all eternity.

He then released a dove, to see whether the waters were receding from the surface of the earth. But the dove, finding nowhere to perch, returned to him in the ark, for there was water over the whole surface of the earth; putting out his hand he took hold of it and brought it back into the ark with him. After waiting seven more days he again released the dove from the ark. In the evening it came back to him, and there in its beak was a freshly picked olive-leaf. After waiting seven more days, he released the dove, and now it returned to him no more.

(Genesis 8:8-12)

I was helpless in the hand of God, and when he said to me, 'Go out into the valley and I will talk to you there', I arose and went, and oh, I saw the glory of the Lord there.

(Ezekiel 3:22-23a)

Dúirt Íosa dá bhrí sin leis an dáréag: 'Cad mar gheall oraibhse, an mian libhse freisin imeacht?' D'fhreagair Síomón Peadar é: 'A Thiarna, cé chuige a rachaimid? Is agatsa atá briathra na beatha síoraí, agus chreideamar agus tá a fhios againn gur tusa Aon Naofa Dé.'

(John 6:67-69)

Leanfad thú, a Thiarna, pé áit dá ngeobhair, de bhrí gur agatsa atá briathra na beatha síoraí.

I shall follow you, O Lord, any place you go, because it is you who have the words of eternal life.

Traditional Prayer before Travelling, County Louth.

Index

Physical disabilities (People who have), 168-170, 219
Pilgrimage, 21, 35
Pioneer Total Abstinence Association, 211
Pluralism, 32-33
Pope Benedict visits three synagogues, 95
Pope John Paul II in Ireland, 35
Pope John Paul II in the Holy Land, 95
Post-Confirmation programmes, 152
Post-primary schools, 7, 204-210, 215, 218
Potential (new culture), 21-22
Prayer, 4, 55, 87-89, 143, 192, 218
Pre-adolescence, 136-140
Pre-evangelisation, 50-51, 150
Presenting the Gospel to adolescents, 148-159
Presenting the Gospel to children, 133-148
Presenting the message of Jesus Christ, 45-46
Priests, 123-127, 192, 194, 197, 213
Primary School Curriculum, 141
Principals, 7, 143, 145, 146, 157, 195, 204, 207-208
Print media, 220
Prisoners, 165
Process, 151
Proclamation, 3, 4, 50-51
Profession of Faith, 4, 55, 75-76
Promoting knowledge of the faith, 55
Provision of materials, 216

R
Radio, 115, 220
RCIA, 51-53, 78, 102-108, 111, 180, 193
Reaching out in Christ's love to all, 161-185
Reconciliation, 79-80, 138, 181
Reflections, 9, 25, 26, 27, 33, 35, 37, 41, 42, 47, 49, 53, 55, 60, 61, 63, 65, 74, 77, 79, 80, 84, 85, 87, 89, 91, 93, 96, 98, 111, 117, 118, 120, 132, 134, 158, 161, 167, 169, 170, 184, 185, 196, 206, 212, 221, 225, 226
Religion and science, 24, 112-113
Religious, 123-127, 200-201, 213

Religious education, 3, 41, 57-59, 74, 140-148, 154-159, 171-172, 204, 209-210
Religious Education Coordinator, 146, 195
Religious Education Department, 204
Religious education in school, 140-148, 154-159
Religious Education Policy, 210
Religious Education Syllabus, 155-157, 203, 217
Religious faith skills, 151
Research, 202
Resources and Implementation, 189-221
Respect for Creation, 23-24
Resurrection, 23, 67, 75, 79, 91, 97, 181
Revelation of God's love, 41-43

S
Sacramental preparation, 145-148, 194, 200, 205, 209, 214, 217
Sacraments, 43, 55, 72, 77-82, 138, 181
Sacraments at the service of Communion, 81-82
Sacraments of Healing, 79-80
Sacraments of Initiation, 43, 77-79, 209
Saint Patrick, 16, 17, 92
Saints, 22
Salvation, 42, 46, 181, 225
Sancti Venite, 79
Schedule for a Catholic Primary School, 143
School, 18, 140-148, 204-210
School chaplains, 5, 7, 195, 215
School ethos, 142-143, 145, 147, 204-207
School principal, 146, 204-210
School provision, 147
Science and religion, 24, 112-113
Sciences, 23-24
Scientism, 24
Scripture, 19, 21, 42, 47, 70-72, 89, 211, 226
Second Vatican Council, 2, 19, 90, 94, 95, 124
Secularism, 31
Seminarians, 213
Sensitivity to adult ways of learning, 108-110